DEUTERONOMY
AND THE
DEATH OF MOSES

OVERTURES TO BIBLICAL THEOLOGY

Editors

A
Theological
Reading

DEUTERONOMY AND THE DEATH OF MOSES

Dennis T. Olson

 FORTRESS PRESS   **Minneapolis**

DEUTERONOMY AND THE DEATH OF MOSES
A Theological Reading

Library of Congress Cataloging-in-Publication Data

Olson, Dennis T.
    Deuteronomy and the death of Moses : a theological reading /
Dennis T. Olson.
        p.   cm. — (Overtures to biblical theology)
    Includes bibliographical references and index.
    ISBN 0-8006-2639-7 (alk. paper)
    1. Bible.   O.T.   Deuteronomy—Criticism, interpretation, etc.
    2. Moses (Biblical leader)—Death and burial.   I. Title.
    II. Series.
    BS1275.2.O47   1994
    222'.1506—dc20   94-12729
                                                            CIP

Manufactured in the U.S.A.   AF 1-2639

98   97   96   95   94   1   2   3   4   5   6   7   8   9   10

In memory of my father,
Toby Roinesdal Olson
And in gratitude to my mother,
Esther Heaak Olson

Contents

Editor's Foreword

Readers familiar with the Overtures series may sense a departure in genre in this volume from Dennis Olson, at least at first glance. The table of contents alone suggests that this volume could pass as quickly for a commentary as for a monograph.

Yet *Deuteronomy and the Death of Moses* is not a commentary, for all its resemblance to that form. Rather, the form of the overture belongs of a piece with the larger thesis: it is only in coming to terms with the richness of the whole book, each part in its given place, with its own unique form and shape, that one can understand Deuteronomy's abiding theological legacy.

But Olson is making more than a sophisticated literary argument for reading the book of Deuteronomy as a whole, in its present shape. Besides, that has been done before, with much in the way of fresh insight and convincing argument for reading the book in the form it has been received. Olson knows this more recent literature well, but feels it has nevertheless not penetrated to the book's theological rationale. It has been an argument for unitary reading for its own sake, mounted largely in defiance of other interpretive approaches concerned with identifying layers and signs of editorial enrichment and modification, and content to treat the book of Deuteronomy as a set of clues from which to reconstruct an elaborate history of religious ideas and institutions.

In some respects, Olson has not turned his back on these sorts of diachronic concerns. He knows the book has an elaborate editorial history, attached to and derived from the actual religious history of the people of Israel, spanning several centuries and more. Three examples treated in convincing fashion by him illustrate this point. First, commentators have seen a tension between the call for one sanctuary and the more abstract conception that God can be called on anywhere, even from foreign soil, so long as the heart is contrite; or, second, between a covenant made at Horeb whose abrogation will lead to permanent curse, and that made in Moab, almost perfectly geared to a heart prone to disobedience; and finally, between a Moses dying on account of the wider generation's sins, and a Moses who dies for his own tragic, even minor, offenses.

Olson knows full well that one can resolve the tension between these alternative themes by assigning them to different editorial hands, hands that betray in some cases opposing (as alleged) theological tendencies, due either to changed circumstances or changed minds. Olson is fully familiar with this rather narrow and sufficiently predictable redactional analysis — once one is trained to read erasures (as a literary science) or sort out divergent ideas (as a theological science) into separate bins. He grants its legitimacy, but then moves beyond it toward another goal: the effort to understand how these themes, several of them in distinct tension, might nevertheless be in intentional juxtaposition. The key to much of the resolution of this tension belongs resolutely in the person of Moses. Moses is both hero and sinner, obedient follower of the first covenant yet embodied foreshadower of a covenant still to come, the second not obviating the first but giving new access to its original intention.

To the extent that Olson has provided an argument for reading themes in tension together in the final form of the book, he has also done just that: read and commented on the book as a whole, even at some of its more prosaic moments. This overture therefore provides the interested reader with a fresh approach to commentary writing, one that engages all the traditional concern with total coverage of the text in question, but with the added feature of uniting that commentary under a single set of larger working concerns. The first-time reader of Deuteronomy is introduced both to the standard critical issues and to the text itself, but within the context of a concern to understand the book's abiding theological legacy.

CHRISTOPHER R. SEITZ

Preface

Translations of the biblical text in this study will follow the New Revised Standard Version (NRSV) unless otherwise indicated. One exception to this practice is my regular use of *torah* in place of the NRSV's *law* in translating the Hebrew word *torah*. Minor differences between English and Hebrew versifications occur at certain points in Deuteronomy. Where they differ, the study will follow English versification. I use the terms *Hebrew Bible* and *Old Testament* interchangeably. Jewish, Christian, and academic communities of interpretation may prefer one label over the other, and I respect each community's preference in designating the biblical text.

I gratefully acknowledge the support of several people and communities who supported me in writing this book. Much of the manuscript was completed during a year-long study leave in 1990–1991. The leave was generously supported by the President and Board of Trustees of Princeton Theological Seminary. I also wish to thank the Center for Theological Inquiry in Princeton, New Jersey, which was my scholarly home during that time. The gracious hospitality, assistance, and intellectual community provided by the director, Daniel Hardy, his able staff, and the other visiting scholars at the Center made writing this book a good deal more enjoyable.

I am also indebted to the editors of the Overtures to Biblical Theology series, Walter Brueggemann and Christopher Seitz, for accepting the manuscript and for their wisdom in editing and shaping the final product. Thanks also to Marshall Johnson, Charles Puskas, and David Lott of Fortress Press for their role in bringing this project to completion and publication. Our student departmental assistant, Kevin Reilly, was a great help in preparing the indices.

I have benefited from the comments and reactions of many people during occasions when I have presented portions of this work on

Deuteronomy in scholarly papers, seminary courses, and other forums. Thanks also to my wife and children who both encouraged me in this project but also provided needed moments of diversion from it and the other duries of a seminary professor.

Finally, I dedicate this book to my parents, Toby and Esther. Like Moses, they faithfully endeavored to pass their faith onto the next generation. For the gift of their love and teaching, I am profoundly grateful.

Abbreviations

AAR	American Academy of Religion
AB	Anchor Bible
AnBib	Analecta biblica
ANET	*J. B.* Pritchard (ed.), *Ancient Near Eastern Texts*
ASTI	*Annual of the Swedish Theological Institute*
BARev	*Biblical Archaeology Review*
BBB	Bonner biblische Beiträge
BETL	Bibliotheca ephemeridum theologicarum lovaniensium
Bib	*Biblica*
BibRev	*Bible Review*
BJS	Brown Judaic Studies
BM	*Beth Mikra*
BN	*Biblische Notizen*
BR	*Biblical Research*
BWANT	Beiträge zur Wissenschaft vom Alten und Neuen Testament
BZ	*Biblische Zeitschrift*
BZAW	Beihefte zur *Zeitschrift für die alttestamentliche Wissenschaft*
CBQ	*Catholic Biblical Quarterly*
CRev	*Clergy Review*
DD	*Dor le Dor*
EgT	*Eglise et Théologie*
ETL	*Ephemerides theologicae lovanienses*
EvQ	*Evangelical Quarterly*
FRLANT	Forschungen zur Religion und Literatur des Alten und Neuen Testaments
FS	Festschrift
GTA	Göttinger theologische Arbeiten
HAR	Hebrew Annual Review
HKAT	Handkommentar zum Alten Testament

HSM	Harvard Semitic Monographs
HTR	*Harvard Theological Review*
HUCA	*Hebrew Union College Annual*
ICC	International Critical Commentary
IDB	G. A. Buttrick (ed.), *Interpreter's Dictionary of the Bible*
IDBSup	Supplementary volume to *IDB*
Int	*Interpretation*
IOS	*Israel Oriental Society*
IRev	*Iliff Review*
JAAR	*Journal of the American Academy of Religion*
JBL	*Journal of Biblical Literature*
JJS	*Journal of Jewish Studies*
JNES	*Journal of Near Eastern Studies*
JQR	*Jewish Quarterly Review*
JR	*Journal of Religion*
JSOT	*Journal for the Study of the Old Testament*
JSOTSup	Journal for the Study of the Old Testament — Supplement Series
MDB	*Le Monde de la Bible*
NCBC	New Century Bible Commentary
NICOT	New International Commentary on the Old Testament
NLH	*New Literary History*
NRSV	New Revised Standard Version
OBO	Orbis biblicus et orientalis
OBT	Overtures to Biblical Theology
OTL	Old Testament Library
PSB	*Princeton Seminary Bulletin*
SBLDS	SBL Dissertation Series
SBLMS	SBL Monograph Series
SBT	Studies in Biblical Theology
ScrHier	Scripta hierosolymitana
SJLA	Studies in Judaism in Late Antiquity
SR	*Studies in Religion/Sciences religieuses*
TBT	*The Bible Today*
TQ	*Theologische Quartalschrift*
TRE	*Theologische Realenzyklopädie*
TUSR	Trinity University Studies in Religion
TynBul	*Tyndale Bulletin*
VT	*Vetus Testamentum*
VTSup	*Vetus Testamentum,* Supplements
WBC	Word Biblical Commentary
YJS	Yale Judaica Series
ZA	*Zeitschrift für Assyriologie*
ZAW	*Zeitschrift für die alttestamentliche Wissenschaft*

Introduction

The book of Deuteronomy forms both the capstone of the Pentateuch (Genesis–Deuteronomy) and the introduction to the Deuteronomistic History (Deuteronomy–2 Kings). The frequent quotations of Deuteronomy in the New Testament and in the classic rabbinical sources testify to its authority within both Jewish and Christian traditions. Contemporary scholars have lauded Deuteronomy as "the theological center of the Old Testament" (Brueggemann), "the middle point of the Old Testament" (von Rad), the "center of biblical theology" (Herrmann) and "the most 'theological' book in the Old Testament" (Reventlow).[1]

Significant theological work has appeared in recent commentaries on the book of Deuteronomy (e.g., Miller, Christensen, Weinfeld).[2] Numerous studies and monographs by Norbert Lohfink and Georg Braulik have helped to illuminate the structure and theology of Deuteronomy (several of their works will be cited in the pages to follow). Many other studies have contributed to the theological interpretation of sections of Deuteronomy. I have noted, however, a relative scarcity of theological readings of Deuteronomy that take seriously the full structure and movement of the book as a whole from beginning to end. For example, theological studies or commentaries often neglect close readings of the "statutes and ordinances" of chapters 12–28 and the interplay between these laws and the narrative material embedded in the reported

---

1. Walter Brueggemann, *The Creative Word: Canon as a Model for Biblical Education* (Philadelphia: Fortress, 1982), 37; Gerhard von Rad, *Studies in Deuteronomy,* trans. David Stalker, SBT 1/9 (London: SCM, 1953), 37; Siegfried Herrmann, "Die konstruktive Restauration: Das Deuteronomium als Mitte biblischer Theologie," in *Probleme biblischer Theologie,* FS Gerhard von Rad, ed. H. W. Wolff (Munich: Chr. Kaiser, 1971), 155–70; and Henning Graf Reventlow, *Problems of Old Testament Theology in the Twentieth Century,* trans. John Bowden (Philadelphia: Fortress, 1985), 131.
2. Patrick D. Miller, Jr., *Deuteronomy,* Interpretation (Louisville: Westminster/John Knox, 1990); Duane L. Christensen, *Deuteronomy 1–11,* WBC 6A (Dallas: Word, 1991); and Moshe Weinfeld, *Deuteronomy 1–11,* AB 5 (New York: Doubleday, 1991).

speech of Moses, particularly in chapters 29–32. The crucial role played by the transition from the legal material that ends with the curses of chapter 28 and the new Moab covenant in chapters 29–32 has not been fully appreciated. Moreover, the role of the recurring theme of the death of Moses throughout Deuteronomy has not been fully explored for the richness of its theological and interpretive implications.

Another dimension that is often absent in the study of Deuteronomy is the application of literary approaches or sensitivities to the book as a whole. Literary methods that focus on plot, character, point of view, and other literary concerns are more readily applied to narratives like Genesis or 1 Samuel than to the mixture of narratives, laws, poetry, and discourse that makes up Deuteronomy. The one significant exception is the literary study of Deuteronomy contained in Robert Polzin's book *Moses and the Deuteronomist.*[3] Polzin's compositional analysis of Deuteronomy focuses on the interplay of three narrative "voices" within Deuteronomy: God, Moses, and the "narrator." In the end, Polzin appears to silence not only Moses (Deuteronomy 34) but also God—the only remaining "voice" is Deuteronomy's "narrator," the "implied author" of the text. This narrator is one voice who continues to speak authoritatively throughout the rest of the Deuteronomistic History (Joshua–2 Kings). In the concluding chapter of this study, I evaluate Polzin's argument in the light of my own conclusions and thereby raise some larger theological and hermeneutical issues.

Like Polzin, I seek to do a close literary reading of Deuteronomy on the basis of the final form and structure of the book as whole. Unlike some practitioners of literary approaches to the Bible, I do not avoid insights from historical-critical perspectives. Such insights are welcomed when they contribute to understanding the final form of the text. Some reliance on historical methods in interpreting an ancient biblical text is unavoidable. Every reading depends at the very least on the historical enterprise of translation from ancient Hebrew to a modern language. The frequent antagonism between literary and sociohistorical methods in biblical studies needs to be replaced by a greater appreciation of the contributions of each to the enterprise of biblical interpretation.

My reading of Deuteronomy seeks to make contributions to a literary and theological interpretation of Deuteronomy in the following areas:

1. I argue that the form of Deuteronomy by the book's own designation is *torah,* which I translate as a program of "catechesis."

---

3. Robert Polzin, *Moses and the Deuteronomist: A Literary Study of the Deuteronomic History,* Part One: *Deuteronomy, Joshua, Judges* (New York: Seabury, 1980), esp. 25–72.

2. The structure of Deuteronomy is built around a series of super-scriptions, with Deuteronomy 5 as the compressed blueprint for the structure of the book as a whole.

3. Beginning with Deuteronomy 1 and extending through the final chapter, I argue that the motif of the death of Moses casts its shadow over the entire book of Deuteronomy with important theological results.

4. I agree with others who suggest that Deuteronomy 6–11 function as a commentary on the first and most important of the Ten Commandments in Deuteronomy, "You shall have no other gods before me." My contribution is to show that Deuteronomy isolates three important "gods" who tempt Israel away from loving God: militarism, self-sufficient materialism, and self-righteous moralism. In other words, the notion of "other gods" in Deuteronomy extends to broader and less culture-specific idolatries that may tempt Israel from its allegiance to Yahweh alone.

5. In regard to the "statutes and ordinances" in Deuteronomy 12–26, other scholars have argued that this collection of miscellaneous laws largely follows the sequence of the Ten Commandments as they appear in Deuteronomy 5. Because no sustained theological interpretation of the Ten Commandments has taken advantage of that insight, however, I have sought to explicate the Ten Commandments in the light of the "statutes and ordinances" in chapters 12–26.

6. I try to demonstrate the role that the "statutes and ordinances" play in the entire structure of the book, particularly in relation to the new Moab covenant of Deuteronomy 29–32.

7. I argue that the Moab covenant in Deuteronomy 29–32 places priority on the mercy and compassion of God. The Moab covenant provides the way by which Deuteronomy addresses the crisis of Israel's exile and the death of an old generation that comes through the curses at the end of the "statutes and ordinances" (chap. 28). The Horeb covenant based on the Ten Commandments and the "statutes and ordinances" is retained; the new Moab covenant expressly functions "in addition" to the Horeb covenant (29:1). Thus, Deuteronomy in the end holds together law and human responsibility with promise and divine mercy. The theology of Deuteronomy's final form is much more nuanced and viable than the simple retributional theology often associated with Deuteronomy, which says "if you obey, you will be blessed" and "if you disobey, you will be cursed." This formula reflects neither the fullness of Deuteronomy's theology nor the reality of human experience.

8. The mechanisms of the "Moab covenant" for continuing faith in God to future generations include a covenant liturgy that is addressed to all members of the community (Deut. 29:10-11), a book of the *torah*

written by Moses, provisions for human priests and elders who will read and teach the text to future generations, and the poetic Song of Moses that strains through human language to express the inexpressible mysteries of the relationships of God, humans, and all creation.

9. The juxtaposition of Moses' final blessing of Israel and Moses' death outside Canaan is significant. Even as the individual Moses dies outside the promised land (chap. 34), the ultimate hope for Israel remains the blessing of God that Moses requests before his death (chap. 33).

10. The final chapter explores some implications of this study for the task of biblical theology in what is often called our present postmodern context.

I am aware that while I employ historical-critical insights, many interesting and important questions of a sociological or historical nature remain unexplored in this study. My assumptions are that the community which shaped and carried the tradition that eventually became Deuteronomy had its roots in northern Israel. After the Assyrian conquest of the north (722 B.C.E.), the Deuteronomists migrated south to Judah, where they exercised some influence under the reigns of Hezekiah and Josiah. The Deuteronomists joined the southern Judahite population in their exile to Babylon in 586 B.C.E. (Deut. 4:26-27; 29:28; 30:3-4). With the loss of the land, kingship, and the temple, the Babylonian exile "deconstructed" Judah's foundations of power, ideology, and understandings of reality. The Deuteronomistic tradition provided the exilic community an alternative theological and social vision for the survival of its faith. The persuasive viability of Deuteronomy eventually caused it to become the capstone of an otherwise largely southern Judahite Pentateuch or Torah (Genesis–Numbers).

The power and endurance of Deuteronomy's vision have been tested not only in biblical times but throughout the history of church and synagogue. We cannot simply and uncritically adopt Deuteronomy's program without adaptation, interpretation, and reflection. But Deuteronomy may point us in the direction of what a viable vision of God, humans, and the world ought to be. The vision should be persuasively taught rather than forcefully dictated. It ought to offer realistic hope rather than impossible idealism. It ought to accommodate plurality while also finding a common center that can bind communities together. It should embrace an ethic that moves beyond simple self-interest and the absolute priority of individual rights to embrace the values of self-sacrifice, community virtues, and a reasonable balance between individual and community well-being. It should cause us to rethink the old arrogance of science as mastery of nature, recognizing instead our interdependence with nature and its capacity to turn in judgment upon us.

This vision will recognize the limits and provisional character of all human constructions, ideas, systems, and powers. It will be open to the existence of a transcendent reality in our world, a reality that is disclosed in down-to-earth and real ways but also hidden and beyond full human comprehension. This vision provides a process for ongoing interpretation and adaptation, knowing that humans have only partial access to the knowledge of God, themselves, and the world.

I offer the following interpretation as *a* theological reading of Deuteronomy. I acknowledge the possibility and viability of other readings, theological and otherwise. Whether this theological reading is a helpful and persuasive one is finally up to the reader.

CHAPTER 1

Torah, Superscriptions, and the Death of Moses: Deuteronomy's Form, Structure, and Recurring Theme

> When Moses had finished writing down in a book the words of this *torah* to the very end, Moses commanded, . . . "Take this book of the *torah* and put it beside the ark of the covenant of the LORD your God."
> —Deut. 31:24-26

> The Torah is eternal; it refers to all times and to every person . . . Torah is so called because it teaches or points the way.
> —Manahem Nahum of Chernobyl, nineteenth-century Jewish mystic[1]

I argue in this chapter for three dimensions in the interpretation of Deuteronomy that will guide our reading of the book as a whole. First, I argue that the *form* of the present book of Deuteronomy is *torah,* a genre designation that might best be translated in its use in Deuteronomy as a program of "catechesis." In its present form Deuteronomy is intended to function as a foundational and ongoing teaching document necessitated by the reality of human death and the need to pass the faith on to another generation.

Second, I argue that the *structure* of Deuteronomy is marked by a series of superscriptions that divide the book into sections. These sections trace a literary and theological movement from the story of the past (chaps. 1–4) to the commandments, statutes, and ordinances for the present (chaps. 6–28), to the covenant for the future (chaps. 29–32), and on to the future blessing that Moses prays will come after his death (chaps. 33–34). Deuteronomy 5 is a key structural chapter in so far as

---

1. Manahem Nahum of Chernobyl, *The Book of the Enlightenment of the Eyes,* trans. Arthur Green (New York: Paulist, 1982), 249. For a more contemporary discussion of recurring typologies or patterns in the Torah, cf. Michael Fishbane, "The Sacred Center: The Symbolic Structure of the Bible," in *Texts and Responses: Studies Presented to Nahum N. Glatzer,* ed. M. A. Fishbane and Paul Mendes-Flohr (Leiden: Brill, 1975), 6–27.

it provides a summation and road map of this overall structure of the book.

Third, I argue that the death of Moses in Deuteronomy 34 is an important *recurring theme* that weaves its way into the fabric of the entire book. Deuteronomy repeatedly intertwines the death of Moses with the death and exile of the people of Israel as a whole. The theme of Moses' death functions in two ways. On the one hand, it provides a paradigm by which Israel may understand its own human limits, struggles, and failures as the people of God. On the other hand, Moses' death provides a metaphor for the possibilities of moving through the agony of exilic death and loss to the hope of life and blessing.

FORM: DEUTERONOMY AS CATECHESIS

Past attempts to define the form or genre of the text of Deuteronomy have typically focused either on the form of some earlier stage in the formation of the book or on one major part of the book that ignores other crucial parts. Biblical scholars have offered primarily four options for describing the basic form of Deuteronomy: covenant, sermon, law code, and constitution. Each of these proposals for the genre or form of Deuteronomy reflects some but not all of the truth about Deuteronomy in its present form.

The word covenant (Hebrew *běrît*) does occur in Deuteronomy in two contexts. Deuteronomy 9:9, 11, 15 refer to the Ten Commandments as "the tablets of the covenant." Deuteronomy 29:1 functions as a title for chapters 29–32 and calls that particular section of Deuteronomy a covenant: "These are the words of the covenant . . . in the land of Moab." Nowhere, however, does Deuteronomy use the term *covenant* to refer to itself as a whole book. Some parts of Deuteronomy reveal traces of influence probably from Neo-Assyrian treaty or covenant forms dating from the eighth or seventh century B.C.E. But the present form of Deuteronomy as a whole is not a covenant.[2]

---

2. Discussions of Deuteronomy and the ancient Near Eastern treaty or covenant form were sparked in large part by George Mendenhall, *Law and Covenant in Israel and the Ancient Near East* (Pittsburgh: Biblical Colloquium, 1955). A comprehensive survey of the topic is Dennis J. McCarthy, *Treaty and Covenant,* AnBib 21A, 2d ed. (Rome: Pontifical Biblical Institute, 1978).

Because of the identification of Deuteronomy with the story of King Josiah's reform in 2 Kings 22–23, many scholars in the past have assumed that the bulk of Deuteronomy was written during Josiah's reign. This, they argue, would have been an opportune time for the Deuteronomists to become acquainted with Neo-Assyrian treaty forms. But archaeological evidence from the excavation of an Israelite shrine at Tel 'Arad has confirmed that the Deuteronomic call for the centralization of worship in Israel and the

Gerhard von Rad argued that Deuteronomy was a homiletical summary or sermon based on vestiges of an actual liturgy of covenant renewal from the northern Israelite sanctuary at Shechem. This liturgical material was reworked into sermons preached by rural Levitical priests who traveled throughout the nation. Deuteronomy represents a summary of such preaching put into the mouth of Moses.[3] This proposal has little historical evidence to support it. Moreover, the present form of Deuteronomy sees itself more as a written document rather than simply oral proclamation. Finally, Deuteronomy's present form moves from being the sole possession of Levitical priests to entrusting "all the elders of Israel" with the teaching of *torah* (31:9; cf. 27:1).[4]

Other scholars have proposed the Hebrew term *torah* as the best description of Deuteronomy's form and function as a book. Deuteronomy is in fact the only book of the Pentateuch that refers to itself as *torah* (cf. 1:5; 4:8, 44; 17:18-19; 27:3, 8, 26; 28:58, 61; 29:28; 31:9, 11, 12, 24; 32:46; and "this book of the *torah*" in 29:20; 30:10; and 31:26). But how is *torah* best translated in the context of Deuteronomy? Some have taken a cue from the common name of the book, Deuteronomy. "Deuteronomy" derives from the Greek (Septuagint) translation of the Hebrew phrase in 17:18. This verse commands the king of Israel to study "a copy of this *torah*" (cf. the same phrase in Josh. 8:32). The Greek translators rendered this phrase somewhat inaccurately as *deuteronomion touto,* "this second [or repeated] law." The Hebrew word *torah* came to be translated by the Greek word *nomos,* or "law." The book of Deuteronomy was thus understood as a second law, a repetition and updating of the first law given in the

---

destruction of other competing sanctuaries (Deuteronomy 12) occurred not only in the reign of Josiah but also in the reign of Hezekiah. Thus, influence from Neo-Assyrian covenant forms may date at least from the time of Hezekiah. Cf. Norbert Lohfink, "Deuteronomy," *IDBSup,* 229-32; Moshe Weinfeld, *Deuteronomy and the Deuteronomic School* (Oxford: Clarendon, 1972); idem, "Traces of Assyrian Treaty Formulae in Deuteronomy," *Bib* 46 (1965): 417-27.

3. Gerhard von Rad, *Deuteronomy,* trans. Dorothea Barton, OTL (Philadelphia: Westminster, 1966); idem, *Studies in Deuteronomy,* trans. David Stalker, SBT 1/9 (London: SCM, 1953).

4. Some scholars have argued that Deuteronomy was not produced by Levites but more broadly by the elders in Israel. Cf. Leslie J. Hoppe, "The Levitical Origins of Deuteronomy Reconsidered," *BibRev* 28 (1983): 27-36; idem, "Elders and Deuteronomy: A Proposal," *EgT* 14 (1983): 259-72. Hoppe argues that after the exile the elders were the only group who remained with sufficient authority to administer governing functions in the exilic and postexilic periods. For a somewhat different perspective, cf. Joachim Buchholz, *Die Ältesten Israels in Deuteronomium,* GTA 36 (Göttingen: Vandenhoeck & Ruprecht, 1988).

book of Exodus at Mount Sinai, also known as Mount Horeb.[5] In some ways, this understanding is literally true. About fifty percent of the laws in the so-called Book of the Covenant in Exod. 20:23 − 23:33 are repeated in Deuteronomy. But only chapters 12–28 of Deuteronomy may properly be described as anything like a law code. This designation ignores much of the rest of the book, which includes narratives, liturgical material, poetic songs, and blessings.

In a more recent proposal, S. Dean McBride, Jr. uses as a starting point the observation of the Jewish historian Josephus (late first century C.E.) that Deuteronomy was the "*torah*" in the sense of being the national "polity" or "constitution" of the people of Israel.[6] In the light of some apparent parallels between Deuteronomy's laws and the reforms of religious centralization under King Hezekiah (2 Kings 18:1-8) and King Josiah (2 Kings 22–23), it is probable that some *earlier* form of Deuteronomy did influence political and religious policies in Judah and in this extended sense functioned as a national constitution. But the loss of the nation and the editing of Deuteronomy during Judah's exile to Babylon in 587 B.C.E. conspired to shift Deuteronomy's function away from its role as a political constitution. In exile, Judah as a political state evaporated, and Deuteronomy became something else.[7]

5. The identification of "the book of the law" found by King Josiah in 2 Kings 22–23 prompted some scholars to translate the Deuteronomic book of the *torah* by "the book of the law." This was the conclusion of Julius Wellhausen, *Die Composition des Hexateuchs und der historischen Bücher des Alten Testaments,* 3d ed. (Berlin: Georg Reimer, 1899); idem, *Prolegomena to the History of Ancient Israel,* trans. J. S. Black and A. Menzies (Edinburgh: A. & C. Black, 1885).

Wellhausen was dependent in this regard on the work of Wilhelm M. L. de Wette, *Dissertatio critica qua Deuteronomium a prioribus Pentateuchi libris diversum, alius cujusdam recentioris auctoris opus esse monstratur* (Jena: Etzdorf, 1805). While de Wette was one of the first modern scholars to identify Deuteronomy with the law book found in 2 Kings 22–23, others long before him, including the church father Jerome, had entertained such thoughts.

Notable parallels with Josiah's reform program in 2 Kings 23 are found in Deut. 12:1-7; 16:21-22; 17:3; 18:1-11; 23:17-18.

6. Josephus, *Antiquities of the Jews,* 4.176–331. Cf. S. Dean McBride, "Polity of the Covenant People," *Int* 41 (1987): 229–44; idem, "Deuteronomium," *TRE* 8:531.

7. Udo Rüterswörden (*Von der politischen Gemeinschaft zur Gemeinde: Studien zu Dt. 16,18 − 18,22,* BBB 65 [Frankfurt am Main: Athenaeum, 1987]) argues from his study of the laws concerning political authorities in Deuteronomy 16–18 that these laws functioned at an earlier stage in Deuteronomy as a kind of national constitution. But the Babylonian exile caused a dramatic reinterpretation of Israel as it moved from a political state with territory to a community or association of people, constituted in the exile not by a political constitution but by a *torah* whose meaning became something other than a national constitution.

McBride is correct to focus on the term *torah*. But the identification of *torah* with "constitution" misses the connotations of "teaching" and "instruction" that are part of the semantic range of *torah* and part of the central didactic concern of the present form of Deuteronomy.[8] A constitution is not so much taught as it is legislated and enforced. The present book of Deuteronomy does not legislate as much as it teaches. Some influence from the wisdom tradition within ancient Israel may be responsible for Deuteronomy's strong emphasis on teaching and learning.[9]

The proposals of covenant, sermon, law code, and constitution have all highlighted important aspects of the book of Deuteronomy. The notion of covenant contributes the sense of a structure to the relationship between God and the people envisioned by Deuteronomy. Von Rad's emphasis on the sermon highlights Deuteronomy's concern for proclamation and exhortation; its words seek to move a people to faith and obedience. The focus on the book as a law code places the spotlight on one important part of the book but leaves out other narrative and poetic sections. The proposal that Deuteronomy is a constitution comes closest among all the preceding proposals in laying out its form and function. Deuteronomy is intended to be the basis for a community's identity and life. The book does provide a succinct and condensed summation of what the community is to be. Some interest in the structures of governance is evident as would be expected in a constitution.

But is there a translation of the rich term *torah* that more fully captures its meaning in Deuteronomy? How could one describe the unique form of Deuteronomy that includes these elements (structured relationship, proclamation, the role of law, summation of the community's identity and practice) as well as other important features left out by earlier proposals (the role of teaching, passing the faith from one generation to the next, the focus on the family as well as the larger national community, the focus on theology and its practical implications for daily life)? In my judgment, Deuteronomy as *torah* is best

8. Barnabas Lindars, "Torah in Deuteronomy," in *Words and Meanings: Essays Presented to David Winton Thomas,* ed. Peter Ackroyd and Barnabas Lindars (Cambridge: Cambridge Univ. Press, 1968), 117–36. Of the term *torah,* Lindars writes: "The term retains its didactic overtones, and to say 'the book of the divine instruction' might represent the real meaning better than the usual translation 'the book of the law'" (p. 131). Cf. also A. D. H. Mayes, *Deuteronomy,* NCBC (repr. Grand Rapids: Eerdmans, 1981), 116–17. Walter Brueggemann also notes that Deuteronomy is "intentionally a teaching literature" (*The Creative Word* [Philadelphia: Fortress, 1982], 37).
9. See Weinfeld, *Deuteronomy and the Deuteronomic School,* esp. 244–306.

understood as a program of *catechesis.* What do I mean by this designation?

Catechesis in this broad sense is the process of education in faith from one generation to another based on a distillation of essential tradition. As noted above, the meaning of the word *torah* includes this catechetical dimension of teaching and guidance. So when Deuteronomy calls itself *torah,* it calls itself a teaching book. Apart from the word *torah,* synonyms for the word *teach* occur at least seventeen times in Deuteronomy.[10] More importantly, one of the primary functions of Moses in Deuteronomy is to be a model teacher (1:5; 4:1, 5; 4:14; 5:31; 31:19, 22). Deuteronomy gives specific instructions and mechanisms for transferring this teaching function in later generations from Moses to the priests, Levites, and elders (31:9-13) and to parents who are enjoined to teach their children this *torah* (4:9, 10; 6:7; 11:19).

The overall framework and literary setting for the present form of Deuteronomy likewise exemplify this catechetical purpose. The structure of the book focuses on passing the story, law, and covenant from one old generation to another new generation of God's people. Whatever its previous functions, Deuteronomy in its present form functions as Moses' last words before his death to a new generation standing on the edge of the promised land (1:1-5; 4:14). The structure of this catechism of Deuteronomy provides the paradigm or model for the life of faith in every new generation of God's people. Since the creation story of Genesis 1, the narrative of the Pentateuch has told the story of the world and of the people of God. But in Deuteronomy, the narrative pauses to teach what this foundational story means for every new generation.

Catechesis in the Deuteronomic mode implies a number of corollaries beyond interest in educating or socializing a new generation in the community's tradition. Deuteronomic catechesis is theologically centered, humanly adaptable, form-critically inclusive, socially transformative, and communally oriented.

1. *Catechesis is theologically centered.* The term *catechesis* implies education from a theological perspective. Deuteronomy is primarily a word of and about God and the implications which spring from that word for human relationships to God, to other humans, and to the wider world of nature. Deuteronomy is the closest thing we have in the Old Testament to a systematic catechism or theology. Deuteronomy

---

10. Hebrew verbs meaning "to teach" or its equivalent occur in Deut. 1:5; 4:1, 5, 10, 14; 5:31; 6:1, 7; 11:19; 17:11; 20:18; 24:8; 31:19, 22; 33:10.

presents itself as the mature and final summation of the wisdom and insight of an individual, Moses. But the scholarly acknowledgment of multiple authors and editors of Deuteronomy suggests that Moses here stands not only for the important leadership of one individual but also for the authority and accumulated experience of a community that has spanned generations of life experience under God. It is a theology forged in the hot fires of suffering and loss and cooled in the soothing waters of the grace and hope given by God. Deuteronomy knows that faith in God forms the only realistic basis of hope for God's people. Even the remarkable Moses must die outside the promised land, leaving God to continue the journey with God's people.

2. *Catechesis is humanly adaptable.* The image of an ongoing journey is central to Deuteronomy's vision of catechesis. Moses dies without entering the promised land (Deuteronomy 34). The end or goal remains for him and the community he leads an elusive and future-oriented vision of hope. Deuteronomy does contain a fixed core of tradition, expressed most clearly by the Ten Commandments (chap. 5). The Ten Commandments are the only words spoken directly by God to the people. The rest of Deuteronomy is a secondary interpretation of the Decalogue, humanly mediated through the prophet-teacher Moses. Deuteronomy does not claim to be the final and exhaustive catechism for all time. A new prophet like Moses will come with new words of interpretation (18:15). Mechanisms for ongoing human teaching and interpretation in future generations are established (chaps. 29–32). Catechesis is an ongoing and adaptive process. The rabbinic saying is true: "What is Torah? It is the exposition of Torah."[11] Deuteronomic catechesis is an ever-changing process of exposition and exploration of *torah* for new times and places.

3. *Catechesis is form-critically inclusive.* The use of catechesis as a genre designation for Deuteronomy takes advantage of its capacity to include a variety of other subforms or genres found in individual sections of Deuteronomy. The form of Deuteronomy as a whole includes elements of a law code, a covenant, and a constitution. The term *catechesis* or *catechism* is able to incorporate elements of these prior forms under its umbrella, elements that are clearly present in the final form of Deuteronomy: words/narratives, commandments, statutes and ordinances, speeches, covenant, song, blessing, and so on. Deuter-

11. Quoted in Jacob Weingreen, *From Bible to Mishnah: The Continuity of Tradition* (New York: Holmes and Meier, 1976), 153.

onomic catechesis uses a variety of methods and forms to achieve its goals.

4. *Catechesis is socially transformative.* Like a law code, an effective catechetical program has power to shape and transform the thoughts, attitudes, and behaviors of individuals and whole communities. Unlike a law code, however, catechesis attains such power not through enforcement but through persuasion and conviction. Hence, even among the laws in Deuteronomy, the reader frequently finds motive clauses that provide reasons why the laws should be followed.[12] Deuteronomy provides a persuasive and compelling model for understanding God, humans, and the world. This theological understanding in turn has quite specific and practical implications for daily life, exemplified in the commandments and laws of chapters 5–28. The interplay of faith and obedience, worship and social ethics, lies at the heart of a mature theology as exemplified in Deuteronomy.

5. *Catechesis is communally oriented.* In contrast to the rampant illusion of individualism in much of contemporary society, Deuteronomy is passionately communal and relational.[13] The individual is intimately tied to and interdependent in his or her relationship to God, to the community, and to the world at large. Deuteronomy deals with the wide variety of relationships—God's relationship to humans, human relationships within the faith community, the relationship of the people of God to other peoples and nations, and the relationship of humans to creation. The various functions of community are treated: worshiping, witnessing, marrying, parenting, governing, adjudicating, loving, rejoicing, learning, farming, buying, selling, cooking, and working. Deuteronomy even creates communities across generational lines: the present-day community becomes one with generations past and generations future (4:25-31; 5:3-5; 28:36-46).

To call Deuteronomy communal catechesis is not to suggest that

---

12. See Pinchas Doron, "Motive Clauses in the Laws of Deuteronomy: Their Forms, Functions and Contents," *HAR* 2 (1978): 61–77.

13. Cf. Robert Bellah et al., *Habits of the Heart: Individualism and Commitment in American Life* (New York: Harper & Row, 1985); and Christopher Lasch, *The Culture of Narcissism* (New York: Warner Books, 1979). I stress the "illusion" of modern individualism since it is often the corporate and structural ethos of modern society that subtly imposes its self-serving values of individualism upon people. We are in part inevitably enslaved to psychological, social, economic, and political forces whose communal or institutional sources transcend the individual. As we will see, Deuteronomy would name such forces as false gods of death that oppose its alternative vision of interdependency.

Deuteronomy swallows up or makes invisible the individual human being. Indeed, Deuteronomy often alternates in addressing the rea ler both as a plural "you" (communal) and as a singular "you" (individual). Although this alternation is not always apparent in English translations, it is clear in the original Hebrew text. The alternation between singular and plural "you" occurs at times within a single verse (e.g., 6:3; 7:4) or often within an otherwise coherent single section (e.g., 4:1-40; 6:13-19).[14] The language of Deuteronomy seems able to move easily and fluidly between individuals and the community as a whole in its address without obliterating the viability of one or the other.[15]

The emphasis of Deuteronomy is not only on how people relate as individuals to others within a given community. This communal catechesis is also concerned to shape the structural and institutional life of the community. Fully aware of individual human fallibility, Deuteronomy sets up specific mechanisms and structures to regulate community life and governance to curb systemic evil and widespread unfaithfulness (e.g., the centralization of worship in chap. 12, the slave laws of chap. 15, or the laws concerning the authority of kings, prophets, priests, and judges in chaps. 17-18). From beginning to end, Deuteronomy envisions the life of faith as a communal enterprise. It is for the nurture of that community that Deuteronomy sets out its programmatic *torah*.

STRUCTURE: DEUTERONOMY'S FIVE SUPERSCRIPTIONS

The book of Deuteronomy is *torah,* a program of communal catechesis. But what is the structure of this *torah?* Does Deuteronomy provide any clear markers of how one may divide the book as an aid to discerning the movement of its thought and theology? Reading through the book, one notices five important editorial superscriptions that mark the major sections of Deuteronomy:

14. Some scholars have assumed that these alternations between singular and plural address signal different sources, editorial hands, or stylistic clues to distinguish thematic sections. On sources, cf. C. Steuernagel, *Das Deuteronomium,* HKAT, 2d ed. (Göttingen: Vandenhoeck & Ruprecht, 1923), 4. On editorial layers, cf. G. Minette de Tillesse, "Sections 'tu' et sections 'vous' dans le Deutéronome," *VT* 12 (1962): 29-87. On the use of the alternations to distinguish thematic sections on stylistic grounds, cf. Norbert Lohfink, *Das Hauptgebot: Eine Untersuchung literarischer Einleitungsfragen zu Dtn 5-11,* AnBib 20 (Rome: Pontifical Biblical Institute, 1963), 239-60.

15. Other related ancient Near Eastern documents outside the Old Testament exhibit a similar fluidity in moving between sinfular and plural address. Cf. Klaus Baltzer, *The Covenant Formulary,* trans. David Green (Philadelphia: Fortress, 1971), 33 n. 71.

- "These are the words" (1:1)
- "This is the *torah*" (4:44)
- "This is the commandment—the statutes and the ordinances" (6:1)
- "These are the words of the covenant" (29:1)
- "This is the blessing" (33:1)

These editorial superscriptions have a similar form and are typically accompanied by notations that situate the time or place when Moses spoke the words which follow.[16] The other ingredient in discerning this structure is Deuteronomy 5. As our exploration of Deuteronomy unfolds, we will discover that the structure of Deuteronomy 5 functions as a miniature version of the structure of the whole book. Chapter 5 is the *torah* of Deuteronomy *en nuce*. I explore the significance of that feature in chapter 3, which is devoted to a study of Deuteronomy 5. For now, however, I may depict the structure of Deuteronomy in the light of the superscriptions and their relation to Deuteronomy 5 as in diagram 1 (p. 16).

Diagram 1 corresponds visually to the image of the relationship of the Ten Commandments (chap. 5) and the rest of the book of Deuteronomy as portrayed in 31:26. There Moses commands the Levites to place the written book of the *torah* (Deuteronomy) "beside" the ark of the covenant. While the book of the *torah* is *beside* the ark, the stone tablets containing the Ten Commandments (corresponding to chap. 5) are *inside* the ark (10:5). The Decalogue's placement inside the ark suggests its primal and authoritative character. Therefore, in relation to the Ten Commandments in chapter 5, the rest of Deuteronomy is

---

16. An early example of a commentator who noted the structuring role of the editorial superscriptions in Deuteronomy is Paul Kleinert, *Das Deuteronomium und der Deuteronomiker* (Leipzig: J. C. Hinrich, 1872), 167. The significance of the superscriptions has been developed more thoroughly in some recent studies, including Robert Polzin, *Moses and the Deuteronomist* (New York: Seabury, 1980), 30; McBride, "Polity," 231; and Norbert Lohfink, "Der Bundesschluss im Land Moab: Redaktionsgeschichtliches zu Dt 28, 69−32,47," *BZ* 6 (1962): 35−56. An interesting analysis of the significance of these editorial superscriptions for Lohfink's interpretive strategy is Robert Robinson, *Roman Catholic Exegesis Since Divino Afflante Spiritu: Hermeneutical Implications* (Atlanta: Scholars Press, 1988), 105–48. On the basis of form, Gottfried Seitz (*Redaktionsgeschichtliche Studien zum Deuteronomium* [Stuttgart: Kohlhammer, 1971]) distinguished two stages in the addition of these editorial superscriptions. The earliest stage involved the addition of the superscriptions in 4:45; 6:1; and 12:1, largely associated with the law code. A second set of superscriptions was edited into Deuteronomy as other material was added to the law code: 1:1; 4:44; 29:1 (Hebrew 28:69); and 33:1. In the present form of Deuteronomy, the superscriptions function together at the same semantic level to structure the book as a whole.

Diagram 1

"This is the
torah" — 4:44

	Chapter 5 Torah in a Nutshell	
	5:1-5 — Deuteronomy's overall theme: "for you" "today"	
Chaps. 1–4 "These are the words" — 1:1 PAST STORY	5:6 — "I am the LORD who brought you out of Egypt"	
	5:7-21 — The Ten Commandments	Chaps. 6–28 "This is the commandment — the statutes and the ordi- nances" (6:1) LAW FOR THE PRESENT
	5:22-31 — Moses as future covenant mediator	Chaps. 29–32 "These are the words of the covenant" (29:1) NEW COVENANT FOR THE FUTURE
	5:32-33 — "so that you may live, and that it may go well with you"	Chaps. 33–34 "This is the blessing" (33:1) BLESSING FOR FUTURE GENERATIONS: THROUGH DEATH TO LIFE

visualized as extended and secondary commentary or exposition of the primal Decalogue.

The significance of this structure of Deuteronomy will emerge as we work through the chapters in sequence. But the global structure of the book already reveals at this preliminary stage some major movements. The past is recalled in order to shape the present life of the community and in order to thrust the community always toward the future, both a future near at hand and a future more distant. The community of faith is rooted in the past, active in the present, but always open to and yearning for God's new future.

The superscriptions and their correlation with the structure of Deuteronomy 5 give us the key to the overarching structure and movement of the book of Deuteronomy as a whole. Thus, Deuteronomy's form is *torah,* catechesis cast as Moses' last words to a new generation standing on the edge of the promised land. This *torah* (summarized in Deuteronomy 5) moves from

1. the community-forming story of God's grace from the past in chapters 1–4 to
2. the community-shaping law to guide the present in chapters 6–28 to
3. the community-sustaining provisions for a new covenant with future generations in chapters 29–32 to
4. God's ultimate blessing of the community as it moves through death to life in chapters 33–34.

In both form and structure, the book of Deuteronomy intends to bring readers of every age to claim its *torah* as their own. Moses' words to the ancient Israelites beckon each new generation: "Not with our ancestors did the LORD make this covenant, but with us, who are all of us here alive today" (5:3). The contemporary reader is invited to join Deuteronomy in a transformative journey that leads from past to present and on to a future yet to be revealed.

RECURRING THEME: THE DEATH OF MOSES

The final scene in the book of Deuteronomy is the death and burial of the leader Moses outside the promised land (chap. 34). In my judgment, the importance of this theme for the entire book of Deuteronomy has not been fully appreciated in previous studies or commentaries on Deuteronomy. Moses' death outside the land of promise is a central metaphor for the reality of human finitude at both an individual and a corporate level. For each Israelite and for Israel as a whole, Moses was a reminder that the full experience of the promised land would always in some way be beyond their grasp. Moses' demise is a metaphor for the necessary and inevitable losses and limits of human life and power before God.

But at the same time, Moses' death functions in Deuteronomy in a positive sense. It is a paradigm for the vocation of sacrificial giving. Moses gave his life for the sake of the community's future. Moses' death outside the land in some way opened the path for the rebellious Israelites to continue their journey toward the promised land. But Moses' death is not the final word. God's compassion and blessing continue and provide a basis for ultimate hope in the midst of death and loss.

In the following chapters I work out the full significance of the recurring theme of Moses' death for Deuteronomy. But a preliminary glimpse of some important contact points between Moses' death in chapter 34 and the rest of Deuteronomy will help orient the reader.

DEUTERONOMY 1–4 AND THE DEATH OF MOSES

The first narrative in the book of Deuteronomy is a brief account of Moses giving up some of his authority by appointing a large number of other leaders for the people (1:9-18). This is Moses' first act recounted in Deuteronomy. It is an act of letting go, relinquishing, a kind of dying.

The next major narrative is a retelling of the spy story from Numbers 13–14 (Deut. 1:19—2:25). In the spy story, God condemns the old wilderness generation of rebellious Israelites to wander for the rest of their lives in the wilderness. God denies them entry into the promised land. The last major narrative at the end of the book (chap. 34) is the account of Moses' death outside the land. As this study will show, these two narratives at the beginning and end of Deuteronomy have numerous parallels in the way they are told. They form a key interpretive framework as an inclusio for the entire book. Moses' death is explicitly linked several times with the fate of all Israel. Negatively, Moses' death is associated with the judgment on the old generation of Israelites (1:37; 3:23-27). Positively, Moses' death in some way opens up the possibility that a new generation of Israelites will be able to enter the land (4:21-22). But Moses' fate of dying outside the land remains an ongoing possibility for future generations (4:25-31).

DEUTERONOMY 5 AND THE DEATH OF MOSES

This key chapter recounts the giving of the Ten Commandments at Mount Horeb, where Moses is put at risk for the sake of the people. The Israelites say to Moses, "Why should we die? . . . If we hear the voice of the LORD our God any longer, we shall die. . . . Go near, you yourself, and hear all that the LORD our God will say" (5:25-27). The implication is clear. Any human who hears the voice of the holy God will die. Afraid of such a death, the people ask Moses to stand in their stead as a mediator between them and God. Moses stands in the place of death for the sake of the people.

In the end, Moses will die outside the land. The burden of mediating God's word will lead to the premature death of the greatest prophet Israel ever had (34:10-12).

DEUTERONOMY 6–11 AND THE DEATH OF MOSES

Deuteronomy 6–11 are an extended commentary on the first of the Ten Commandments, "you shall have no other gods before me" (5:7). God, not Moses, is the one whom the people must worship: "Hear, O Israel: The LORD is our God, the LORD alone" (6:4). One of the "other gods" whom Israel and its neighbors were tempted to worship were dead ancestors, the cult of the dead. But 34:6 notes that Moses' burial place is unknown and thus incapable of becoming a cultic site for the worship of the ancestor Moses.

In this section one may also see the motif of Moses' death in Moses' retelling of the golden calf story (9:8 – 10:11). Although Moses' death is not explicitly noted, Moses does relinquish his own glory for the sake of the people. After the people worship the golden calf, an angry God tells Moses that the Israelites will be destroyed. God promises to make Moses alone into a nation mightier and greater than the Israelites (9:14). But Moses chooses to let his own ambitions die in order that the people might live. In a posture resembling death, Moses lays prostrate before God for forty days and forty nights. He eats no bread and drinks no water, denying himself the basics of life (9:18). Moses intercedes on behalf of the life of the people and of Aaron. Remarkably, God listens to Moses and allows the Israelites to live (9:19, 20; 10:10).

DEUTERONOMY 12–28 AND THE DEATH OF MOSES

In a series of introductory observations to the study of the statutes and ordinances in Deuteronomy 12–28, I will note how the language of "death" and "dying" saturates these laws. Indeed, many of the laws speak of the need to relinquish the gifts from God. Paradoxically, such giving or "dying" to one's self leads to joy and blessing. Moses gave up his dearest wish of setting foot on the land and so brought life and blessing to a new generation. Many of the laws have been shaped to follow this same Mosaic paradigm: through death and letting go comes life and blessing for others and joy for oneself.

One important and specific reference to Moses' death occurs in Deut. 18:15–19. Here Moses promises that God will raise up a new "prophet like me" in the future after Moses' death. This promise is understood as a continuing response to the people's request at Mount Horeb that Moses be a mediator. The people did not want to hear God's word directly, lest they die. Thus, God will raise up again after Moses another prophet like Moses. Such a prophet in the mold of Moses will also presumably die outside the promised land. Among the Old Testament prophets, Jeremiah comes most readily to mind as a candidate for the role of "a prophet like Moses." Jeremiah suffers as a mediator of

God's word. Like Moses, Jeremiah ends up outside the promised land in Egypt, not knowing whether his prophecies of hope and restoration would ever be fulfilled (Jeremiah 43).

I will note other laws among the statutes and ordinances that resonate with the theme of Moses' death outside the land. Many of the laws have to do with giving something up, letting go, dying, or acknowledging the limits of human abilities, knowledge, and laws. The laws themselves are humanly mediated words that one must see as provisional, subject to interpretation, and not the final word. God alone remains the judge and sovereign over all things, even over God's laws. Like Moses and all human creations or activities, the laws are not gods or idols. They are subject to the ebb and flow of time and history and the forces of death. They are necessary, but they will not enable the people of Israel to arrive at the promised land. As we shall see in the movement of Deuteronomy's structure, the law in itself will lead ultimately to curse, exile, and death outside the land (Deut. 28:45-68).

DEUTERONOMY 29–32 AND THE DEATH OF MOSES

Deuteronomy 29:1 introduces a new covenant at Moab "in addition to" the covenant made at Horeb with the Ten Commandments. This new covenant of Moab divides into three section in chapters 29–32: (1) Chapters 29–30—a ritual of covenant making; (2) chapter 31—the transfer of leadership from Moses to Joshua and the writing of the book of the *torah;* and (3) chapter 32—the Song of Moses. Each of the three sections follows a similar movement of thought from the limits of humans to the unlimited compassion of God that transcends the boundaries of human time, space, and mortality. In the Song of Moses, God proclaims God's sovereign power over life and death:

> There is no god beside me.
> I kill and I make alive;
> I wound and I heal;
> and no one can deliver from my hand. (32:39)

Yahweh's divine power is not arbitrary but moves God's people through death to life. Divine love and deliverance come as human power is relinquished:

> Indeed the LORD will . . . have compassion on his servants,
> when he sees that their power is gone,
> neither bond nor free remaining. (32:36)

Deliverance and blessing come as God's people are catechized not only into the death of the rebellious and self-serving community but also into the emergent life of obedience and trust in God alone. The covenant-making liturgy in chapters 29–30 moves through the future exile and death of the community to the promise of restoration and God's shaping of the people into obedient doers of God's will. The Song of Moses likewise recounts the movement of Israel through judgment and death to life and hope.

Situated between these two communal portraits of Israel's death and life is Deuteronomy 31. This chapter highlights the crisis of leadership and direction created by the imminent death of Moses. Deuteronomy 31 notes repeatedly the nearness of Moses' death (31:2, 14, 16, 27, 29). Moses is a unique leader and prophet. He will be replaced not just by another human leader but by a combination of a human leader (Joshua in addition to all the elders, Levites, and parents responsible for catechizing the young), a written normative text ("the book of the *torah*"), and a song (the Song of Moses). The transfer of Moses' leadership to Joshua, a book, and a song involves a kind of dying for Moses, a letting go of identity and power.

DEUTERONOMY 33–34 AND THE DEATH OF MOSES

Deuteronomy 34 is the actual account of Moses' death on top of Mount Nebo. This account is the culminating episode of the present book of Deuteronomy; all the recurring allusions to Moses' death throughout Deuteronomy finally flow into this last scene. I will say more about the significance of this climactic scene in chapter 8. But even Moses' blessing of the twelve tribes of Israel in Deuteronomy 33 participates in this theme of Moses' death. The act of prayer and the request that God bless some person or group is an acknowledgment of human limits and finitude. Intercessory prayer to God recognizes human limitations in working for and ensuring the well-being of others. Moses' last words are a prayer of blessing to the God who alone transcends the limits of human power and mortality.

The *theme* of Moses' death outside the promised land is also integrally tied to the book's present form and larger structure. The *form* of catechesis is a multifaceted strategy for passing faith on from one generation to the next. An old generation in the process of dying teaches faith to another generation maturing into life. Deuteronomy presents Moses as Israel's first formal catechist, teaching on the eve of his death what is essential for life. The catechesis of a new generation is a tacit confession that he will soon die.

The *structure and theological movement* of Deuteronomy also participate in the theme of Moses' death. The structure moves from past story to present imperatives to a new covenant and a prayer for future blessing. In each of the major sections, the experience of God's people moves through death to life. Human limits and the press of death are overcome only through the God who "kills and makes alive," "wounds and heals" from generation to generation. Thus, form, structure, and theme serve one another in the overall movement of Deuteronomy from death to life.

CHAPTER 2

"These Are the Words" —
Deuteronomy 1–4: A Story
of Faithfulness and Rebellion

You were angry with [our ancestors] to the point of destroying them but you had compassion on them in your love for them on account of your covenant because Moses atoned for their sin.

— A prayer from the Dead Sea Scrolls[1]

Deuteronomy 1–4 begin by relating the community-forming story of God's mercy and the people's disobedience. This first section of Moses' address to the Israelites may be outlined as follows:

I. Situating the time and place (1:1-5)
II. A rehearsal of the past story of God's grace and human failure from Mount Horeb to the edge of the promised land (1:6 – 3:29)
III. Interpreting the past story for the sake of the future of God's people (4:1-40)
IV. The concluding frame to Moses' first address: the cities of refuge (4:41-43)

This introductory narrative section in Deuteronomy 1–4 appears to have been artfully reconstructed out of material that already existed elsewhere in literary form. For example, all the stories in chapters 1–3 have parallels in the book of Numbers, with some allusions to material in the book of Joshua as well.[2] But this disparate material has been shaped in new ways by the later editors of Deuteronomy into a new and

---

1. A prayer found as part of the Dead Sea Scrolls in Qumran Cave 4 – 4Q505, F1-2.2 published in M. Baillet, *Qumran grotte 4 III, Discoveries in the Judaean Desert, VII* (Oxford: Clarendon, 1982), 139-40.
2. See Lothar Perlitt, "Deuteronomium 1-3 im Streit der exegetischen Methoden," in *Das Deuteronomium: Entstehung, Gestalt und Botschaft,* ed. Norbert Lohfink, BETL 68 (Leuven: Leuven Univ. Press, 1985), 149-63.

coherent narrative that defines the community's foundational identity, values, behavior, and future hopes.

DEUTERONOMY 1: MOSES, DEATH, AND THE OLD GENERATION

DEUT. 1:1-8: THE IMAGE OF A COMMUNITY ON THE WAY

Verses 1-8 set the stage and define the essence of this new generation of God's people who now stand poised on the edge of the promised land. Moses begins his last words to this new community by reminding them of the events that began around Mount Horeb (or Mount Sinai as it is called in the book of Exodus). They could not stay around the security and comfort of that mountain, but God sent them out on a journey. "The LORD our God spoke to us at Horeb, saying, 'You have stayed long enough at this mountain. Resume your journey. . . . See, I have set the land before you; go in and take possession of the land that I swore to your ancestors, to Abraham, to Isaac, and to Jacob, to give to them and to their descendants after them'" (vv. 6-8). Like their ancestors, this new generation is a pilgrim people called to journey into the future.

DEUT. 1:9-18: SHARED LEADERSHIP

Moses next chooses one of the stories that capture the nature of leadership in this community. Deuteronomy praises Moses as the greatest of all the leaders and prophets of God's people (34:10-12). Yet the human Moses acknowledges the limits of what he can do as a leader: "I am unable by myself to bear you. . . . How can I bear the heavy burden of your disputes all by myself? Choose for each of your tribes individuals who are wise, discerning, and reputable to be your leaders" (1:9-13).

The last story in the book of Deuteronomy is the story of the death and burial of Moses. The first story in Deuteronomy is the story of another kind of dying by Moses. It is a dying to exclusive claim on authority, a dying to self-glorification, a dying to hoarding power for oneself rather than sharing and trusting others with it. It is the first stroke of the theme of Deuteronomy—the dying of the old voice of Moses and the rising of the living voice of God for a new generation. Tradition is necessary and defines the community, but it is always tradition that is living and creative. Here a new circumstance is encountered: the growing population makes the present system of leadership untenable. The tradition embodied in Moses' sole leadership gives way to a new solution of sharing power, and the journey moves on.

DEUT. 1:19-46: THE DEATH OF THE OLD
AND THE BIRTH OF THE NEW

The next story captures the foundational experience, both positive and negative, of the community of God. Next to the narrative of the exodus out of Egypt, it is the key story in the whole Pentateuch. It is recounted for the first time in Numbers 13–14. Like the Ten Commandments in Deuteronomy 5, this story is repeated for the benefit of the new generation of God's people as they are about to enter the promised land. It is the spy story of the first entry into Canaan, an entry that was unsuccessful.[3] The story differs in some details and is more condensed in comparison to Numbers 13–14, but the basic plot remains the same.

The outline of the story is as follows:

A. The mission of the spies into Canaan and their report (1:19-25)
B. The response of the people—fear and a yearning for the security and safety of slavery in Egypt (1:26-28)
C. Moses' appeal and the people's refusal (1:29-33)
D. The old generation will die (including Moses) (1:34-40)
E. The people try to take the promise into their own hands (1:41-46)

Verses 19–25 recount the spy mission into Canaan when the Israelites first stood on the southern boundary of the promised land. The Israelites had traveled from Egypt through the desert to reach the edge of the land of Canaan. Before going to receive the land, the Israelites sent in twelve spies to scout out the native cities and inhabitants. The spies return and report, "It is a good land that the LORD our God is giving us." Everything looks hopeful and the excitement mounts as one expects the people to enter the land with confidence and anticipation.

The surprising twist in verses 26-28 is that in spite of the good report and the excitement of the moment, the people refuse to go into the promised land. The spies reported not only that the land was good but also that in Canaan "the people are stronger and taller than we; the cities are large and fortified up to heaven!" The people fear death and defeat at the hand of the Canaanites more than they fear God (v. 27). The spies even mythologize the enemy, saying, "We actually saw there the offspring of the Anakim!" (v. 28). The Anakim were a legendary people of giant proportions (cf. Num. 13:33; Deut. 2:11, 21). The

---

3. For a study of the important role which the earlier version of the spy story in Numbers 13–14 plays in the book of Numbers, cf. my *The Death of the Old and the Birth of the New: The Framework of the Book of Numbers and the Pentateuch,* BJS 71 (Chico, Calif.: Scholars Press, 1985).

people ascribe to these Anakim more power than to their own God, Yahweh. Hence, they refuse to accept God's gift of the land.

In *verses 29-33,* Moses exhorts the Israelites, "Have no dread or fear of them." Moses reminds the people of God's past faithfulness in the old foundational story of the exodus (v. 30) and God's care of Israel in the wilderness: "you saw how the LORD your God carried you, just as one carries a child, all the way that you traveled until you reached this place" (v. 31). But the memory of God's dramatic deliverance or ongoing blessing could not shake loose people's fear: "In spite of this, you have no trust in the LORD your God" (v. 32).

Verses 34-40 outline the punishment for the people's refusal to trust God and to enter the promised land. This old wilderness generation will wander for forty more years in the wilderness until the entire generation dies out (except Joshua and Caleb). Only the new generation ("your little ones . . . your children") will enter the promised land. Ironically, the people's fear of death brings on the very death they feared.

Verses 41-45 relate the people's sudden change of heart. After hearing of Yahweh's anger, they decide to march in and invade the promised land after all. But Moses warns them that God is not "in the midst of you" and thus the invasion will surely fail. The promised land is a gift from God. It is not a human achievement. As Moses warned, Israel is soundly defeated and condemned to wander forty years in the wilderness.

One important note not included in the earlier version of the spy story in Numbers 13–14 but highlighted in Deut. 1:37 is the inclusion of Moses among those who will die in the wilderness. This is a unique Deuteronomic addition to the story. In the book of Numbers, Moses and Aaron were denied entrance into the promised land because of a somewhat unclear violation of God's command at Meribah (Num. 20:12). But in this retelling of the spy story in Deuteronomy 1, the denial of Moses' entry into the land is joined with the spy story in a new combination of motifs. The important theme of Moses' death outside the promised land appears again at the end of chapter 3 at a strategic point in the narrative (vv. 23-29) as well as in the important interpretive section in chapter 4 (vv. 21-22).

The spy story reminds the Israelites that although God has acted as their savior and ally in the past, they cannot take God's compassion for granted. The result of the people's rebellion in the spy story was an "anti-exodus" and an "unholy war" directed by God against Israel.[4]

4. See Norbert Lohfink, "Darstellungskunst und Theologie in Dtn 1,6–3,29," *Bib* 41

Because of its sin, Israel experienced God as enemy, not as friend and deliverer. Yet God could not let the people go. The old wilderness generation will die in the wilderness, but God will lead this new generation into the promised land. In the end, God will find a way to ensure that God's promise and hope have the final word. But the path to that hope and promise is through death and judgment. As we shall see, this movement of the past story will also shape Israel's future hope (Deuteronomy 29–32).

DEUTERONOMY 2–3: ISRAEL AMONG THE NATIONS AND FORETASTES OF THE CONQUEST

In Deut. 1:6, God commanded the people to leave Mount Horeb and resume their journey. In 2:3, God commands the people to leave Kadesh and resume their journey. In the course of the next thirty-eight years in the desert, the entire old wilderness generation dies (2:14–16).

DEUT. 2:1-25: ISRAEL AMONG THE NATIONS

As the people wander through the wilderness, they encounter three other peoples or nations: the people in Seir (also known as Edom), the nation of Moab, and the nation of Ammon. The people in Seir descended from Esau, who was the brother of Jacob, the father of the twelve tribes of Israel (Gen. 25:19-27). These descendants of Esau came to be identified with the area next to Canaan known as Seir or Edom (Gen. 36:8-9). The Moabites and Ammonites were said to be descendants of Lot, the nephew of Israel's ancestor Abraham (Gen. 11:31; 13:1-18). All three of these nations were neighbors to Israel on its eastern border across the Jordan River.

God commands the Israelites not to fight with the people of Seir, Moab, and Ammon since God had already promised them their land as their own possession (Deut. 2:5, 9, 19). In the light of the preceding spy story, chapter 2 plays an important role in reinforcing the themes of chapter 1. God cares for other families and nations of the earth besides Israel. If God can be Israel's enemy as in chapter 1, the corollary in chapter 2 is that God can be friend and ally to peoples and nations other than Israel. This claim is all the more striking since these nations had often been bitter enemies of Israel in the course of its history (Numbers 22–24; 2 Samuel 8; 10; 1 Kings 11; 2 Kings 3; 14).

(1960): 105-34, esp. 110-14, 119-20. Additional insights into the "anti-exodus" and "unholy war" themes, particularly in relation to Deut. 2:14-16, are provided by W. L. Moran, "The End of the Unholy War and the Anti-Exodus," *Bib* 44 (1963): 333-42.

The prophets of Israel sometimes spoke harsh oracles of God's judgment against these and other nations (Amos 1:11 — 2:3). Yet here God protects their land. Israel is reminded again that it cannot presume upon God's favor too easily and too casually. God has other nations and peoples for whom God cares. But God's firm commitment to the promise of land for these other nations of Seir, Moab, and Ammon also has a positive meaning for Israel. God's faithfulness to these three nations gives confidence to the new generation of Israelites that God will likewise make good on the promise of the land given to them.

God's protection of the three foreign nations encourages God's people to recognize the broad horizons of God's work in the world. The stories of creation and all humankind in Genesis 1-11, Israel's vocation as a blessing to "all the families of the earth" (Gen. 12:3), and other witnesses such as Ruth and Jonah echo this inclusive and global concern of God toward peoples and communities other than Israel. Deuteronomy 2 reminds the community of God that it exists for the sake of the larger community and in fact depends on it. Israel will buy food and water from the offspring of Esau (2:6).

DEUT. 2:26 — 3:29: FORETASTES OF THE CONQUEST

Moses next recalls for the new generation the victories that God had won over two kings named Sihon and Og. Their defeat was a common item in Israel's national memory (29:7-8; Num. 21:21-35; Ps. 136:17-22). Although the story of Og's defeat follows the same outline as the defeat of Sihon, the conquest of Og emphasizes more his massive fortresses and high walls, which seemed unconquerable (3:5). The reader hears an echo of the spies' report about the Canaanites in Deuteronomy 1 that led to the people's refusal to enter the promised land: "The cities are large and fortified up to heaven" (1:28). But this time it was different. The people trusted in God in spite of the apparent invincibility of the enemy. And this time God gave them the victory.

The stories of a successful conquest in Deuteronomy 2-3 offer a positive counterbalance to the disobedience and defeat of the spy story in chapter 1. They are glimpses of the future that inspire hope and courage (3:21-22). But glimpses and foretastes are not always enough. Moses confesses his yearning not only to glimpse the promised land but actually to set foot in it:

> At that time, too, I entreated the LORD, saying: "O LORD God, you have only begun to show your servant your greatness and your might; what god in heaven or on earth can perform deeds and mighty acts like yours! Let me cross over to see the good land

beyond the Jordan, that good hill country and the Lebanon." (3:23-25)

Although Moses' prayers on behalf of the people had changed God's mind before (e.g., Exod. 32:11-14; Num. 14:13-25), this time God would not grant Moses' request. Moses recalls:

> But the LORD was very angry with me on your account and would not heed me. The LORD said to me, "Enough from you! Never speak to me of this matter again! Go up to the top of Pisgah and look around you to the west, to the north, to the south, and to the east. Look well, for you shall not cross over this Jordan." (Deut. 3:26-27)

Following this definitive refusal of Moses' request, the narrative returns to the theme sounded at the very beginning of Deuteronomy 1, the relinquishment of Moses' leadership to others (1:9-18). God instructs Moses, "But charge Joshua, and encourage and strengthen him, because it is he who shall cross over at the head of this people and who shall secure their possession of the land that you will see" (3:28).

The Torah or Pentateuch ends with the book of Deuteronomy and a new generation of God's people on the edge of the promised land. But the land is not in their full possession. Like Moses, who here functions as a paradigm, the people remain outside the land and still on their journey. Of course, Israel eventually enters the land, as the book of Joshua recounts. Yet Deuteronomy marks a definitive canonical break as the end of the foundational Pentateuch. This image of the ongoing journey that concludes the Pentateuch remains Israel's defining posture and essence. Like Moses, this fragile community of God could never feel for long that it had fully and finally arrived in the land of Canaan.

DEUTERONOMY 4:1-40: INTERPRETING THE PAST FOR THE SAKE OF THE FUTURE

Moses' first address moves from narration of the past (chaps. 1–3) to application to the future (chap. 4). Some scholars have argued that all or part of Deuteronomy 4 was probably written during the exile of the people of Judah to Babylon in 587 B.C.E. Most consider this chapter one of the latest sections of Deuteronomy to be written,[5] although the

---

5. The exilic dating of Deuteronomy 4 is upheld by most critical scholars; for example, see Jon Levenson, "Who Inserted the Book of the Torah?" *HTR* 68 (1975): 203–33. Chapter 4 is typically considered one of the latest additions to the book of Deuteronomy and thus represents a later reflection and interpretation of its earlier form and themes in the light of the exile. One contested issue is whether chap. 4 is a unified composition written all at once or a text containing older material that has been subsequently edited

words of chapter 4 have been placed in the mouth of Moses as if he was speaking many centuries earlier. Thus, chapter 4 functions as an updated and authoritative interpretation of the book of Deuteronomy and of chapters 1–3 in particular for the time of exile. The primary evidence for this late dating is the apparent reference to an exile and scattering of the people in 4:26-28 and the more developed monotheism of this chapter in relation to other parts of Deuteronomy.[6] The chapter provides a model of ongoing interpretation and reflection on past tradition that keeps the tradition alive and adaptable.

Diagram 2 (p. 31) displays the carefully crafted structure and movement of thought evident in Deuteronomy 4.

The body of the chapter in 4:9-31 is bracketed by an *outer frame* comprised of an introduction (4:1-4) and conclusion (4:40) as well as by an *inner frame* made up of two proclamations of the uniqueness and singularity of Israel and Israel's God (4:5-8 and 4:32-39). But the heart of the chapter is a set of *three teaching paradigms* from past, present,

---

one or more times. Those arguing against the unity of Deuteronomy 4 include von Rad, *Deuteronomy,* trans. Dorothea Barton, OTL (Philadelphia: Westminster, 1966), 48–52; and S. Mittmann, *Deuteronomium 1,1 – 6,3: Literarkritisch und traditionsgeschichtlich Untersucht,* BZAW 139 (Berlin: de Gruyter, 1975), 115–28. The primary evidence for disunity is the laternation of singular and plural second person pronouns, sometimes "you" singular and sometimes "you" plural. The difference is not evident in English translations, but the Hebrew clearly distinguishes between "you" singular and "you" plural. Von Rad and Mittmann would argue that the alternation of pronouns corresponds to an alternation of writers or editors.

Those arguing for the unity of Deuteronomy 4 include Norbert Lohfink, *Höre, Israel! Auslegung von Texten aus dem Buch Deuteronomium* (Düsseldorf: Patmos, 1965), 92–97; Georg Braulik, *Die Mittel deuteronomischer Rhetorik: Erhoben aus Deuteronomium 4,1-40,* AnBib 68 (Rome: Pontifical Biblical Institute, 1978), 91–100; idem, "Literarkritik und archäologische Stratigraphie: Zu S. Mittmanns Analyse von Deuteronomium 4,1-40," *Bib* 59 (1978): 351–83; and A. D. H. Mayes, "Deuteronomy 4 and the Literary Criticism of Deuteronomy," *JBL* 100 (1981): 23–51. In response to the alternating of singular and plural pronouns, these scholars would argue that the writer of chap. 4 is simply imitating the earlier Deuteronomistic style of sections of Deuteronomy where the alternation of pronouns occurs and that may well originally reflect differences in literary or editorial layers (e.g., chaps. 6 or 8). Studies on the phenomenon of pronominal alternation include Christopher Begg, "The Significance of the *Nummerwechsel* in Deuteronomy: The 'Pre-history' of the Question," *ETL* 55 (1979): 116–24; and G. Minette de Tillesse, "Sections 'tu' et sections 'vous' dans le Deutéronome," *VT* 12 (1962): 29–87. More recent discussion on Deuteronomy 4 is provided in C. Begg, "The Literary Criticism of Deut 4,1-40: Contributions to a Continuing Discussion," *ETL* 56 (1980): 10–55, and Dietrich Knapp, *Deuteronomium 4: Literarische Analyse und Theologische Interpretation,* GTA 35 (Göttingen: Vandenhoeck & Ruprecht, 1986).

6. Georg Braulik, "Das Deuteronomium und die Geburt des Monotheismus," in *Studien zur Theologie des Deuteronomiums* (Stuttgart: Katholisches Bibelwerk, 1988), 257–300.

Diagram 2

4:1-4 — Introduction — "Give heed to the statutes and ordinances . . . so that you may live to enter and occupy the land that the LORD . . . is giving you

4:5-8 — The unique greatness of Israel's wisdom and God's nearness

4:9-31 — THE BODY OF THE CHAPTER: THREE TEACHING PARADIGMS OF THE MOVEMENT FROM DEATH AND JUDGMENT TO LIFE AND HOPE CENTERED ON THE FIRST COMMANDMENT, "YOU SHALL HAVE NO OTHER GODS"

1. 4:9-20 — The Horeb-Creation-Egypt paradigm from the past
2. 4:21-24 — The Moses-People paradigm of the present
3. 4:25-31 — The Exile-Return paradigm of the future

4:32-39 — The unique greatness of Israel's God, the God of heaven and earth

4:40 — Conclusion — "Keep his statutes and his commandments . . . so that you may long remain in the land that the LORD . . . is giving you for all time"

and future that exemplify the recurring movement of God's people through judgment to hope, curse to blessing, life to death.

DEUT. 4:1-4 AND 4:40: THE OUTER FRAME —
INTRODUCTION AND CONCLUSION

The introduction in 4:1-4 and conclusion in 4:40 call upon Israel to heed the statutes and the ordinances that Moses is teaching for two reasons: "so that you may live to enter and occupy the land" and "so that you may long remain in the land." The material between these introductory and concluding frames makes clear that the obedience of the law enhances the quality and viability of life in the land. But obedience to the law does not supply the basis for the relationship between God and the people. Even if the people disobey the law, as they surely will, "because the LORD your God is a merciful God, he will neither abandon you nor destroy you; he will not forget the covenant with your ancestors that he swore to them" (4:31). That irrevocable relationship between God and God's people began long before the Ten Commandments and laws were given. The relationship began when

God rescued Israel from slavery in Egypt "to become a people of his very own possession, as you are now" (4:20).

The introduction in 4:2 goes on to warn that "you must neither add anything to what I command you nor take away anything from it, but keep the commandments of the LORD your God with which I am charging you." The commandments mentioned here refer above all to the Ten Commandments or Decalogue in Deuteronomy 5. These are fixed, unchangeable, and always and everywhere in force. God spoke these Ten Commandments or "ten words" directly to the people and "wrote them on two stone tablets" (4:13; cf. 5:22). In contrast to these commandments, which can in no way be altered, Moses is directed to teach the people "statutes and ordinances," which are interpretations and applications of the commandments for new times and places (4:1, 5, 14).[7] The statutes and ordinances (largely chapters 6–28) serve as provisional explications of the Ten Commandments. The Ten Commandments cannot change, but the "statutes and ordinances" invite further study and exploration and argument as an ongoing tradition of interpretation.

The last part of the introduction in 4:3-4 recalls a past event from Israel's history involving the first and fundamental commandment of the Decalogue, "you shall have no other gods before me." The story is recounted in Numbers 25. The Israelites bowed down and worshiped the gods of Moab or Midian. One of the foreign deities was also known as the Baal of Peor. This encounter with another culture and its gods led to the death of twenty-four thousand Israelites, presumably the last of the old wilderness generation who died in the desert (Num. 25:1-18). The writer of Deuteronomy 4 recalls this story from the past and makes the point: obedience to the first commandment leads to life; disobedience leads to death (4:3-4).

This use of a past story functions as a paradigm for the new generation as they are about to enter the promised land of Canaan. The Israelites will again face an alien culture and foreign gods in Canaan, just as they had faced them with the Midianites in Numbers 25. If this text was indeed written during the Babylonian exile, the same temptation to worship the impressive array of Babylonian gods and culture would be present. The paradigm of the past would again apply directly to the exiles, as it had for the Israelites in the wilderness. Both the introduction and conclusion stress this actualization of the past for the

---

7. Georg Braulik, "Die Abfolge der Gesetze in Deuteronomium 12–26 und der Decalog," in *Das Deuteronomium, Entstehung, Gestalt und Botschaft,* ed. Norbert Lohfink (Leuven: Leuven Univ. Press, 1985), 252–72, esp. 253–54, 271.

sake of the present through their repetition of the word *today* (4:4, 40; cf. 5:3).[8]

DEUT. 4:5-8 AND 4:32-39: THE INNER FRAME —
THE UNIQUENESS OF ISRAEL'S GOD

Just as the introduction and conclusion form an outer frame, the two sections that speak of the uniqueness of Israel and Israel's God in 4:5-8 and 4:32-39 form an inner frame surrounding the main body of chapter 4. The two sections of the inner frame hold together paradoxical qualities of God's character. The combination of these opposing characteristics within one God forms the basis for the claim of God's uniqueness and singularity.

Thus, the intimate nearness of God (4:7) is balanced by the terrifying majesty and power of God (4:34-35). God's ongoing and quiet guidance through the wisdom of statutes and ordinances (4:8) is matched by the bold and dramatic saving events in the rescue from Egypt and the conquests at the edge of the promised land (4:37-38). God's disciplining voice sounds from above in the heavens (4:36a), yet God also walks among the people on earth as the divine form is veiled in fire (4:36b). Sinful people hear the voice of the holy God speak out of the consuming fire, an experience that should lead to their death. Yet the people live (4:33). The paradox is extended even to God's relationship to other nations outside Israel. This relationship oscillates between admiration and terror. On the one hand, the statutes and ordinances given by God will lead other nations and peoples to look in admiration at God's people, saying, "Surely this great nation is a wise and discerning people" (4:6). On the other hand, God's power and destructive force will lead other nations to look in terror as God fights against those who oppose the divine will (4:34, 37-38).

This inner frame is an extended reflection on the unique qualities of God. The God of Israel defies any one description or form. Yet this incomparable and incomprehensible God wills to be known and trusted, as the inner frame of Deuteronomy 4 concludes: "So acknowledge today and take to heart that the LORD is God in heaven above and on the earth beneath; there is no other" (4:39). As we move into the main body of chapter 4, the mystery of God remains even as God's intimate nearness is affirmed.

---

8. On the actualizing function of the frequent use of the word *today* in Deuteronomy, cf. J. van Goudoever, "The Liturgical Significance of the Date in Dt 1,3," in *Das Deuteronomium: Entstehung, Gestalt und Botschaft,* 145–48.

DEUT. 4:9-31: THE CHAPTER'S MAIN BODY—
THREE TEACHING PARADIGMS

The speech of Moses in Deuteronomy 4 uses three teaching models of how God has acted and will act in the future. The underlying argument or lesson is that the oneness of God implies a consistency in the way in which God's people experience life under this one God. God's people have always moved through judgment and death to promise and life. Moreover, the primary problem that has led Israel into communal death and judgment is making and worshiping idols, going after other gods.

The first paradigm in 4:9-20 uses the past to establish the Creation-Egypt-Horeb paradigm. One of the central events of the past was the revelation of God at Mount Horeb when the Ten Commandments were given. Moses asks the hearers to reflect on how that revelation from God was given: "Then the LORD spoke to you out of the fire. You heard the sound of words but saw no form; there was only a voice" (4:12). The story is recounted, and then the lesson is drawn: "Since you saw no form when the LORD spoke to you . . . ," the people are not to make "an idol for yourselves, in the form of any figure" (4:15-16).

As part of the Creation-Egypt-Horeb paradigm, Deuteronomy 4 moves from the story of Mount Horeb to an allusion to the creation story of Genesis 1. No single part of the creation can be used as an idol or representation of God. In precisely the reverse order in which they appear in Genesis 1, Moses names all the creatures that cannot be made into idols to represent God: the human likeness of either male or female, animals, birds, creeping things, fish, sun, moon, stars, and all the host of heaven (4:16-19; cf. Gen. 1:1-27).[9] To all peoples everywhere God has allotted these created things, which many people worship as their gods. But Israel worships Yahweh alone.

The first paradigm from the past moves from Horeb to creation to the deliverance out of Egypt. A humanly constructed idol cannot be worshiped as God. Yet 4:20 suggests that the closest one can get to the image of God in the world is to look at the people of Israel. Israel is the people God has chosen and saved out of the hot fires of death and slavery, the "iron-smelter" of Egypt (4:20). Israel is God's "very own possession" (Hebrew *naḥălāh*). Deuteronomy uses the term most often for the promised land of Canaan as Israel's "possession" or "inheri-

---

9. Michael Fishbane, *Biblical Interpretation in Ancient Israel* (Oxford: Clarendon, 1985), 321-22.

tance," which is given as a gift from God (4:21, 38).[10] But if the promised land is Israel's "possession" or "inheritance," God's "inheritance" is the people of Israel, who have been chosen as God's own people from among all the peoples of the earth (4:29; 7:6; 9:26, 29; 14:2). The Creation-Egypt-Horeb paradigm teaches that no human can construct an idol that captures the incomparable God of creation and history. Yet God is tangibly present and at work in a specific and historical people whom *God* has created and chosen as God's "very own possession" (cf. 32:6).

The second paradigm moves from the experience of Israel as a community in the past to the experience of an individual in the present. In the Moses-People paradigm in 4:21-24, Moses recalls again God's judgment that Moses must die outside the promised land. The reason for the prohibition is the predominant one in Deuteronomy: "the LORD was angry with me because of you" (4:21). Thus, the death of Moses outside the land is in some way a vicarious act of atonement for the sake of the people: "I am going to die in this land without crossing over the Jordan, but you are going to cross over to take possession of that good land" (4:22). The Moses-People paradigm again underscores the consistent pattern of moving through death to life, through judgment to promise.

The death of Moses and the crossing over of the new generation into Canaan then leads to the lesson: "So be careful not to forget the covenant that the LORD your God made with you, and not to make for yourselves an idol" (4:23). The lesson is two-sided. On the one hand, follow the covenant that *God* made. On the other hand, don't follow any idols that *you* make. But what do idols have to do with Moses' dying outside the promised land? The connection is subtle but suggestive. The narrative preceding chapter 4 made clear Moses' dearest wish to set foot on the promised land (3:23-27). Had the land itself in a sense become Moses' idol? Did the land threaten to become more important to Moses than Moses' relationship and trust in God? Or more importantly, did Moses have to die outside the land as a reminder that he himself was not a god, an object of worship for the people? Moses' death shifts Israel's allegiance from a human like Moses to Yahweh, the true God of Israel.

The third and final paradigm in chapter 4, the Exile-Return para-

---

10. Gerhard von Rad, "The Promised Land and Yahweh's Land in the Hexateuch," in *The Problem of the Hexateuch and Other Essays,* trans. E. W. Trueman Dicken (Edinburgh: Oliver & Boyd, 1966), 79–93; and P. Diepold, *Israels Land,* BWANT 95 (Stuttgart: Kohlhammer, 1972), 83ff.

digm, moves from the past and present to the distant future, a time "when you have had children and children's children." In the future if and when the people make idols and forget the convenant God had made with them, Moses warns that the covenantal curses will come into force: "I call heaven and earth to witness against you today [cf. 30:19; 32:1] that you will soon utterly perish from the land that you are crossing the Jordan to occupy; you will not live long on it, but will be utterly destroyed" (4:26). In a probable reference to the historical exile to Babylon that Judah experienced in 587 B.C.E., the text notes: "The LORD will scatter you among the peoples; only a few of you will be left among the nations where the LORD will lead you" (4:27). Ironically, in exile the people will be forced to do the very thing that led them into exile; they will serve idols, "other gods made by human hands" (4:28). The text scorns these idols as simply "objects of wood and stone that neither see, nor hear, nor eat, nor smell." This mocking of idols and the denial of the existence of other gods represents a later development in the history of Israel's religion.[11] The closest parallel to Deuteronomy 4 in this regard stems from the exilic text of Second Isaiah (Isa. 40:19-20; 44:19-20; 46:6-7).

But as the paradigms of the past and present have shown, there is hope for life in the midst of exilic death, promise in the midst of judgment. The turning point is 4:29: "From there [the place of exile and judgment] you will seek the LORD your God, and you will find him if you search after him with all your heart and soul." This new hopeful finding and returning to God is not grounded in the people's character and activity but in the character and activity of God: "Because the LORD your God is a merciful God, he will neither abandon you nor destroy you; he will not forget the covenant with your ancestors that he swore to them" (4:31). Israel's confidence and hope rest in the mercy of the one, incomparable God.

---

11. Compare the early Israelite poem in Deut. 32:8-9, where the original text outlines the following scenario at the creation of the world's nations: "the Most High" God apportioned the nations "according to the number of the gods"; "the LORD" (Yahweh) received Jacob or Israel as "the LORD's own portion." Implied here is a view of a pantheon of several gods to whom "the Most High" God distributed the various nations on the earth. "The LORD" (Yahweh) is allotted Israel while other gods were allotted other peoples. This text represents one perspective in Israel's understanding of God that is in tension with views expressed elsewhere in the Old Testament. I return to this question of Yahweh, Israel, and the other nations in the study of Deuteronomy 32. Two recent overviews of the development of Israel's understanding of its God in relation to other gods are Mark Smith, *The Early History of God* (San Francisco: Harper & Row, 1990); and J. C. de Moor, *The Rise of Yahwism: The Roots of Israelite Monotheism* (Leuven: Leuven Univ. Press, 1990).

Deuteronomy 4 summarizes many of the important themes of Deuteronomic catechesis. The word *teach* (Hebrew *lmd*) occurs four times
(4:1, 5, 11, 14). Mention of "children" and "children's children" (4:9,
25) stresses the intergenerational dimensions of this catechetical
process. This process joins together in community generations stretch-
ing from "your ancestors" (4:1, 31, 37) to "your descendants after you"
(4:40). References to learning, wisdom, discernment, and not forget-
ting weave their way throughout the chapter. The constant movement
in the chapter from past and present stories to implications and lessons
for the future characterizes the essence of the catechetical enterprise.
A consistent pattern of movement through death to life characterizes
the relationship of God and Israel.

DEUTERONOMY 4:41-43: THE CITIES OF REFUGE

Chapter 4 ends with a transitional piece in which Moses establishes
cities of refuge, sanctuaries for those who accidently kill another person (cf. Numbers 35).[12] Manslaughter or unintentional homicide is a
gray area of the law, one difficult to prove. The judge must discern not
only physical evidence but also deeper intentions and motivations. Was
the killing only an accident? How much responsibility should the defendant assume? Should a relative of the dead man's family be allowed to
take blood revenge and kill the defendant, as was customary in early
Israel? The cities of refuge provided a place where those who accidently
killed another human being could flee and live. In these designated
cities they were safe from relatives, who typically took vengeance into
their own hands on behalf of the deceased.

The provisions for the cities of refuge in 4:41-43 provide a stepping-
stone into the next large section of Deuteronomy, chapters 5-28, which
has to do with the commandments for the community in the present.
The cities of refuge have to do with a legal matter, a matter of the commandments. But provision is made here at the outset for an exception
or gray area in the commandment "you shall not kill." The exception
signals the living and dynamic quality of existence in this community.
This is a people who will wrestle with ambiguity and new circumstances. Here is a signal of the openness of the community to new interpretations; in a sense the book of Deuteronomy is itself a new interpretation of the *torah* to a new generation of God's people. The cities
of refuge have to do with issues of death and life, guilt and responsi-

---

12. Alexander Rofé, "The History of the Cities of Refuge in Biblical Law," *BM* 31
(1985/86): 110-33 (Hebrew).

bility, judgment and hope. They represent an acknowledgment that life and community often force us into uncharted areas where clear answers, easy solutions, and happy endings are not possible. But the provision for cities of refuge provides enough of a reasonable compromise for life to go on.

The development of the cities of refuge was probably a long and complex one in the history of ancient Israel. Worship sites may have functioned originally as sanctuaries for people guilty of unintentional homicide. But when Deuteronomy prescribed only one proper place of worship for the whole nation of Israel ("the place that the LORD your God will choose" — 12:1-28), some alternate provisions for the unintentional killer had to be made through the designation of special cities of refuge. According to Rofé, these cities of refuge eventually came to be seen not so much as places of refuge but as places of exile.[13] They came to represent a kind of imprisonment and punishment that was harsh but less so than the ultimate death of capital punishment. In the light of Israel's own future exile in Babylon, the juxtaposition of this provision for a place of exile for accidental killers (4:41-43) immediately after the extended interpretation of God's judgment and promise in 4:1-40 is suggestive. The Babylonian exile may be seen as a compromise that both punishes Israel for its grave rebellions and sin and yet avoids the ultimate judgment of total death and annihilation. As in the spy story in Deuteronomy 1, God's prople will be punished, but the judgment will not be the end of the story. God's promise and hope always have the final word.

SUMMARY: DEUTERONOMY 1-4 AND THE DEATH OF MOSES

The narratives of Deuteronomy 1–3 and Deuteronomy 34 form a key interpretive framework for the entire book of Deuteronomy. The story of the death of the old wilderness generation in chapters 1–3 contains a number of echoes with the account of Moses' death in chapter 34:

- Same geographical setting (plains of Moab) (1:1, 5; 34:1)
- Moses relinquishing leadership (1:9-18; 34:9)
- Survey of the whole land of Canaan (1:22-25; 34:1-3)
- God's denial of entry into the promised land (1:34-36; 34:4)
- Recounting the death and God's involvement (2:14-15; 34:5-6)
- God's promise that a new generation would enter the land (1:38-39; 34:4, 9)

13. Ibid.

- God's continuing activity beyond the finite horizon of personal, national or generational boundaries (1:39; 2:5, 9, 19, 24; 3:1-2; 34:4, 9)

Beyond these, Deut. 1:37 and 3:23-29 make the most important connections, where the themes of the wilderness generation's death outside the land and Moses' death are explicitly brought together. The note in 1:37 is a unique Deuteronomic addition to the spy story recounted in Numbers 13-14. Deuteronomy 3:23-29 is an explicit foretelling of the narrative of Moses' death in chapter 34. The theme of Moses' death is inextricably woven into these opening narrative chapters of Deuteronomy.

Deuteronomy 4 incorporates the theme of Moses' death, most directly in 4:21-24. Moses recounts again God's verdict that Moses would die outside the promised land "because of you [the people]." Moses' death is linked here with the prohibition of idols and the jealousy of God (4:23-24). Had the land become Moses' idol? Or did the humanity of Moses require his death outside the land so that later generations would not worship or idolize him? This linking of Moses' death and the first commandment's prohibition of other gods joins together two important and recurring themes throughout Deuteronomy.

Deuteronomy 4 also weaves into its tapestry the broader themes associated with Moses' death: the failure of human faithfulness as well as the limitations of human abilities to comprehend the full and seemingly paradoxical qualities of God. God requires obedience yet promises to restore a disobedient people. God is both intimately near and yet terrifyingly transcendent. God is both mysterious and yet knowable.

Finally, the note about the cities of refuge in 4:41-43 again touches upon the theme of the movement through death and exile to promise and hope. Immediately preceding the Horeb covenant in Deuteronomy 5, the provision for the cities of refuge reminds the reader of the inherent limitations of law and the inevitable gray areas of human decision and action where resolutions are sometimes less than perfect. Both Moses' death outside the promised land and the cities of refuge provide a note of realism about the struggles and ambiguities of human existence and action.

CHAPTER 3

"This Is the Torah" — Deuteronomy 5: The Blueprint of Deuteronomy's Structure and Themes

This is the *torah* that Moses set before the Israelites.

—Deut. 4:44

Deuteronomy as a whole is called "the book of the *torah*" (Deut. 31:26). Deuteronomy 5 presents itself as a capsule form of this "book of the *torah*," as the superscription to chapter 5 begins, "this is the *torah*" (Deut. 4:44). This superscription and the details of the setting in time and place that follow in Deut. 4:45-49 mark the transition to the next section of Moses' words in Deuteronomy 5. In its structure and themes, Deuteronomy 5 provides a condensed version of the *torah* of Deuteronomy. A look at the structure of Deuteronomy 5 reveals the parallels in structure and theme to the rest of Deuteronomy:

I. 5:1-5: The overarching theme of Deuteronomy—Actualizing the covenant for "us, who are all of us here alive today." The story, the commandments, and the covenant of the past become the reader's story, commandments, and covenant.

II. 5:6-33: The structure of the covenant relationship between God and the people
    A. 5:6: The story of the past—God's gracious election of Israel: "I am the LORD your God"
    B. 5:7-21: The law for the present—The Ten Commandments
    C. 5:22-31: Provisions for extending the covenant into the future—God's commission of Moses' unique role as teacher and interpreter
    D. 5:32-33: Blessing as the last word—"that you may live, and that it may go well with you"

As I already noted in chapter 1, these four sections of 5:6-31 correspond to the four parts of Moses' last words in the book of Deuteronomy as a whole:

A. The story of the past — Deuteronomy 1-4
B. The law for the present — Deuteronomy 5-28
C. Provisions for extending the covenant into the future —
   Deuteronomy 29-32
D. Blessing: Through death to life — Deuteronomy 33-34

Deuteronomy 5 is not the earliest section of Deuteronomy nor is it the latest.[1] But those who shaped chapter 5 did so in light of the emerging structure and themes of the entire book of Deuteronomy as it was written and edited. Thus, a careful look at chapter 5 gives important insights into the message of the whole book in its present form.

DEUTERONOMY 5:1-5: THE CENTRAL CONCERN OF DEUTERONOMY

Moses begins, "The LORD our God made a covenant with us at Horeb" (5:2). But Moses is speaking to a new generation of Israelites born *after* the events of the exodus and Mount Horeb. Yet Moses insists, "Not with our ancestors did the LORD make this covenant, but with us, who are all of us here alive today" (5:3). God renews the covenant for a new generation "who are all of us here alive today." The phrase "this day" or "today" occurs twenty-seven times in Deuteronomy. In this narrative context it refers first to the time of Moses. But as the book of Deuteronomy was read and carried from one generation to another, "this day" came to mean any festival or liturgical day on which these same words were read and heard throughout Israel's history, whether in the time of King Hezekiah or King Josiah, or in the time of the Babylonian exile, or at any other time of worship.

Verses 4-5 wrestle with the paradox of the intimate and mediated presence of God.[2] Moses reminds his hearers that the Lord "spoke to

---

1. A succinct summary of scholarly arguments about the literary and editorial history of chap. 5 is provided by Chr. Brekelmans, "Deuteronomy 5: Its Place and Function," in *Das Deuteronomium: Enstehung, Gestalt und Botschaft,* ed. Norbert Lohfiink, BETL 68 (Leuven: Leuven Univ. Press, 1985), 164-73.
2. Verse 4 seems to say that God spoke "face to face" with the people, while v. 5 emphasizes that Moses stood between the people and God. Because of this apparent difference in perspective, scholars often suggest that v. 5 is a later insertion into the text. Cf. Brekelmans, "Deuteronomy 5," 165. In any case, vv. 4 and 5 now serve in their

you face to face," in a personal and intimate way, yet Israel did not see the form of God (4:12). The image of intimacy is joined with another cluster of images. God speaks "at the mountain" and "out of the fire." In the ancient Near East, looming mountains and blazing fires were associated with the terrifying presence of the gods. Together these conflicting images of intimate kindness, awesome power, and an untamed fire portray the reality and the mystery of the God of Deuteronomy. Thus, Moses reports that the people "were afraid because of the fire and did not go up the mountain."

DEUTERONOMY 5:6: A PAST STORY CAPTURED IN A SNAPSHOT

Deuteronomy 5:6 is a snapshot of one crucial and defining narrative event in Israel's already long past "I am the LORD your God, who brought you out of the land of Egypt, out of the house of slavery." Israel's community identity is based on the story of slaves freed by God. This is the theme of the narratives of Deuteronomy 1-4: the faithfulness and compassion of God.

DEUTERONOMY 5:7-21: THE LAW FOR THE PRESENT – THE TEN COMMANDMENTS

I will deal in detail with Deuteronomy's interpretation and expansion of each of the individual commandments later, in the study of Deuteronomy 6-28. For now, however, I will make some general observations about the list of the Ten Commandments in Deuteronomy 5. The importance of the Ten Commandments is underscored by the fact that they are presented twice in the Bible, first in Exodus 20:1-17, and then here in Deuteronomy 5. The commandments are largely the same in Exodus 20 and Deuteronomy 5 with a few minor exceptions and one major alteration with the sabbath commandment.

One issue that we face with the Ten Commandments is their division and numbering. Jewish and Christian groups throughout the centuries have differed in the way in which they divide and arrange the commandments. The number ten is fixed because Deut. 10:4 explicitly names the commandments "the ten words." But which are the Ten Commandments? Table 1 (p. 43) shows how different traditions arrange and number them.

---

present form to complement one another concerning the intimate but mediated way in which the people receive God's words.

Table 1

	Jewish	Lutheran/Roman Catholic	Reformed
1st	I am the LORD your God	no other gods	no other gods
2nd	no other gods	LORD's name in vain	no graven image
3rd	LORD's name in vain	remember sabbath day	LORD's name in vain
4th	remember sabbath day	honor parents	remember sabbath day
5th	honor parents	not kill	honor parents
6th	not kill	no adultery	not kill
7th	no adultery	not steal	no adultery
8th	not steal	no false witness	not steal
9th	no false witness	not covet neighbor's house	no false witness
10th	not covet	not covet neighbor's wife, etc.	not covet

This variation in the traditional division of the Ten Commandments reflects the ambiguity within the texts of Exodus 20 and Deuteronomy 5 themselves. The Jewish arrangement of the commandments is unique in that it includes the promise or declaration, "I am the LORD your God, who brought you out of the land of Egypt, out of the house of slavery," as the first commandment. Our first obligation is to remember what God has already done for us. This declaration is theologically suggestive, but it does seem to fall outside the list of imperatives or commands. As I try to demonstrate, Deuteronomy highlights the commandment "you shall have no other gods before me" as the first and foremost of the Ten Commandments. Thus, it seems preferable to begin with the first imperative as the first commandment.

The major wrinkle in the arrangement in the Reformed tradition is to highlight the prohibition of the graven image as a separate commandment. In contrast, the Jewish, Lutheran, and Roman Catholic lists would understand the prohibition of graven images as in some way an interpretation or expansion of the commandment "you shall have no other gods before me." The writer of Deuteornomy seems to agree in seeing the graven image prohibition in 5:8-10 as a further commentary on the first and most important commandment, "you shall have no other gods."[3] We will see that Deuteronomy 6-11 is itself a much larger expansion and interpretation of the first commandment that mirrors the expansion we find here already within 5:8-10. Given these

---

3. This was the conclusion drawn by Walther Zimmerli, "Das zweite Gebot," in *Festschrift für Alfred Bertholet zum 80. Geburtstag,* ed. Walter Baumgartner, et al. (Tübingen: J. C. B. Mohr, 1960), 550-57.

observations, I use the Lutheran and Roman Catholic system of enumerating the Ten Commandments at least here in the context of Deuteronomy. In any case, the system of numbering the Ten Commandments is not crucial. More important is our understanding and interpretation of the commandments, however they are numbered.

Most of the commandments in Deuteronomy 5 are very brief and to the point. Indeed, in the original Hebrew most of them consist of only two words, and some scholars argue that originally all ten commandments appeared in this shortened form.[4] But in their present form in chapter 5, three of the Ten Commandments are expanded with additional specifications, motivations, and justifications. The first commandment in 5:7, "you shall have no other gods before me," is expanded with a further interpretation in 5:8-10 that prohibits the making of idols and provides the foundation for the commandment. The two positive commandments about observing the sabbath and honoring parents are also expanded with further specifications, justifications, and motivations beyond the simple commandment (5:12-15, 16). These interpretations and expansions of the commandments already within chapter 5 serve to prefigure more elaborate expansions and interpretations of the Decalogue in the succeeding chapters of Deuteronomy 6–28. As we shall see, these chapters (Deuteronomy 6–28) follow roughly the sequence of the Ten Commandments and thus function as interpretations and expansions of the Ten Commandments in Deuteronomy 5.

These expansions and interpretations already in chapter 5 suggest that Deuteronomy understands the law and the commandments primarily in the context not of a courtroom but of a classroom. The writers of Deuteronomy scattered additional motivations and justifications among many of the laws of Deuteronomy. Deuteronomy is more a catechetical book than a law book. Elders, teachers, and parents are to use this book more than lawyers and judges.[5] Deuteronomy is primarily aimed at a new generation in need of growth and maturity.

---

4. For a discussion of the possible origins and early forms of the Ten Commandments, see J. J. Stamm and M. E. Andrew, *The Ten Commandments in Recent Research,* SBT 2/2 (Naperville, Ill.: Allenson, 1967). A more recent survey is provided by Bernhard Lang, "Neues über den Dekalog," *TQ* 164 (1984): 58–65.

5. This point is made by Bernard S. Jackson, "Legalism and Spirituality: Historical, Philosophical, and Semiotic Notes on Legislators, Adjudicators, and Subjects," in *Religion and Law: Biblical-Judaic and Islamic Perspectives,* ed. Edwin Firmage, et al. (Winona Lake, Ind.: Eisenbrauns, 1990), 244–61. Jackson argues that the role of judges in ancient Israel was to render judgments not so much on the basis of a set of rules or laws as on a sense of God's justice and the practical wisdom of local tradition (Deut. 16:18-20). The commandments or law codes were more teaching documents for the general populace, including even the king (17:18-20; cf. 2 Chron. 17:9).

These expansions teach how and why these commandments should be obeyed. They tell how past history shapes the present community. For example, the sabbath commandment in 5:12 commands that slaves or workers be allowed to rest on the sabbath and then gives the basis for the commandent: "Remember that you were a slave in the land of Egypt" (5:15). Memory of the past shapes and motivates present action. This is law not so much enforced as taught and persuasively encouraged.

DEUTERONOMY 5:22-31: THE COVENANT FOR THE FUTURE – MOSES' COMMISSION AS MEDIATOR AND TEACHER

Deuteronomy 5:22-31 tells how the Ten Commandments were given, their relationship to the other laws of Deuteronomy, and the role of Moses as mediator and teacher of the laws for the future. This unit may be divided into three sections:

- The Ten Commandments: Yahweh speaks to the people (5:22)
- The people speak to Moses (5:23-27)
- Yahweh speaks to Moses (5:28-31)

The first scene (v. 22) recounts how "these words" (the Ten Commandments) were given. The Decalogue was spoken directly from God to the people at the mountain. The fire, the cloud, and the thick darkness all hid the form of God from sight, but the people heard the voice of God directly in the Ten Commandments ("The LORD spoke with you face to face" — 5:4). The scene continues with God writing the Decalogue upon two stone tablets and giving them to Moses. The Ten Commandments thus contain the direct words of God, written in stone and preserved for all future generations. This first scene heightens the uniqueness and authority of the Ten Commandments over all other laws. No other laws are spoken directly by God to the people. No other laws are written in stone by the divine hand. But even this giving of the Ten Commandments is a one-time event in the past. Thus, some mechanism must be provided for carrying the commandments into the future. Moses becomes the link to that future as the stone tablets are entrusted into his care.

The second scene (vv. 23-27) recounts the request by the people that Moses mediate all future words from Yahweh. Here fundamental themes of Deuteronomy emerge: the awesome power of the divine word, the need for a mediator, and the subtle but crucial intimation of the imminent death of Moses for the sake of the people. Scholars have noticed a tension in these verses. On the one hand, the people hear directly the words of God (v. 24). On the other hand, the people claim that to hear the voice of God will lead to their death (v. 25). As a result, some scholars argue that these verses come from two different writers or editors working at different times with different theologies. Although this may be the case, the effect achieved in the present text is to hold together three important affirmations: (1) God wills to speak intimately and directly to God's people; (2) such direct divine speaking leads eventually to the death of the human hearers; and (3) God's powerful word must therefore be communicated through a human intermediary like Moses.

Now the people fear for their own lives and tell Moses to go in their place: "Go near, you yourself, and hear all that the Lord our God will say. Then tell us everything that the Lord our God tells you, and we will listen and do it" (5:27). But will Moses then have to die for the sake of the people as he mediates God's word to them? And if Moses dies, how will God's word continue to live and work within the community of God's people? The shadow of Moses' death in Deuteronomy 34 creeps again upon the stage. There is no direct word here about Moses' death. But the intimations of the necessity of his death are again clear.

The third scene (vv. 28-31) relates Yahweh's approval of the people's request that Moses be their mediator. God then directs the people to return to their tents while God tells Moses, "But you, stand here by me, and I will tell you all the commandments, the statutes and the ordinances, that you shall teach them." Deuteronomy gives the "commandments" a unique and fixed authority as God's direct words to the people. God then mediates a series of additional "statutes and ordinances" orally to Moses. These "statutes and ordinances" are secondary and humanly mediated through Moses. In this way, Deuteronomy marks the "statutes and ordinances" as less authoritative, less fixed, and more in need of interpretation and adaptation.

The juxtaposition of "commandments" (the Decalogue) on the one hand and "statutes and ordinances" on the other hand (5:31) provides a key to the organization of the laws of Deuteronomy. The Ten Commandments in chapter 5 provide the sequential framework for understanding the sequence of laws that follow in chapters 6–28. It is this expanded collection of "statutes and ordinances" based on the Decalogue that Moses proclaims in subsequent chapters.

DEUTERONOMY 5:32-33: THE BLESSING—
"THAT IT MAY GO WELL WITH YOU"

Chapter 5 concludes, "You must therefore be careful to do as the LORD your God has commanded you; you shall not turn to the right or to the left. You must follow exactly the path that the LORD your God has commanded you." These words transpose the image of Israel's journey through the wilderness into another kind of journey. The wilderness sojourn of the Israelites becomes now the journey of obedience of every future generation as it struggles to walk "the path that the LORD your God has commanded you."

Moses concludes in 5:33 with the reason Israel should follow the commandments "so that you may live, and that it may go well with you, and that you may live long in the land that you are to possess." God's intention for the commandments is that they be a gift which gives life and blessing. Obedience of the commandments is not the means of salvation or the prerequisite for belonging to God's people. The people belong to God before the commandments are given (5:6). But the commandments provide the space and the structure that make blessing and life possible. For all its talk of commandments and judgment and disobedience, Deuteronomy is finally a book about God's faithfulness, God's compassion, and God's promise of life and blessing. Thus, Moses' last words to the Israelites before his death will be words of blessing and hope (chaps. 33–34).

SUMMARY: DEUTERONOMY 5 AND THE DEATH OF MOSES

A hermeneutical issue is at the center of this chapter and of the entire book of Deuteronomy: How will God's word be mediated to the people and to succeeding generations so that the relationship of God and Israel may be continued? The people have a divinely written text, the two stone tablets with the Ten Commandments scrawled by the hand of God. This primal text requires interpretation and expansion. Moses becomes the mediator and interpreter of God's word to the people, but in so doing becomes susceptible to the death that must come to a human who comes face to face with God's holiness. "For who is there of all flesh that has heard the voice of the living God . . . and remained alive?" The office of mediator carries with it the price of premature death, a death Moses will experience while still strong and vigorous in Deuteronomy 34.

The impending death of Moses will create another hermeneutical crisis comparable in urgency to the crisis when the Horeb covenant was made. The crisis will be addressed by another covenant, the covenant of Moab, in Deuteronomy 29–32. The theme of Moses' death weaves into itself hermeneutical concerns of overcoming boundaries of space (carrying texts from Horeb to the promised land), of time (interpreting authoritative texts from one generation to another), and of divinity and humanity (communicating and relating between God and people). No one human individual, not even Moses, can overcome such boundaries of finitude and limitation. In the face of Moses' death, a new strategy must be enacted in order to keep the covenant alive with "us, who are all of us here alive today."

"This Is the Commandment" — Deuteronomy 6–11: The Great Commandment for the Present

Thus did the Sages say: All the commandments in the Torah are based on two verses: one, "you shall love the LORD your God" and the second "you shall love your neighbor as yourself."

—Medieval Jewish Midrash[1]

He asked him, "Which commandment is the first of all?" Jesus answered, "The first is 'Hear, O Israel: The LORD our God, the LORD is one; you shall love the LORD your God with all your heart, and with all your soul, and with all your mind, and with all your strength.' The second is this, 'You shall love your neighbor as yourself.' There is no other commandment greater than these."

—Mark 12:28-31

The first and most important of the commandments and the one that Deuteronomy spends the most time expanding and explaining is "you shall have no other gods before me." Already within the "Small Catechism" of Deuteronomy 5, this first commandment receives an expansion (Deut. 5:8-10). This expansion in Deuteronomy 5 is developed further in chapters 6–11, which function as an interpretation of the first commandment, "you shall have no other gods before me."[2] Deuter-

---

1. Cited in Ephraim Urbach, "The Decalog in Jewish Worship," in *The Ten Commandments in History and Tradition,* ed. Ben-Zion Segal and Gershon Levi (Jerusalem: Magnes Press, 1990), 175.
2. The classic critical study of Deuteronomy 5-11 and its history of formation is Norbert Lohfink, *Das Hauptgebot: Eine Untersuchung literarischer Einleitungsfragen zu Dtn 5-11,* AnBib 20 (Rome: Pontifical Biblical Institute, 1963). Brian Peckham has proposed a redactional layering based on the assumption of two Deuteronomistic editors, a so-called Dtr[1] redactor (at the time of Josiah) and a Dtr[2] redactor (at the time of the Babylonian exile); see his "The Composition of Deuteronomy 5-11," in *The Word of the Lord Shall Go Forth,* FS David Noel Freedman, ed. C. L. Meyers and M. O'Connor (Winona Lake, Ind.: Eisenbrauns, 1983), 217-40.

onomy 6–11 has been reworked and edited in the course of its history, but one may discern a clear structure and movement throughout these chapters:

   I. The Great Commandment: Love the One LORD Alone (Deut. 6:1-9)
  II. The Giftedness of Israel's Existence (Deut. 6:10-25)
 III. Three Gods of Death: Militarism, Materialism, and Moralism (Deuteronomy 7–10)
 IV. Motivations and Strategies for Remembering the Great Commandment (Deut. 11:1-32)

DEUTERONOMY 6:1-9: THE GREAT COMMANDMENT –
LOVE THE ONE LORD ALONE

Deuteronomy 6 begins, "Now this is the commandment – the statutes and the ordinances." The "statutes and ordinances" refer to the various expansions on the Ten Commandments that we find in chapters 12–28. But "*the* commandment" refers in this context above all to the first and the great commandment, "you shall have no other gods before me," which chapters 6-11 interpret. Deuteronomy 6:1-3 portray Moses again in the exemplary teaching role that seeks to cross generational boundaries: "so that you and your children and your children's children, may fear the LORD your God . . . so that your days may be long."

In the traditions of Judaism and Christianity, one of the most important Old Testament texts is *Deut. 6:4-5,* the so-called Shema (the Hebrew word for "Hear!") "Hear, O Israel: The LORD is our God, the LORD alone." The Shema functions as a positive restatement of the first commandment.[3] Deuteronomy 6:4 begins not with a commandment but with a proclamation or affirmation: "Hear, O Israel: The LORD is our God." The next phrase in the Shema consists of two Hebrew words, *yhwh 'ḥd.* The Hebrew form of the divine name (*yhwh*) is customarily rendered as "Yahweh" or (in the NRSV) as "the LORD," following an ancient tradition of not pronouncing the divine name. The two Hebrew

3. S. Dean McBride, "The Yoke of the Kingdom: An Exposition of Deuteronomy 6:4-5," *Int* 27 (1973): 290. For other discussions of the Shema and its relationship to the first commandment, cf. Patrick D. Miller, Jr., "The Most Important Word: The Yoke of the Kingdom," *IRev* 41 (Fall 1984): 17–29; Norbert Lohfink, "The Great Commandment," in *The Christian Meaning of the Old Testament,* trans. R. A. Wilson (Milwaukee: Bruce Pub. Co., 1968), 87–102; J. Gerald Janzen, "The Yoke That Gives Rest," *Int* (1987): 256–68; idem, "On the Most Important Word in the Shema (Deuteronomy vi, 4-5)," *VT* 37 (1987): 280–300.

words together (*yhwh 'ḥd*) may be translated either as "the Lord alone" or "the Lord is one." The meaning of the Hebrew is ambiguous, and scholars have debated which meaning is best.[4] The translation "the Lord alone" places the spotlight on the people and their loyalty toward Yahweh among all the other possible gods that Israel may be tempted to worship. Israel's God is Yahweh and no other god. This translation leaves open the question whether other gods may be the proper gods of other nations (cf. 32:8-9).

In contrast, the second translation — "the Lord is one" — places the spotlight not on the people's devotion but on the nature of God. "The Lord is one" makes a claim about the unity of the divine. God is singular, not divided. God acts in a consistent way. The relationship between Yahweh and Israel has a particular congruity or pattern that one may glimpse in and through the varied contingencies of its history and life. As catechesis, Deuteronomy struggles to distill the pattern of God's consistent activity in the past, present, and future, a pattern rooted in the memory of the one God "who brought you out of the land of Egypt, out of the house of slavery" (5:6).

"The Lord alone." "The Lord is one." The ambiguity of the translation of the Shema captures both the call to Israel's fidelity to the Lord and the confession of the Lord's oneness or singularity as the one God of all. Both dimensions play an important role in Deuteronomy's understanding of the first and great commandment and the multifaceted ways in which its concerns touch every aspect of a community's life and faith.

The affirmation of the Shema in Deut. 6:4 about the nature of God and Israel's allegiance leads into an imperative response. The command is the positive form of the first commandment expressed in the command to "love": "You shall love the Lord your God."[5] Israel's "love" of God in Deuteronomy involves both "obeying" *and* "holding fast" (11:22; 30:20). In personal relationships, the Hebrew verb translated as "holding fast" to someone often denotes passion, romantic love, and sexual attraction (Gen. 2:24; 34:3; 1 Kings. 11:2). Obedience *and* passionate relationship characterize the full love of God in Deuteronomy. The totality of the commitment and love commanded in the Shema is explicitly underscored with three terms: Love the Lord with

4. McBride, "Yoke of the Kingdom," 291–97, outlines the linguistic and contextual evidence for the alternate translations.
5. That the Shema is a positive restatement of the first commandment has often been observed, e.g., John Calvin, *Commentaries on the Four Last Books of Moses,* vol. 1, 420; and Martin Luther, *Lectures on Deuteronomy,* 67.

all your "heart" (*lēbāb*), "soul" (*nepeš*), and "might" (*mĕ'ōd*). The Shema calls the community of Israel to love Yahweh with its inner will and mind ("heart"), which in turn extends to its whole being or self ("soul"), and reaches finally to the uttermost boundaries of its existence and activity ("might"). The commandments that follow in chapters 6–26 are exploratory probes into the many areas where this love of God is made public and concrete as it extends into every crevice of Israel's corporate and personal life.

DEUTERONOMY 6:10-25: THE GIFTEDNESS OF ISRAEL'S EXISTENCE

This section proceeds in reverse chronological order as it traces a pattern in three specific and important times in Israel's history. The characteristic pattern is God as giver and Israel as receiver.

1. Immediate future—God's gift of the land of Canaan without human effort (6:10-15)
2. Immediate past—God's gracious provision in the wilderness (6:16-19)
3. The primal event of the past—God's deliverance of Israel out of slavery (6:20-25)

Each of these events emphasize the giftedness of Israel's life as the people of God. Israel ultimately owes its past and its future not to its own human efforts but to God alone.

DEUTERONOMY 7-10: THE GODS OF DEATH— MILITARISM, MATERIALISM, AND MORALISM

After exploring the love of God alone as the positive meaning of the first commandment and the grounding of that love in the giftedness of Israel's existence, Deuteronomy names and reflects upon some of the other gods who will threaten Israel's allegiance to Yahweh. Modern biblical scholarship has tended to focus on the Canaanite gods El, Baal, and Asherah, the cults of the dead, or the Assyrian, Babylonian, or Egyptian deities and their relationship to the history of ancient Israelite religion. Deuteronomy 7-10 reflect not upon these gods but upon three other gods or idols who were more insidious and more universal threats to the singular commitment to Yahweh. They are less culture-specific and thus apply not only to the time of ancient Israel but to every generation.

Chapters 7-10 contain three sections that revolve around three themes: militarism and the worship of military might (7:1-26), materialism and the worship of wealth (8:1-20), and moralism and the worship of self-righteousness (9:1 – 10:11). The three sections are marked by and circulate around three formulaic statements that serve as organizing centers for chapters 7-11. The statements all have the same form "to say in your heart" (a literal translation of the Hebrew – the verb *'āmar* + the preposition *b-* + the noun *lēbāb* + a pronominal suffix). The NRSV translates the phrase as "to say to yourself." The construction "to speak in your heart" is scattered throughout the Hebrew Scriptures and is not specific to any one tradition. The triad of three temptations (political or natural powers, self-sufficient materialism, and self-righteous moralism) appear together in the same text once in the prophets (Isa. 47:5-7, 8-9, 10-11), once in the wisdom tradition (Eccl. 2:1; 3:17, 18), and once in the Psalms (Ps. 10:3-4, 5-6, 10-13).

The only other example where the triad of temptations occurs together is Deuteronomy 7-10 where the formula "to say in your heart" (NRSV "say to yourself") occurs three times:

1. "If you say in your heart, 'These nations are more numerous than I; how can I dispossess them?'" – bowing down to the god of military might (7:17)
2. "Do not say in your heart, 'My power and the might of my own hand have gotten me this wealth'" – bowing down to the god of self-sufficient wealth (8:17)
3. "Do not say in your heart, 'It is because of my righteousness that the LORD has brought me to occupy this land'" – bowing down to the god of communal self-righteousness (9:4)

These inner voices speak to the communal "heart" of Israel and seek to claim Israel's allegiance from Yahweh. The Shema enjoins Israel to love the LORD with all its "heart." But Deuteronomy warns against other gods who will gnaw at Israel's "heart" and tempt the community away from its true God.

DEUT. 7:1-26: FALSE ARROGANCE AND FALSE DESPAIR –
THE ILLUSORY GOD OF MILITARISM AND NUMERICAL STRENGTH

Chapter 7 begins by naming seven nations or peoples who occupy the promised land and thereby resist God in his promise to give Israel the land of Canaan. The chapter opens with two affirmations. First, these other nations or people are "mightier and more numerous than you" (7:1). This phrase "more numerous than" recurs throughout chapter 7 (vv. 1, 7, 17, and 22). Second, Yahweh, not Israel, will be the one who will ultimately defeat the enemies (7:1-2). The ideology of holy war in ancient Israel clearly stands behind this chapter.[6] Yahweh, the Divine Warrior, fights Israel's enemies on behalf of the people. Deuteronomy 7 outlines two unacceptable responses that Israel will constantly be tempted to make.

The first unacceptable response is the claim that Yahweh chose Israel because it was militarily stronger and more numerous than the other nations. But Moses reminds the people that "it was not because you were more numerous than any other people that the LORD set his heart on you and chose you—for you were the fewest of all peoples" (7:7). The people were chosen by Yahweh because, says Moses, "the LORD loved you" and because the LORD kept the promise given to the ancestors (7:8).

A second unacceptable response to an enemy who appears militarily stronger is despair. Israel will be tempted to bow down in fear before the power and numbers of its enemies, saying in its heart, "These nations are more numerous than I; how can I dispossess them?" (7:17). The remedy for such despair is memory: "Do not be afraid of them. Just remember what the LORD your God did to Pharaoh and to all Egypt. . . . The LORD your God will do the same to all the peoples of whom you are afraid" (7:18-19). Both despair and arrogance are simply other facets of the wrongful worship of the false god of militarism and numerical strength. Despair does not trust God enough; arrogance trusts too much in its own human ability and calculation.

DEUT. 8:1-20: FALSE SELF-SUFFICIENCY:
THE ILLUSORY GOD OF WEALTH

Deuteronomy 8 is an artfully constructed treatise on how wealth and prosperity drain the mind of memory, causing it to forget the God who has given the gifts necessary for life.[7] Chapter 8 may be outlined as follows:

---

6. A standard treatment of the subject is Gerhard von Rad, *Holy War in Ancient Israel,* trans. Marva J. Dawn and John H. Yoder (reprint, Grand Rapids: Eerdmans, 1991). This translation includes a helpful introduction and bibliography on the topic of war and peace in the Hebrew Bible. Another important work in this area is Patrick D. Miller, Jr., *The Divine Warrior in Early Israel,* HSM 5 (Cambridge: Harvard Univ. Press, 1973).

7. Raymond Van Leeuwen, "On the Structure and Sense of Deuteronomy 8," *Proceedings of the Eastern Great Lakes Midwest Biblical Societies* 4 (1984): 237-49, esp. p. 237. Van Leeuwen builds upon and expands the outline of Deuteronomy 8 offered by Lohfink (*Hauptgebot,* 195), who discerns an artful chiasm of wilderness and promised land within the chapter. Van Leeuwen adds the interplay of the admonitions to "remember" and "don't forget" along with attention to specific key words at important transition points within Deuteronomy 8. The outline presented is an adaptation of Van Leeuwen's work.

I. 8:1: Introductory Frame — Observe the commandment so you may live
II. 8:2-17: Remember/Do not forget
   A. 8:2-10: Remember
     1. 8:2-5: The wilderness journey in the past
      (Result of remembering: obedience to God — 8:6)
     2. 8:7-9: The promised land in the future — echoes of the Garden of Eden[8]
      (Result of remembering: praise of God — 8:10)
   B. 8:11-17: Do not forget
     1. 8:11-13: The promised land in the future
      (Result of forgetting: exalt yourself — 8:14)
     2. 8:15-16: The wilderness journey in the past
      (Result of forgetting: claim self-sufficiency — 8:17)
III. 8:18-20: Closing Frame — Remember and live; forget and perish

One of the better-known phrases of Deuteronomy 8 is verse 3: "One does not live by bread alone, but by every word that comes from the mouth of the LORD." After fasting for forty days in the wilderness, Jesus quoted these words from Deuteronomy to counter the temptation to use his power to turn stones into bread and thus satisfy his hunger (Matt. 4:4; cf. Luke 4:4). The central point of these words in Deuteronomy is not to uphold a kind of "spiritual" or ascetic ideal over against a "material" or physical world. Rather, the chapter urges acknowledgment that all the gifts that make for life come from the hand (or here "the mouth") of God.[9]

DEUT. 9:1 – 10:22: FALSE SELF-RIGHTEOUSNESS: THE ILLUSORY GOD OF MORALISM

Chapter 9 begins with the reminder that Israel is about to cross over into the promised land to dispossess "nations larger and mightier than you" (9:1). But why has God chosen the people of Israel to receive the promised land now occupied by the Canaanites? It was not because of their numerical or military superiority. They "were the fewest of all

---

8. Some interesting relationships between the Garden of Eden in Genesis and the descriptions of the promised land in Deut. 6:10-11 and 8:7-10 are discussed in M. Ottoson, "Eden and the Land of Promise," VTSup 40 (1986): 177–88; and Werner Berg, "Israels Land, der Garten Gottes: Der Garten als Bild des Heiles im alten Testament," *BZ* 32 (1988): 35–51.

9. Raymond Van Leeuwen, "What Comes Out of God's Mouth: Theological Wordplay in Deuteronomy 8," *CBQ* 47 (1985): 55–57.

people" (7:7). It was not because of Israel's great wealth. The people were destitute slaves with nothing except what God had given to them (8:3, 14-16). A third possible explanation is that Yahweh chose the people of Israel because they were morally and ethically superior to any other people, including the Canaanites. Israel may be tempted to believe that its moral obedience and superiority had earned for them the blessings of the promised land.

It is often held that Deuteronomy reflects such a mechanical and moralistic view of reality: if you obey, you will be blessed; if you disobey, you will be cursed. Some scholars argue that the book of Job, for example, was written to refute this allegedly "Deuteronomistic" and mechanical understanding of retribution, sin, and suffering (e.g., Job 21; 23; 42:7). Under this supposedly Deuteronomistic understanding, the Canaanites lost the land because they sinned, and Israel received the land because it was obedient. But the present form of Deuteronomy joins Job in refuting such a mechanical view of retribution and reward. "Do not say to yourself, 'It is because of my righteousness that the LORD has brought me in to occupy this land'" (Deut 9:4). The temptation to claim higher righteousness, superior morality, and greater commitment to God and justice as the basis for God's blessing and election is simply misguided (9:5).

Why then is God clearing out the other nations from Canaan and bringing Israel into the land to possess it? Two reasons are given. First, the wickedness of these other nations in Canaan has disqualified them from any inalienable right to the land (9:5). Beginning from the time of Abraham, the sin of the "Amorites" who inhabit the land has been accumulating to the point that now they will be dispossessed from the land (cf. Gen. 15:16). But Israel has shown itself to be no less sinful or disobedient than these other nations. Thus, the second reason and the *only* positive basis for Israel's claim to the promised land is that God promised to give the land to Israel's ancestors (9:5). God's choice of Israel rests on God's gracious promise, not on any inherently superior moral quality of Israel.[10]

The rest of Deuteronomy 9 is an extended remembrance of particular key rebellions in Israel's past story that function as a paradigm for Israel's understanding of itself and its God. Moses reminds Israel "You have been rebellious against the LORD from the day you came out of the land of Egypt until you came to this place" (9:7). Later in the

---

10. For a more extended discussion of this theme in Deuteronomy, see Georg Braulik, "Law as Gospel: Justification and Pardon According to the Deuteronomic Torah," *Int* 38 (1984): 5–14.

chapter, Moses repeats the same conclusion, "You have been rebellious against the Lord as long as he has known you" (9:24). These conclusions are illustrated by one paradigmatic event in Israel's past, the worship of the golden calf at Mount Horeb. Even as the Ten Commandments were being written by God upon the stone tablets (9:10), Israel rebelled and broke the first and most important commandment, "you shall have no other gods before me" (9:8 — 10:11). Moses retells an abbreviated version of the golden calf story recounted in Exodus 32–34.

This golden calf rebellion was symptomatic of Israel's continual disobedience. Israel repeatedly rebelled at various sites throughout the journey in the wilderness "at Taberah also, and at Massah, and at Kibroth-hattaavah" (Deut. 9:22). Moses recalls the spy story of Numbers 13–14 as part of this series of rebellions (Deut. 9:23; cf. chap. 1). The bulk of Deut. 9:1 — 10:11 recounts the one story of the golden calf apostasy. But 9:6-7 and 9:22-24 recognize this one rebellion as characteristic of Israel's entire history.

The seriousness of Israel's sin in the golden calf story is underscored by Moses' repeated reminder to the people, "The Lord was so angry with you that he was ready to destroy you" (Deut. 9:8; cf. also 9:14, 19, 20 [Aaron], and 25). The one factor that kept Yahweh from destroying Israel was the vicarious suffering, self-denial, and intercession of Moses. Deuteronomy 9:1 — 10:11 schematizes the intercession of Moses into two phases. In the first phase, Moses ascends Mount Horeb to receive the Ten Commandments. Moses remains on the mountain forty days and forty nights, neither eating bread nor drinking water (9:9). The significance of this first reference to Moses not eating and drinking is not explored with any interpretive comment; in this way it resembles the uninterpreted note about Moses not eating and drinking in Exod. 34:28.

In the second reference *after* the golden calf debacle, however, Moses "lays prostrate" (literally in Hebrew, "makes himself to fall") before Yahweh, a posture resembling death and connoting humility (9:18). In this second phase Moses again does not eat and drink for forty days and nights. But this time it is done explicitly for a reason: "because of all the sin you had committed" (9:18). Moses' abstinence from food and drink and his laying prostrate before the Lord are unique elements of Deuteronomy's retelling of the golden calf story — they are not found in the Exodus version. These elements form part of the larger theme of Moses' death and denial that runs throughout the book of Deuteronomy and climaxes with the final death and burial of Moses in chapter 34.

Another feature of the motif of Moses' self-denial is God's offer to

Moses in 9:14 and the prayer of intercession in 9:25-29. In 9:14, God in effect "tempts" Moses with the god of numerical strength and might, the false god that Moses had just discussed in chapter 7. The LORD says to Moses, "Let me alone that I may destroy them [the Israelites] and blot out their name from under heaven; and I will make of you a nation mightier and more numerous than they" (9:14). But Moses refuses to bow down or lay prostrate before this false god of his own self-exaltation. Instead, Moses prays that God's inclination to destroy the people be changed in line with God's merciful and forgiving nature. The prayer in 9:25-29 is a bold act of intercession. It uses much the same tactic to change God's heart and soul as Moses had used to change the heart and soul of Israel: Moses asks God to remember the story of the past and to act accordingly.

Remarkably, Moses succeeds in changing God's plans about destroying Israel. At the beginning, the LORD "was ready to destroy you" (9:8). In the end, Moses reports that "the LORD listened to me. The LORD was unwilling to destroy you" (10:10). Moses appeals to God's consistently gracious intentions, which always outweigh God's judgmental side (cf. 5:9-10). Moses' "death" in chapter 9 (fasting, self-denial, laying prostrate, interceding for others) made possible the life and continuing journey of the people of God (10:10-11).

Given this long history of rebellion, Moses implores the people, "Circumcise then, the foreskin of your heart, and do not be stubborn any longer" (10:16). Chapter 10 concludes by extending the obligation to love God (10:12-13) to include love of the stranger "You shall also love the stranger, for you were strangers in the land of Egypt" (10:19).

DEUTERONOMY 11: LIFE AND DEATH, BLESSING AND CURSE

Deuteronomy 11:1-17 outlines two motivations for loving and obeying God "today." The first motivation stems from God's mercy in the *past,* exemplified in the dramatic rescue from Egypt and in God's ongoing care and guidance in the wilderness (11:1-7). It is important to note here that God's activity involves both the forces of history (defeat of Egypt, journey through the wilderness) and the forces of nature (the water of the Red Sea and the swallowing of the earth—11:4, 6). God integrates the historical and the natural forces of the world as God works in the world. The second motivation looks to the *future:* the dramatic and saving act of God (past exodus, future conquest—11:8-12) and the ongoing care and blessing of the people (past blessing in the wilderness, future life in the land—11:13-17).

Deuteronomy 11 ends with the options that are open to the people in regard to the commandment to love God alone. Moses proclaims, "See, I am setting before you today a blessing and a curse: the blessing, if you obey the commandments of the LORD your God . . . and the curse, if you do not obey the commandments of the LORD your God" (11:26-28). Obedience of any of the commandments is ultimately expressed as the love of God with all one's heart and soul (11:22). Disobedience of any of the commandments ultimately comes down to breaking the first commandment, following "other gods that you have not known" (11:28). The Jewish *Sifre* to Deuteronomy interprets 11:28 this way: "Hence the Sages have said that anyone who acknowledges idolatry denies the entire Torah, and anyone who denies idolatry acknowledges the entire Torah."[11] With different words but similar intent, the church reformer Martin Luther called the first commandment "the most important" of the Ten Commandments, for "where the heart is right with God and this commandment is kept, fulfillment of all the others will follow of its own accord."[12]

Moses instructs the people that when they enter the promised land, they should establish a bold and visible reminder of the two options that lie before them. They are to set the blessing on Mount Gerizim and the curse on Mount Ebal, two mountains in the middle of the land of Canaan near the town of Shechem. Standing from the perspective of inside the land and looking east, Mount Gerizim is the southernmost of the two mountains and thus on the right hand, the position of favor and blessing (cf. Gen. 48:17-19). Moreover, the two mountains were topographically distinct. Gerizim was a mountain green with vegetation, a sign of God's blessing, and Ebal was a starkly barren and dry mountain, a sign of curse and death.[13] Like two billboards with neon lights flashing, the two mountains were visible and tangible reminders of the competing paths that Israel could walk: disobedience and following after other gods, which leads to curse and death, versus obedience and the love of Yahweh alone, which leads to blessing and life.

The theme of the alternative paths that Israel may travel (obedience or disobedience) and the instruction to set the blessing and the curse upon Mount Gerizim and Mount Ebal are repeated later in chapters

11. Reuven Hammer, *Sifre: A Tannaitic Commentary on the Book of Deuteronomy,* YJS 24 (New Haven: Yale Univ. Press, 1986), 112.
12. Martin Luther, "The Large Catechism," in *The Book of Concord,* trans. Theodore Tappert (Philadelphia: Fortress, 1959), 371.
13. Cf. A. D. H. Mayes, *Deuteronomy,* NCBC (reprint, Grand Rapids: Eerdmans, 1981), 218.

27–28. Thus, chapter 11 and chapters 27–28 form a frame or envelope surrounding the "statutes and the ordinances" of chapters 12–26. At this point in chapter 11, the alternative ways of obedience and disobedience are simply presented as equal possibilities even as Moses urges Israel to walk the path of obedience. The theme will be picked up in chapters 27–28. But the perspective will begin to look more to the future in these later chapters. It will focus much more on the side of curse and judgment as it moves into the section beginning with chapter 28 and its decidedly future orientation with the Babylonian exile in view. But for now chapter 11 looks toward the laws of chapters 12–26 as Moses concludes, "you must diligently observe all the statutes and ordinances that I am setting before you today" (11:32).

SUMMARY: DEUTERONOMY 6–11
AND THE DEATH OF MOSES

The explication of the first commandment in Deuteronomy 6–11 explores more fully the commandment's positive meanings to love Yahweh alone. Israel owes its very existence and life to the promise and gifts of God, not to its own achievements. Deuteronomy launches an explicit critique of other gods in whom Israel may be tempted to trust. Each of the three "gods" involves trusting ultimately in human powers and claims to superiority: political and military might (the god of militarism and numerical strength—Deut. 7:1-26), self-sufficient economic power (Deut. 8:1-20), or self-righteous moral or ethical power (Deut. 9:1 — 10:11). Each of these has a rightful place as a gift of God: the numerical increase of Israelites, the gifts of food and prosperity, and the obedient life of righteousness and justice. But such gifts can also become gods, objects of ultimate concern. Investing total allegiance in these human gods will lead to disobedience and death.

The theme of Moses' death outside the promised land has already been linked with the concerns of the first commandment in Deut. 4:21-24. Part of the meaning of Moses' death is that Moses is not God. Moses' burial place is not known, a deliberate check against establishing a shrine or worship of the dead for Moses (Deut. 34:6). But in light of Deuteronomy's emphasis on the first commandment, Moses' death extends beyond the life of one individual as a metaphor for human finitude and limitation even while celebrating the marvelous ways in which God worked through a human being like Moses (Deut. 34:10-12).

Moses' death has both a negative and a positive meaning. On the negative side, Moses' death is a critique of all attempts to idolize or divinize human achievements. Like Moses, all human creations will finally fall short and flounder on the rocks of time and mortality. But on the positive side, Moses' death functions as a model of how life is to be lived. In Deuteronomy's retelling of the golden calf episode (Deuteronomy 9), Moses "dies" to advancing his own self-interest and instead advocates before God on behalf of a rebellious Israel. God in effect tempts Moses with an offer of an ideal promised land "Let me alone that I may destroy them [the Israelites] . . . , and I will make of you [Moses] a nation mightier and more numerous than they" (9:14). Moses resists the temptation and persuades God to preserve Israel. Just as Moses died outside the land of Canaan so that the people could enter it (Deut. 4:21-22), so too Moses resisted the temptation of a mighty and numerous nation of his own so that God would not destroy the people. In both cases, Moses "dies" in order that the people might live.

CHAPTER 5

"These Are the Statutes

and the Ordinances" —

Deuteronomy 12–18: Expansions of

the Ten Commandments, Part One

Hananiah the son of the brother of R. Joshua said: Just as in the case of the sea there are small waves between one big billow and another, so between one commandment and another came the detailed interpretations and signs of the Torah.

—Palestinian Talmud, *Sheqalim* 6.1[1]

The story of the past in Deuteronomy 1–4 began with the editorial superscription "These are the words" (1:1). Chapter 5 was introduced by another superscription in 4:44, "This is the *torah*." Chapter 5 functioned as a "small *torah*" or a "Small Catechism" of Deuteronomy, a blueprint for the rest of the book. Chapter 6 began with the superscription "Now this is the commandment — the statutes and the ordinances," which served as an overarching superscription for all of chapters 6–28. This Mosaic address could in turn be broken down into two subsections, with "This is the commandment" introducing chapters 6–11 (the first commandment) and the second subsection beginning with "the statutes and the ordinances," which introduce chapters 12–28.[2] Having journeyed through chapters 1–4, 5, and 6–11, we consider the next section of the book, chapters 12–28. This chapter of our study will examine Deuteronomy 12–18, the first half of the statutes and ordinances, while

1. Quoted in Ephraim E. Urbach, *The Sages: Their Concepts and Beliefs,* trans. Israel Abrahams, 2d ed., 2 vols. (Jerusalem: Magnes, 1979), 1:361.
2. Earlier scholars had understood the phrase "statutes and ordinances" in Deut. 12:1 to function primarily as a designation for two different kinds of laws within chaps. 12–26 (obligations to Yahweh vs. civil law, apodictic vs. casuistic law, cultic vs. judicial law). But Norbert Lohfink (*Das Hauptgebot,* AnBib 20 [Rome: Pontifical Biblical Institute, 1963], 56–57) has shown that the primary function of the phrase in the present form of the book is not to designate two different forms of laws. Rather, the two words in the phrase, "statutes" and "ordinances," mean essentially the same thing. The phrase is simply a word pair that functions as a superscription or title for the section of laws in chaps. 12–26. The phrase in Deut. 12:1 and 26:16 serves to frame the collection of laws. Cf. also Georg Braulik, "Die Ausdrücke für 'Gesetz' im Buch Deuteronomium," *Bib* 51 (1970): 39–66.

the next chapter will be devoted to the second half in Deuteronomy 19–28.

The Ten Commandments of chapter 5 are terse and compressed statements, begging for further interpretation and elaboration. Chapters 6–11 are an interpretation and expansion of the first and most important of the commandments, "you shall have no other gods." Chapters 12–28 function in a similar way as interpretations and extensions of the Ten Commandments. The "statutes and ordinances" in these chapters are exemplary applications of the Decalogue into the concrete and everyday life of the community. Their concerns include worship, economics, politics, judicial practice, marriage and sexuality, family life, business practices, and relations with other nations and communities.

Studies by Stephen Kaufman and Georg Braulik among others have argued that chapters 12–28 lay out these legal applications in roughly the same sequence of themes as in the Ten Commandments.[3] Adapting

3. Attempts to account for the sequence of the statutes and ordinances in Deuteronomy 12–26 have been many and varied. Some scholars have discerned no order or organization in these laws. An example is A. C. Welch (*The Code of Deuteronomy: A New Theory of Its Origin* [London: Clarke, 1924]), who concluded that "while any order into which the laws may be placed is sure to be unsatisfactory, none can be quite so bad as the order in which they appear in Deuteronomy today" (p. 23). The suggestion that the sequence of laws in chaps. 12–26 is organized according to the sequence of topics in the Ten Commandments has had some support among commentators in the history of Deuteronomy's interpretation. One of the earliest forerunners of such an approach was the Jewish philosopher Philo of Alexandria (first century C.E.) who sought to organize all the laws of the Torah (not just the laws of Deuteronomy 12–26) according to the sequence of topics in the Ten Commandments. Cf. Yehoshua Amir, "The Decalogue according to Philo," in *The Ten Commandments in History and Tradition,* ed. Ben-Zion Segal and Gershon Levi (Jerusalem: Magnes, 1990), 121–60. Sixteenth-century reformers such as Calvin and especially Luther understood the laws of chaps. 12–26 as sequential explications of the Ten Commandments.

Although some nineteenth- and early twentieth-century commentators suggested such an arrangement, a more systematic argument for the sequence of the Ten Commandments as the key to the sequence of laws in Deuteronomy 12–26 was put forth by Stephen Kaufman, "The Structure of the Deuteronomic Law," *Maarav* 1/2 (1979): 105–58. Kaufman used the organizing principles of ancient Near Eastern law codes as evidence for the ways in which laws were gathered together into collections as the basis for understanding how seemingly unrelated laws were brought together under a given topic. Kaufman is particularly indebted to the insights of H. Petschow, "Zur Systematik und Gesetzestechnik im Codex Hammurabi," *ZA* 57 (1965): 146–72; idem, "Zur 'Systematik' in den Gesetzen von Eschunna," *Symbolae juridicae et historicae M. David dedicatae,* vol. 2 (Leiden: Brill, 1968), 131–43.

Also using Petschow, Georg Braulik has modified some of Kaufman's divisions and arrangements of Deuteronomy 12–26 while agreeing that overall chaps. 12–26 are arranged according to topics that largely follow the Ten Commandments. In making his divisions between sections of laws, Braulik depends more than Kaufman on internal criteria of changes in theme, introduction of casuistic law, changes in forms of laws, concluding formulae, and framing devices. Cf. Braulik, "Die Abfolge der Gesetze in Deuteronomium 12–26 und der Decalog," in *Das Deuteronomium, Entstehung, Gestalt und Botschaft,* ed. Norbert Lohfink (Leuven: University Press, 1985), 252–72; idem, "Zur Abfolge der

some of the conclusions of these studies and allowing for overlap in some divisions, I outline chapters 6–28 in the following way:

Deuteronomy 12–28: The Statutes and Ordinances
Deut. 12:1: "These are the statutes and the ordinances"

1. 12:2 – 13:18: Explication of the first commandment – no other gods
2. 14:1-21: Explication of the second commandment – God's name
3. 14:22 – 16:17: Explication of the third commandment – sabbath
4. 16:18 – 18:22: Explication of the fourth commandment – parents
5. 19:1 – 22:8: Explication of the fifth commandment – killing [22:5: transitional unit in anticipation of the upcoming laws on adultery and sexuality]
6. 22:9 – 23:18 (Heb. 23:19): Explication of the sixth commandment – adultery [23:15-16 (Hebrew 23:16-17): transitional unit in anticipation of the upcoming laws on stealing]
7. 23:19 (Heb. 23:20) – 24:7: Explication of the seventh commandment – stealing [24:1-5: transitional unit hearking back to the preceding law on adultery and sexuality]
8. 24:8 – 25:4: Explication of the eighth commandment – bearing false witness
9. 25:5-12: Explication of the ninth commandment – coveting your neighbor's wife
10. 25:13 – 26:15: Explication of the tenth commandment – coveting anything that belongs to your neighbor

---

Gesetze in Deuteronomium 16,18 – 21,23. Weitere Beobachtungen," *Bib* 69 (1988): 63–92. Braulik's first article provides a helpful summary of the history of research in this area.

Within the broader framework of the thematic sequence of the Ten Commandments, other factors are at work in the arrangement of the laws such as associations of word, sound, or theme or literary patterns or chiasms. Cf. Alexander Rofé, "The Arrangement of the Laws in Deuteronomy," *ETL* 64 (1985): 265–87; Calum Carmichael, "A Common Element in Five Supposedly Disparate Laws," *VT* 29 (1979): 129–42; G. J. Wenham and J. G. McConville, "Drafting Techniques in Some Deuteronomic Laws," *VT* 30 (1980): 248–51; and Lyle Eslinger, "More Drafting Techniques in Deuteronomic Laws," *VT* 34 (1984): 221–26. The question of whether such careful arrangement is evidence of a unitary redaction or authorship is an open one. In my judgment, one must reckon with the possibility of a long history of collection and arrangement of these laws along with a definitive editing of the collection as a whole at some point. A few other laws may have been inserted after this definitive editing; this sequence may account for some of the apparent disjunctures in the sequence of laws. My own conclusions involve a selective use of both Kaufman and Braulik with some modification.

A useful image for picturing how the statutes and ordinances follow in the sequence of the Ten Commandments is the image of ocean waves suggested by Hananiah in the quotation that opened this chapter. Each of the ten sections outlined has one of the Ten Commandments as the primary swell that underlies it. The smaller waves, the statutes and ordinances, flow in and out of this larger commandment. But often no major breaks occur between one section of the statutes and ordinances and the next. The smaller waves, the statutes and ordinances, flow like rippling water into one another and often overlap with no decisive demarcation between them. These more detailed statutes, which are in some way connected to the Ten Commandments in succession, flow together on the basis of associations of topics, key words, motifs, and even similar-sounding words.[4]

In these next two chapters of this study, I move through these ten sections of Deuteronomy 12:1 – 26:15, noting in brief how each of the Ten Commandments is extended or reinterpreted in various directions. I then consider the concluding frame to this section in 26:16 – 28:68 as an interpretation of the purpose of "the statutes and ordinances" in the preceding chapters.

PRELIMINARY OBSERVATIONS ON THE STATUTES AND ORDINANCES

Six preliminary observations about the character and function of these laws may help orient us as we move into this large and varied collection of laws.

1. *Centrality of the first commandment.* References to the first commandment, loving the LORD alone and not following other gods, reappear frequently like a unifying thread running through many of the statutes and ordinances (12:30, 31; 13:2, 3, 6, 7, 13; 17:3; 18:20; 19:9; 20:18; 26:16-19).

2. *Remembrance of Israel's origin as slaves in Egypt.* The remembrance of Israel's past as slaves in Egypt and the LORD's gracious deliverance from slavery forms a primary motivation and basis of

4. Cf. Kaufman, "Structure," 115. Cf. also Rofé, "Arrangement," 265–87. I find helpful many of Rofé's suggestions for why some laws are associated with others, but I do not find compelling his contention that an accidental tearing of scrolls resulted in an error in the arrangement of the Deuteronomic laws. Other attempts to account for arrangements of particular sections of the Deuteronomic laws include Carmichael, "Common Element," 129–42, dealing with laws in Deuteronomy 21; Wenham and McConville, "Drafting Techniques," 248–51, dealing with laws in 22:13-29; and Eslinger, "More Drafting Techniques," 221–26, dealing with laws in 25:4-12.

obedient action throughout the laws (13:5, 10; 15:15; 16:1, 3, 6, 12; 17:16; 20:1; 23:4; 24:9, 18, 22; 25:17; 26:5-9).

3. *The recurring triad of relationships throughout the statutes and ordinances: God, humans, and creation.* Each of the ten clusters of statutes and ordinances in chapters 12-26 that correspond to the series of Ten Commandments contain laws pertaining to three community relationships: (a) the relationship to God, (b) the relationship to other humans (particularly caring for the powerless or dependent and avoiding the idolatrous practices of other nations), and (c) the relationship to the nonhuman creation or world of nature. For example, the statutes and ordinances in 12:2 – 13:18, which explicate the first commandment's prohibition against other gods, include laws not only about worshiping Yahweh and avoiding all other gods. The statutes in this section also include laws about caring for humans who are powerless in society (children, slaves, dependent Levites – 12:12, 18-19) and laws pertaining to the gifts of creation in harvested grain and firstborn animals, which are to be offered back to God and then eaten and shared with others (12:6). Moreover, when animals are slaughtered, the blood is not to be eaten as a kind of reverence for life in all its forms: "for the blood is the life" (12:23). This interpenetrating triad of relationships – God, other humans, and creation – recurs throughout *each* of the ten sections of the statutes and ordinances.

4. *The language of death throughout the statutes and ordinances.* Language of "death" saturates these statutes and ordinances. The words "death" and "die" (Hebrew *mwt*) occur thirty-two times in the statutes and ordinances of chapters 12-26. The occurrences include death penalties for disobedience, issues of human killing and war, an important reference back to 5:25 and the issue of a future prophet like Moses, and laws for cases when a person dies. The words *death* and *die* occur only four times in chapters 1-11 but at four key points: the death of the old wilderness generation (2:16), the future death of Moses (4:22), the people's fear of dying when they hear the voice of God at Mount Horeb (5:25), and the death of Aaron (10:6). How one lives in the light of this reality of death in the past and in the future is the concern of the statutes and ordinances. This concern over issues of life and death weave the laws of Deuteronomy into the larger tapestry marked by the distinctive theme of the death of Moses.

5. *Obedient life as faithful dying.* In his study *Law and Theology in Deuteronomy* J. G. McConville observes that many laws in Deuteronomy

> are in some way costly to the one who obeys. . . . The principle involved is in fact a paradox. Enjoyment of the land and its benefits

depends upon a readiness to relinquish them. We have noticed that blessing was promised for the act of self-denial involved in slave release or the remittance of debts. But it is actually a regular principle that where blessing is promised it is in the context of self-restraint.[5]

The statutes and ordinances in chapters 12–26 speak of death and giving and letting go. But as they do so, they also call the faithful to rejoice in all that God has given (12:7, 12, 18; 14:26; 16:11, 14, 15; 26:11; 27:7).

Obedience in the statutes and ordinances is fundamentally giving away a portion of what God has given (money, property, crops, power, life, freedom, time, space) as acknowledgment of dependence on God. Such relinquishment is done in relation to *God* (e.g., tithes, sacrifices, sacred space and time, purity restrictions, singular devotion to God that transcends commitment even to one's family). Such relinquishment is done in relation to the *neighbor* (e.g., release of debts and slaves; no bribes; justice for the poor, the widow, the orphan, and the landless; crops left for the needy; maintenance of some restrictive boundaries of clean and unclean in regard to interpersonal, sexual, agricultural, dietary, and other matters). Or it is done in relation to *nature* (e.g., saving lost or fallen animals, not muzzling an ox, letting the mother bird go while only taking the young, restrictions on the cutting of trees). Obedience is learning to let go of the gifts God has given. Disobedience is grasping and clinging to God's gifts, making them into idolatrous objects of ultimate allegiance, desire, and trust.[6] This theme resonates with the portrayals of *Moses* dying outside the land for the sake of the people (4:21-22) and his "dying" to his own self-interests in the golden calf story (9:14-20).

DEUTERONOMY 12:1 – 13:18: NO OTHER GODS
(FIRST COMMANDMENT) – GOD'S PRESENCE AND WORD

Deuteronomy 12–13 interpret the first commandment, "you shall have no other gods before me," in two ways. First, the *place* of worship where God's presence will dwell is centralized; all other cultic sites and practices are to be destroyed (12:1-28). Second, the people should hear and follow the *voice* of Yahweh alone: all other voices claiming priority over the word of God are to be resisted and destroyed (12:29 – 13:18).

5. J. G. McConville, *Law and Theology in Deuteronomy*, JSOTSup 33 (Sheffield: JSOT Press, 1984), 15, 17.
6. Ibid., 12–13.

DEUT. 12:1-28: THE PLACE THAT THE LORD WILL CHOOSE

The significance of the phrase in chapter 12, "the place that the LORD your God will choose as a dwelling for his name," has been a much-discussed issue in modern biblical scholarship. This phrase is first found here in Deuteronomy, but it recurs throughout chapters 12–26.[7] Deuteronomy never names "the place," but most scholars have equated it with the city of Jerusalem, Judah's political and religious capital since the beginning of the monarchy under David and Solomon.[8] The Deuteronomistic History explicitly makes the identification in 1 Kings 8. As King Solomon prays to God, he dedicates the temple at Jerusalem as "the place of which you said, 'My name shall be there'" (1 Kings 8:29; cf. also 1 Kings 8:44, 48).

While Jerusalem certainly came to be identified with "the place that the LORD your God will choose," the focus of Deuteronomy 12 is not on the identification of one particular site (Jerusalem). Rather, the focus is on the insistence that the central worship place (in whatever city it is located) be the one that God *chooses*.[9] Deuteronomy 12:8 makes the point clearly: "You shall not act as we are acting here today, all of us according to our own desires." God will choose where the divine presence and power will be accessed and available; humans alone cannot contain or capture the divine presence and power in any place they choose.

---

7. Longer or shorter variations of the formula "the place that the LORD your God will choose" occur in Deut. 12:5, 11, 14, 18, 21, 26; 14:2, 23, 24, 25; 15:20; 16:2, 6, 7, 11, 15, 16; 17:8, 10, 15; 18:6; 26:2; 31:11.

8. The exclusive identification of Jerusalem with "the place that the LORD your God will choose" in Deuteronomy 12 was supported by Julius Wellhausen (*Prolegomena to the History of Ancient Israel,* trans. J. S. Black and A. Menzies [Edinburgh: A. & C. Black, 1885], 32–33, 492) and has been carried forward by more recent studies, e.g., Ronald Clements, "Deuteronomy and the Jerusalem Cult Tradition," *VT* 15 (1965): 300–312; E. W. Nicholson, "The Centralization of the Cult in Deuteronomy," *VT* 13 (1963): 380–89; and Jon D. Levenson, "From Temple to Synagogue: 1 Kings 8," in *Traditions in Transformation,* FS Frank Moore Cross, ed. Baruch Halpern and Jon D. Levenson (Winona Lake, Ind.: Eisenbrauns, 1981), 143–66. It is this call to centralization of worship in one place (presumably Jerusalem) that most clearly suggests some link between Deuteronomy and the cultic reforms of King Josiah in 2 Kings 22–23 as he destroyed the altars and worship sites outside the temple of Jerusalem.

9. Given that Deuteronomy may contain traditions which are earlier than the monarchy and the rise of Jerusalem as Judah's religious capital and given that Deuteronomy has roots in northern Israelite soil, then it is at least possible that "the place that the LORD your God will choose" may have once referred to a northern cult center like Bethel or more probably Shiloh. The strongest evidence for this possibility is the prophet Jeremiah as he speaks in God's name of Shiloh as the place "where I made my name dwell at first" (Jer. 7:12). Cf. McConville, *Law and Theology in Deuteronomy,* 21–38. Gerhard von Rad (*Studies in Deuteronomy,* trans. David Stalker, SBT 1/9 [London: SCM, 1953], 38–39) notes that the identification of the "place" with the city of Jerusalem is "only one possibility" since "Deuteronomy never speaks of the city of Jerusalem."

Later Jewish and Christian traditions sought to maintain this delicate balance between affirming God's transcendent freedom and God's self-imposed limitation of a specific, concrete, and earthly place in which the Deity was present and revealed to human worshipers. For the Jewish tradition, Robert Cohn concludes his study of biblical mountains and cities (Mount Zion, Jerusalem) as centers of divine presence with observations about later biblical and rabbinic reactions to the Babylonian destruction of Jerusalem and the exile of its inhabitants:

> When Jerusalem was destroyed by the Babylonians, the paradoxical attitude toward the holy place was manifested in the differing responses of the survivors. On the one hand, men from the north came to worship Yahweh on the ruins of the temple (Jer. 41:4f.), testifying to the belief in the ongoing sanctity of the site. On the other hand, exiles in Babylon saw Yahweh to be a *miqdāš mĕ'at,* "little sanctuary" (Ezek. 11:16), wherever they were in exile. Yahweh had been liberated from the sacred place with which he had been identified. When the second temple fell, the rabbis debated whether or not the Shekhinah [the presence of God] had fled with the flames into heaven and forsaken them but decided, rather, that the presence of God had accompanied them into exile (*Mekilta* 1:114f.). Jerusalem remained the ambiguous center, partaking of but not wholly containing the holiness of Yahweh. The center for Judaism was sacred but not ultimate.[10]

God's presence is both free and yet paradoxically bound through self-imposed and specific limitation and choice.

Deut. 12:29 – 13:18: Hearing the Singular Voice of God among the Competing Choruses of Falsehood

Deuteronomy 12 designated the proper *place* of worship as the one chosen by Yahweh. Deuteronomy's expansion of the first commandment goes on to specify the one *voice* or word to be obeyed amid all the competing voices that may tempt allegiance away from Yahweh. The section proceeds through a series of expanding concentric circles where the voices become stronger in their tempting power as one moves out. The sections revolve around quotations from an inner voice (12:30), the voices of individual false prophets (13:2), the voices of family members or intimate friends (13:6), and the voices of an entire community or town (13:13). In each case, the tempting voice speaks the same words: "Let us follow or worship other gods." Moses then warns

---

10. Cohn, *The Shape of Sacred Space: Four Biblical Studies,* AAR Studies in Religion 23 (Chico, Calif.: Scholars Press, 1981), 79. Cf. also Jonathan Z. Smith, "The Wobbling Pivot," *JR* 52 (1972): 146–49.

the people not to listen to these voices but rather "put [them] to death," "stone them to death," "utterly destroying" them (13:5, 10, 15).

Deuteronomy 12:29-32 begins with one's own inner voice, which may covet the way in which other nations or cultures worship their gods, saying, "How did these nations worship their gods? I also want to do the same." But some practices among other religions are simply abhorrent, such as the sacrificial burning and killing of sons and daughters. Human sacrifice practiced by other nations is something "the LORD hates" (12:31; cf. 2 Kings 3:27; 16:3; 21:6; Jer. 7:31). One should also not unquestioningly heed the voice of an individual prophet with magical or heroic powers of prediction (Deut. 13:1-5), the voice of a close family member or friend (13:6-11), or the voice of an entire community (13:12-18). The powerful voices of self, false prophets, family members, and even whole towns may join in a chaotic cacophony of competing voices to tempt Israel to follow other gods. But to this discordant chorus, Deuteronomy directs the reader to the one overriding voice who will tolerate no rivals: "obey [šĕma'] the voice of the LORD your God" (13:18).

DEUTERONOMY 14:1-21: GOD'S NAME
(SECOND COMMANDMENT) — PURITY, BOUNDARIES,
AND POWER

How do these laws against worshiping the dead (14:1-2) or the dietary laws distinguishing between clean and unclean foods (14:1-21) in any way relate to the second commandment against the misuse of God's name ("you shall not make wrongful use of the name of the LORD your God" — 5:11)? To answer that question, one needs to survey the uses of the "name of Yahweh" in Deuteronomy:

1. The *name* of Yahweh is set apart as holy in contrast to the names of other gods (6:13; 10:20; 18:19-20, 22).
2. The place that Yahweh chooses for the divine *name* to dwell is to be set apart from all other rival cults and worship places, which are to be destroyed (12:5, 11, 21; 14:23, 24; 16:2, 6, 11; 26:2).
3. The Levites are set apart from the rest of the Israelites to minister to and bless the people in the *name* of Yahweh (10:8; 18:5, 7; 21:5).
4. The people of Israel are in turn to be set apart from all the nations and from the *names* of the other gods of those nations (6:13-14; 12:3; 26:19; 28:10).

5. If the Israelites do not fear the glorious and awesome *name* of Yahweh their God, then Yahweh will overwhelm them with afflictions "until you are destroyed" (28:58-61 – a summary at the end of the statutes and ordinances).

In the social world of Deuteronomy, the holiness and dangerous power of God's name threatened Israel with death whenever Israel moved outside its boundary as the chosen people of Yahweh by worshiping other gods and adopting the idolatries of other nations.

If one takes these images associated with the name of God in Deuteronomy and joins them with an understanding of the laws of purity or cleanness in the Old Testament, some important continuities emerge. The laws of purity in Deut. 14:1-21 are probably related in some way to the Priestly laws of purity in Leviticus 11 as well as other texts.[11] Other biblical purity laws that distinguish between clean and unclean matters occur in both early and late legal material (Exod. 23:18-19; 34:11-28; Leviticus 17–26; Numbers 12; 19; 25). The function of these laws of purity or cleanness in the social world of ancient Israel has been a much-debated issue in the history of biblical interpretation. Some argue that the purity laws function as primitive rules of hygiene, as regulations against Canaanite religious practices, or as reflections of deeper ethical principles.[12] Anthropologist Mary Douglas has argued that the purity laws are part of a social symbol system that classifies boundaries within the realm of nature in order to protect the society from destructive powers. Unclean animals are those who in some way mix or cross over perceived boundaries: fish without fins or scales, flying insects with multiple rather than just two legs, animals that either do not chew the cud or do not have divided hooves.[13] Purity regula-

---

11. A. D. H. Mayes, *Deuteronomy,* NCBC (reprint, Grand Rapids: Eerdmans, 1981), 237–38; and W. L. Moran, "The Literary Connections between Lv. 11, 13-19 and Dt. 14, 12-18," *CBQ* 28 (1966): 271–77.

12. Helpful surveys and critiques of various proposals for understanding the biblical purity laws include Brevard Childs, "The Role of the Ritual and Purity Laws," in *Old Testament Theology in a Canonical Context* (Philadelphia: Fortress, 1986), 84–91; and Baruch Levine, "The Meaning of the Dietary Laws," in *Leviticus,* JPS Torah Commentary (New York: Jewish Publication Society, 1989), 243–48.

13. Cf. Mary Douglas, *Purity and Danger: An Analysis of Concepts of Pollution and Taboo* (London: Routledge and Kegan Paul, 1966), 53. Douglas has refined her work on the biblical purity laws in a number of subsequent publications. Cf. Douglas, *Implicit Meanings: Essays in Anthropology* (London: Routledge and Kegan Paul, 1975); idem, "Critique and Commentary," in Neusner, *Idea of Purity,* 137–42; and most importantly, idem, "Deciphering a Meal," *Daedalus* 101 (1972): 61–81.

One of the difficulties in applying Douglas's anthropological work to the biblical text is the question of the level at which she is working. Does this classification scheme reflect ancient Israelite society? In what period? Are the regulation of clean and unclean foods

tions extended not only to food laws. They involve sex and marriage, family relationships, business practices, physical anomalies, and most importantly the rejection of abhorrent worship practices of other gods by other nations.

But what is the connection between these purity laws and the proper use of the divine name within Deuteronomy? Both concerns emphasize the designation of various boundaries in Israel's existence: boundaries of holiness, cleanness, and life that when transgressed bring the Israelite community into dangerous spheres of unholiness, uncleanness, and death. The misuse of the divine name in the second commandment involves Israel crossing boundaries from exclusive devotion to the name of Yahweh into the wrongful worship of the names of other gods of other nations. The purity laws likewise prohibit crossing boundaries from clean to unclean food.

This connection between the concerns of the divine name commandment and the purity laws is further strengthened by noting the introduction and conclusion to this section of laws in Deuteronomy 14. The introduction (14:1-2) reminds the listener, "You are children of the LORD your God" who bear the divine Parent's name (6:13-14). The names of other illicit gods include gods associated with the cult of the dead, the worship of dead ancestors, which is strictly prohibited: "You must not lacerate yourselves or shave your forelocks for the dead" (14:1). Verse 2 connects this exclusive devotion to Yahweh with Israel's status as a people set apart and holy to Yahweh alone: "you are a people holy to the LORD your God; it is you the LORD has chosen out of all the peoples on earth to be his people, his treasured possession." 14:21 likewise affirms Israel's status as a people holy to the LORD.

The section relating to the second commandment, Deut. 14:1-21, concludes with an enigmatic prohibition: "You shall not boil a kid in its mother's milk." Here it appears as a dietary law, but in Exod. 23:19

---

and its rationalizations a product of the Priestly writers of Leviticus that the writers of Deuteronomy have subsequently taken over? David P. Wright, in "Ethical Foundations of the Biblical Dietary Laws," *Religion and Law,* 196, is probably correct in commenting on the debates between Milgrom and Douglas, that these classifications developed over time and had multiple origins: economic competition and preference for some domestic animals over others, hygiene, simple aversions, nationalism, and resistance to the practices of other religions or peoples. The Priestly writers of Leviticus systematized the divisions between clean and unclean and offered their own rationalizations centered on the demand of Israel to be holy before its God. The question that has not been adequately addressed is what happened to these purity and dietary laws in Deuteronomy. What effect does the placement of Deuteronomy 14 under the rubric of the second commandment and the misuse of the name of God have on the meaning of the dietary laws?

and 34:26, the law stands in a sacrificial context. In the realm of sacrifice, some have argued it is a rejection of a particular Canaanite fertility rite.[14] Within the present dietary context of Deuteronomy 14, another suggestion seems more probable: boiling a young kid (an act of killing) should not be mixed with something which gave that same animal life (its mother's milk). To do so would be mixing the boundaries between life and death, thus creating an "unclean" situation.[15] This concluding law ties together the themes of the boundaries associated with the interplay between the sphere of animals and humans: boundaries between the realms of life and death, clean and unclean, the people of God and the other nations, the name of Yahweh and the names of other gods.

DEUTERONOMY 14:22 – 16:17: THE SABBATH
(THIRD COMMANDMENT) – LETTING GO AND SETTING FREE

The statutes and ordinances in Deut. 14:22 – 16:17 reflect the required interruptions in time, work, and ambition that are at the heart of the commandment to keep the sabbath holy. In the cycle of years and annual harvests, the interruptions include structured time to remember the gifts that God has given, time to give offerings back to God, time for worship, time for celebration, time for sharing with those in need, time for releasing debts and slaves and giving to the poor. The laws in this section speak of regular cycles of days, weeks, and years in which offerings, festivals, and releases are to occur: "yearly" (14:22), "every third year" (14:28), "every seventh year" (15:1), "in the seventh year" (15:12) "year by year" (15:20), "the month of Abib" (16:1), "for seven days" (16:3), "on the seventh day" (16:8), "seven weeks" (16:9), "seven days" (16:13, 15), and "three times a year" (16:16). Time is punctuated by interruptions that call the community back to remember their vocation as the people of God.

The set of statutes and ordinances related to the sabbath in Deut. 14:22 – 16:17 breaks down into three groups of laws: (1) regulations concerning the offering of tithes of crops and firstlings of herds (14:22-29); (2) laws governing the sabbatical years of release for debtors, the poor, and slaves (15:1-18); and (3) laws concerning the offering of firstlings of livestock and the celebration of three festivals – Passover, Weeks, and Booths (15:19 – 16:17). The first and

---

14. H. Kosmala, "The So-Called Ritual Decalogue," *ASTI* 1 (1962): 50-53.
15. After surveying a variety of explanations of the law, Jacob Milgrom ("You Shall Not Boil a Kid in Its Mother's Milk," *BibRev* 1 [1985]: 48–55) concludes: "The root rationale behind the kid prohibition is its opposition to commingling life and death."

third group of laws deal more explicitly with "sacred" matters and serve as an inclusio around the more "secular" laws concerning the economic system of social welfare involved in the sabbatical release of debts and slaves. The relationship to God remains intimately tied to economic relationships with other humans.

DEUT. 14:22-29: A STEWARDSHIP BANQUET—
OFFERING TITHES OF CROPS AND FIRSTBORN ANIMALS BACK TO GOD

Israelites are here instructed to "set apart a tithe of all the yield of your seed that is brought in yearly from the field" (14:22). The purpose of this tithe offering is "so that you may learn to fear the LORD your God always" (14:23). The offering *giver* is the primary target of benefit for the tithe, another important beneficiary is the neighbor in need. Every third year each town is to set aside and store up the tithe to be available as food for the Levites, the resident aliens, the widows, and the orphans in order that they "may come and eat their fill" (Deut. 14:29).[15] The Levites function in the community as mentors or teaching examples of what dependence on God means. Their bodily presence in the midst of the community brings to mind the powerful sabbath memory: "Remember that you were a slave in the land of Egypt" (5:15; 15:15; 16:12).

DEUT. 15:1-18: SETTING THE CAPTIVES FREE—
LAWS GOVERNING THE SABBATICAL YEAR OF RELEASE

Deuteronomy 15 sets out a program of social justice related to other biblical laws concerning the sabbatical year for the land and the fifty-year jubilee (seven times seven years) in Leviticus 25 and the slave law in Exodus 21:2. It is also associated with later prophetic texts such as Jeremiah 34, concerning a slave release in Jerusalem just before the Babylonian exile, and a postexilic text with eschatological overtones (Isa. 61:1-2). The Gospel of Luke portrays Jesus using the text of Isaiah 61 for his inaugural sermon on a sabbath day at the beginning of his ministry (Luke 4:16-19). The theme of the sabbatical year has been a powerful vision of hope, but scholars debate whether it was ever implemented in ancient Israelite society.[16]

One may divide the sabbatical law in Deuteronomy 15 into three sections: the release of debts (15:1-6), the care of the needy (15:7-11),

---

16. C. Wright, "What Happened Every Seven Years in Israel?" *EvQ* 56 (1984): 129–38, 193–201. A thorough study of the rhetoric and argumentation of chapter 15 as a whole is Jeffries Hamilton, *Social Justice and Deuteronomy: The Case of Deuteronomy 15*, SBLDS 136 (Atlanta: Scholars, 1992).

and the release of slaves (15:12-18). The release of debts every seven years applies to "a neighbor who is a member of the community" (15:2). Because of this periodic cancellation of all debts in the community, part of the distinctiveness of the people of God is that "there will . . . be no one in need among you" (15:4).

The last statement leads immediately into the next section, which begins, "If there is among you anyone in need, a member of your community" (15:7). The law is realistic and so makes provisions for the existence of needy persons even within the community. Unlike the other parts of the sabbath laws that are structured according to a given time schedule, this provision for the needy is on an ad hoc basis as the need arises. This provision is dependent on the inclination of the hearers. Thus, the law intends to shape not only the actions but also the inner attitudes and emotions of the hearers. This shaping is done through imagery, grammar, and argument.

The imagery in 15:7-11 seeks to shape the attitudes and behavior of the hearer by linking images of the outer bodily limb (the hand) to the inner bodily organ (the heart), which was seen as the seat of the will and intellect. "Do not be hard-hearted or tight-fisted toward your needy neighbor," or literally in Hebrew, "do not harden your heart or close your hand" (15:7). The next two verses urge the opposite reaction in both outward action ("You should rather open your *hand*" — 15:8) and inward thought ("Be careful that you do not entertain a mean thought," literally in Hebrew, "lest there be an evil thought in your heart" — 15:9). Verse 10 continues the appeal to both the inner thoughts and the outer actions of those who give: "Give liberally and be ungrudging when you do so" (literally in Hebrew, "and there should not be evil in your heart when you give to him"). The section concludes with the ultimately desired action, the open palm: "I therefore command you, 'Open your hand to the poor and needy neighbor in your land'" (15:11).

The imagery of the outer hand and the inner heart is joined with powerful grammar. Verses 8, 10, and 11 all contain an emphatic imperative construction in Hebrew that in effect places a strong exclamation point after each command: "*open* your hand!" "*give* liberally!" "*open* your hand!" The emphatic imperative recognizes the typical reluctance of the givers and the special care that one must take to lift up the needs of the poor, urging the advantaged to give to those who are not.

The imagery and the grammar supplement the reasoning and argument of this passage. First, 15:7 reminds the hearers that the land has been given to them by Yahweh; it is a gift that they have received from

God, not a possession they have earned. As God has given freely, so too they ought to give freely. Second, if one refuses to help the poor, "your neighbor might cry to the LORD against you, and you would incur guilt" (15:9). The cry of the poor against the oppressive rich has power to move God to action against the oppressor. In the context of the sabbath and its remembrance of the exodus out of Egypt, this warning recalls the cry of the Israelite slaves in Egypt to God and God's effective crushing of Pharaoh and his oppression (cf. Exod. 3:23-25). To refuse to help the poor is to become another pharaoh who will incur guilt and the wrath of God. Third, in a more positive vein, the Israelite ought to give liberally to the needy "for on this account the LORD your God will bless you in all your work and in all that you undertake" (15:10).

Finally, the fourth argument is often misused: "Since there will never cease to be some in need on the earth, I therefore command you, 'Open your hand to the poor and needy neighbor in your land'" (15:11, author's translation). The premise of the argument is often employed to draw a conclusion opposite to the one in the text: "Since there will always be poor people on the earth, why bother trying to improve the lot of the needy? The problem of poverty will never go away, so why not divert our attention to more easily attainable goals and pursuits?" Such sentiments reflect an inability to come to grips with living in a wilderness world that is not a pure and perfect promised land. Conditions such as persistent poverty tend to be ignored or denied since they call into question naïve optimism in human self-achievement. But Deuteronomy knows the truth: There will always be some in need. And Deuteronomy knows that the proper response which will help lead to some proximate, if not perfect, justice is: open your hand and give generously!

One recalls the injunction to the community of God's people a few verses earlier, in Deut. 15:4: "there will . . . be no one in need among you." The ideal is no one in poverty. Yet 15:11 knows the reality of human greed and oppression that will make the ideal difficult to attain: "There will never cease to be some in need in your land." Deuteronomy's realism, however, does not lead to despair but to energized exhortation and action. The juxtaposition of the structured or institutionalized remission of debts every seven years (15:1-6) with the strong pleas for voluntary giving to the poor as the need arises (15:7-11) suggests that poverty is best fought simultaneously on two fronts: the institutionalized system of structured communal assistance (sabbatical release) and vigorous effort that supplements and fills the holes that institutional care inevitably leaves open.

DEUT. 15:19-23: GIVING THE FIRST AND THE BEST TO GOD —
THE OFFERING OF THE FIRSTBORN LIVESTOCK
Offerings to God and acts of justice for the neighbor necessarily go together. Thus, the laws about releasing slaves and caring for the poor are followed by a law concerning the dedication of the firstborn livestock to God: "Every firstling male born of your herd and flock you shall consecrate to the LORD your God" (15:19). The "firstling" is given to God as a reminder that it and all that is to follow comes from God and will one day return to God. The connection to the commandment for sabbath rest is made in the regulation that "you shall not do work with your firstling ox" (15:19; cf. 5:14).

DEUT. 16:1-17: THREE SABBATH FEASTS
THAT INTERRUPT THE YEAR — PASSOVER, FEAST OF WEEKS,
AND FEAST OF BOOTHS
Under the umbrella of the sabbath and the regular interruption of time and work, the writers of Deuteronomy have collected the three feasts celebrated in the spring and fall: (1) the Festival of Passover and Unleavened Bread in the spring, and (2) the Feast of Weeks and (3) the Feast of Booths in the fall. The *Passover* regulations in 16:1-8 contain numerous echoes of the sabbath commandment in 5:12-15.[17] The Passover law begins, "*Observe* the month of Abib by keeping the passover" (16:1). The verb translated "observe" is the same Hebrew word used to begin the sabbath commandment in 5:12. The Festival of Passover and Unleavened Bread is the primary occasion for remembering the exodus out of Egypt, the central concern of Deuteronomy's form of the sabbath commandment (16:1, 3, 6; cf. 5:15). The Passover is a seven-day festival; on the seventh day of the Passover "you shall do no work" (16:8; cf. 5:14). Just as the sabbath day is a regular interruption in the busy routine of each week, so Passover is a regular interruption in the hectic springtime routine of every year. Passover is celebrated "in the evening at sunset, the time of day when you departed from Egypt" (16:6). Israel commemorates Passover as a time of watching, waiting, and hoping as it peers with anticipation into the darkness of an unknown future. Tradition remembers Passover as "a night of vigil" (Exod. 12:42), a night of expectation and hope for what God would do.
The *Feast of Weeks* is also related to the sabbath commandment. The festival begins "seven weeks from the time the sickle is first put to the standing grain" (16:9). The Feast of Weeks is an interruption after

---

17. McConville, *Law and Theology in Deuteronomy,* 118-19.

the hectic activity of the harvest. Moreover, just as the sabbath commandment's primary concern is to give rest to the dependent and powerless people of the community (Deut. 5:14), so the Feast of Weeks makes special provisions for the community's most vulnerable and dependent members: children, slaves, Levites, strangers, orphans, and widows (16:11).

The third sabbatical festival is the *Feast of Booths*. Its link with the seventh day of the sabbath includes its duration of "seven days" (16:13, 15) as well as its attention to the welfare of the dependent sectors of the community (16:14; cf. Deut. 5:14). The Feast of Booths is a thanksgiving not so much for natural blessings of crops but for manufactured blessings that humans produce through their technology: "when you have gathered in the produce from your threshing floor and your wine press" (16:13). Even products made through human ingenuity and skill are ultimately gifts from God. "The LORD your God will bless you in all your produce *and in all your undertakings*" (16:15).

DEUTERONOMY 16:18 – 18:22: PARENTS AND AUTHORITY (FOURTH COMMANDMENT) – THE LIMITS OF HUMAN POWER

The statutes and ordinances of 16:18 – 18:22 share with the commandment honoring parents a basic set of values concerning the role and purpose of authority, whether exercised in a smaller family context (5:16) or in a larger community or national context (16:18 – 18:22).[18] In ancient Israel, parents were primary holders of authority within the family context and warranted honor and respect. But parents were not gods, and they were not to be worshiped, particularly in a cult of dead parents or ancestors (18:9-14). The primary thrust of the *commandment* concerning parents is that authorities are to be honored. The primary thrust of the *statutes and ordinances* that explicate the parents commandment is that authorities are to be worthy of the honor they receive. Leadership brings responsibilities. Deuteronomy thus moves

---

18. The themes and key words that unify this section of laws in Deut. 16:18 – 18:22 as an explication of the fifth commandment and the question of authorities and leadership within the community are well documented by Georg Braulik, "Zur Abfolge der Gesetze in Deuteronomium 16,18 – 21,23. Weitere Beobachtungen," *Bib* 69 (1988): 63–82. Cf. also Kaufmann, "Structure," 133–34. A detailed redactional study of Deuteronomy's leadership laws is Udo Rüterswörden, *Von der politischen Gemeinschaft zur Gemeinde: Studien zu Dt. 16,18 – 18,22,* BBB 65 (Frankfurt am Main: Athenaeum, 1987). Rüterswörden detects a movement from a layer of preexilic laws that reflected actual historical practice in Israel's history to a later exilic layer that changed as Israel moved from a national-political entity (preexile) to a covenant community (postexile).

beyond what ethicist Paul Lehmann describes as the false opposition between hierarchy and equality to a model of "reciprocal responsibility" involving both those who hold authority and those who are led.[19]

Within the patriarchal context of ancient Israel, the commandment's inclusion of both father *and* mother deserves note. The authority was shared by two parents, not centered in only one individual. This distribution of authority and power carries over into the statutes and ordinances on authority in Deuteronomy 16–18. These chapters outline the decentralization and limitations of authority among judges, kings, priests, and prophets.[20] Deuteronomy's program achieves this distribution of power through the number of different leadership offices as well as the variety of bases by which leaders are legitimated (heredity — kings and levitical priests — 17:20; 18:15; human appointment — judges — 16:18; or a claim to divine appointment and charisma — prophets — 18:15).[21]

---

19. Paul Lehmann, "The Commandments and the Common Life," *Int* 34 (1980): 341–55.

20. This distribution and balancing of human authority envisaged by Deuteronomy 16–18 has been observed in several studies. Norbert Lohfink ("Distribution of the Functions of Power," in *Great Themes from the Old Testament*, trans. Ronald Walls [Edinburgh: T. & T. Clark, 1982], 55–75) concludes that in Deuteronomy "an earlier and greater concentration of power in monarchy and priesthood is scaled down and an attempt is made to create a balance of power between four different authorities: the judiciary, the king, the temple priesthood, and free charismatics" (p. 72). In a study of capital crimes in Deuteronomy's law code, Louis Stulman ("Encroachment in Deuteronomy: An Analysis of the Social World of the D Code," *JBL* 109 [1990]: 613–32) argues that Deuteronomy perceives a grave threat to the community not only from foreigners outside the community but also from leaders within the community itself. Thus, Stulman contends, Deuteronomy is concerned to distribute the base of leadership and power among several competing and varied groups and elements within the community so that exclusive power is not vested in one group or leader alone. Cf. also Leslie Hoppe, "Deuteronomy and Political Power," *TBT* 26 (1988): 261–66; and Moshe Greenberg, "Biblical Attitudes toward Power: Ideal and Reality in the Law and Prophets," in *Religion and Law*, 101–12. Bernhard Lang ("George Orwell im gelobten Land: Das Buch Deuteronomium und der Geist kirchlicher Kontrolle," in *Kirche und Visitation*, ed. E. W. Zeeden and P. T. Lang [Stuttgart: Klett-Cotta, 1984], 21–35) points to Deut. 17:2-7 as a source or precedent for highly centralized oppressive religious control characteristic of Western Christianity. Lang claims that Deuteronomy's system of control is patterned after late Assyrian systems of imperial control. But the larger context of Deuteronomy 17–18 leads to an opposite model — the careful distribution and balance of human power and control, the affirmation of diverse voices, and centralization around one concept alone — strict adherence to the first commandment, "you shall have no other gods before me." On that point, there is no compromise.

21. The Deuteronomic conception of the prophet followed a largely charismatic model. In ancient Israel, however, some prophets from other non-Deuteronomic traditions did have more institutional ties to central establishments of power such as the royal court. Isaiah of Jerusalem is an example of a Jerusalemite court prophet. Cf. Robert R. Wilson, *Prophecy and Society in Ancient Israel* (Philadelphia: Fortress, 1980), 135–308.

In this way, leadership in Deuteronomy's program was distributed over several bases of authority. Human tendencies to make gods of themselves, their leaders, or their institutions are undercut by Deuteronomy's limitations and dispersal of human authority.

DEUT. 16:18−17:13: THE JUDGES

The collection of statutes and ordinances on authority begins with laws pertaining to "judges and officials throughout your tribes, in all your towns that the LORD your God is giving you" (16:18). We often assume that judges simply apply the rules or laws that the legislating body of the nation or other rulers have established. Bernard Jackson has argued that the modern Western model of judges simply applying rules or laws to cases does not apply to the biblical view of the function of judges in ancient Israel. Concerning 16:18-20, Jackson writes,

> The judges are here told simply to act justly and avoid corruption. They are not asked to follow any particular rules. I am not, of course, suggesting that they are being given an entirely free discretion. The passage has clear wisdom connections, as seen by the proverb used as a motive clause [Deut. 16:19]. That seems to me to be a clue as to the kind of criteria which the judge is expected to apply: his sense of justice is to be tempered by the conventional norms of practical wisdom.[22]

Verse 20 proclaims to the judges, "Justice, and only justice, you shall pursue." In the context of early Israelite society and Deuteronomy's world, judges did not mechanically and legalistically apply laws. Rather, they sought intelligently to negotiate and arbitrate disputes and so work toward a consensus of the community. As is common in communities where kinship and tribal forms of alliances exist, the goal of judges is the restoration of the community and relationships involved, not just retaliation or legalistic application of rules.[23] Judges must thus have some status of respect among the populace that accounts for their being appointed by the people (16:18). In 1:13 Moses instructs the people to choose judges to assist him in settling disputes, and he lays out the criteria for judges: "Choose for each of your tribes individuals who are wise, discerning, and reputable to be your leaders."

---

22. Bernard S. Jackson, "Legalism and Spirituality," in *Religion and Law,* 245.

23. Robert R. Wilson, "Israel's Judicial System in the Pre-Exilic Period," *JQR* 74 (1983): 229–48, esp. 235–40. Wilson cites the trial of Achan in Joshua 7 and the account of the rape of the Levite's concubine in Judges 19–21 as two narrative examples of judges seeking to resolve difficult cases through building community consensus and negotiaion. Cf. also Moshe Weinfeld, "Judge and Officer in Ancient Israel and the Ancient Near East," *IOS* 7 (1977): 67–76.

What is the fundamental meaning of this "justice" that the judges are to pursue when they settle disputes between people and groups? "You must not distort justice; you must not show partiality; and you must not accept bribes, for a bribe blinds the eyes of the wise and subverts the cause of those who are in the right" (16:19). Michael Goldberg has suggested that this prohibition of bribes is a unique element in comparison to other ancient Near Eastern conceptions of judges.[24] The practice of offering a gift to the judge in order to have one's case heard or in order for a favorable verdict to be rendered was a common and accepted practice in the culture of the Near East outside of Israel.

Goldberg traces the unique Israelite prohibition of bribes or gifts to judges back to Israel's unique conception of its God, who takes no bribes or gifts (Deut. 1:17; cf. 2 Chron. 19:6-7). Goldberg notes the juxtaposition of the law prohibiting bribes to judges with the preceding laws of tithes and offerings that are given to God only *after* the harvest has taken place.[25] The common practice of fertility cults in the ancient Near East was to give offerings and sacrifices to the gods *before* the crops were harvested in order to encourage or manipulate the gods to give a bountiful harvest. In Deuteronomy, however, the offering is given *after* the harvest as a token of gratitude for what God has already given. Moreover, the offering is returned immediately to the worshiper to be eaten and shared with others. God was a God of justice with no visibly human characteristic that motivated God to choose one people over another. God was not motivated by bribes, offerings, power, wealth, or moral character. The primary example of this was God's election of Israel, despite the absence of any superior qualities over other people (cf. Deuteronomy 7-12). Similarly, the judge was to be as impartial and objective as possible.

The law of the judges is immediately followed by a series of laws concerning forbidden forms of worship, particularly the worship of other gods (16:21 – 17:7). Some scholars have seen these verses about false worship as intrusive into the collection of laws having to do with judges and other leaders of Israel.[26] But the intrusion of this (16:21 – 17:7) and a second group of laws (18:9-14) prohibiting the worship of other gods highlights a consistent feature of the statutes and ordinances.

---

24. Michael Goldberg, "The Story of the Moral: Gifts or Bribes in Deuteronomy?" *Int* 38 (1984): 15-25. Goldberg cites several Near Eastern examples of judges expecting bribes or gifts. Even some of the wisdom sayings in the book of Proverbs affirm this Near Eastern practice of giving gifts as bribes for favorable treatment (Prov. 17:8; 21:14).
25. Ibid., 22-25.
26. An example is Rofé, "Arrangement," 278: "Also significant is the fact that 16,21 – 17,7 are misplaced in their present setting as they disrupt the law of judiciary."

Again and again, the laws that explicate the Ten Commandments are grounded in the first commandment, "you shall have no other gods." One can properly understand the issue of honoring authorities and leaders only in connection with the laws prohibiting false worship of other gods. Yahweh alone is God and worthy of worship. All other human creations, persons, institutions, and powers derive their authority only provisionally and secondarily from God. No human leader is infallible and worthy of worship.

This point is driven home by the laws in the rest of the section that acknowledge the limitations of human judges and thus include other members of the community in the adjudication of difficult and serious cases (Deut. 17:6-13).

DEUT. 17:14-20: THE KING

Early in its national life, Israel was bitterly divided over the issue of whether their nation should be ruled by a king like the other nations around them. Those who opposed kingship argued that Yahweh was their ruler; a human king would only attempt to substitute himself for God. Others argued that this human form of centralized government was a practical necessity required to unify the nation against strong enemies. One finds a taste of this debate in 1 Samuel 8. The law of the king reflects a compromise in this bitter debate, allowing a human king but putting severe limits on the powers and functions of the ruler.[27]

Deuteronomy allows kingship but with important qualifying conditions. First, the king must be one "whom the LORD your God will choose" (17:15), typically through a prophet (1 Samuel 16; 2 Samuel 7). The king was thus subject to a higher divine authority.

Second, the king must be "one of your own commuinty." While the institution of kingship may be borrowed from the other nations, the person occupying the throne may not come from a foreign nation. A foreigner will only bring other gods, other myths, and other laws that will rob Israel of its true identity as the unique people of Yahweh.

Third, the Israelite king must not be tempted to worship the false gods that Deuteronomy 7-10 enumerated under the rubric of the first commandment: the gods of *militaristic power, materialism, and self-righteous moralism*. Deuteronomy 17:16-20 cover these false gods in the same order as they appear in chapters 7-12:

---

27. On these verses as a balanced critique of Israelite kingship, see Werner H. Schmidt, "Kritik am Königtum," in *Probleme biblischer Theologie,* FS Gerhard von Rad, ed. Hans Walter Wolff (Munich: Chr. Kaiser, 1971), 440-61.

- no stockpiling of military chariots or horses; no diplomatic marriages or alliances with foreign nations and gods for political power (militarism, numerical strength) (Deut. 17:16-17a)
- no acquisition of gold and silver in great quantity (materialism) (Deut. 17:17)
- study a copy of the *torah,* no exalting of oneself or turning aside from the commandment (self-righteous moralism) (Deut. 17:18)

Much of the Deuteronomistic History is concerned with documenting the abuses of kings throughout the history of Israel precisely along the lines set out in this law of the king. King Solomon is a notable example. He acquired large numbers of horses for chariots from Egypt (1 Kings 4:26; 10:26-29), returned to Egypt in the sense of marrying Pharaoh's daughter (3:1; 9:16, 24) and instituting slave labor (5:13-18), married many foreign wives (chap. 11), and accumulated vast wealth (10:14-22). The most important redeeming quality of Solomon was his early request to God not for riches or power but for wisdom in order "to discern between good and evil" and thus govern the people well (chap. 3). But in his old age, Solomon's wives "turned away his heart after other gods" so that "the LORD was angry with Solomon" (11:4, 9). The fundamental problem was a first commandment issue: following after other gods. According to the Deuteronomistic History, this basic problem plagued kings and people throughout the history of Israel and Judah (e.g., Josh. 24:14-19; Judg. 2:16-17; 1 Sam. 8:8; 1 Kings 12:28-30; 14:9; 2 Kings 17:5-23; 21:1-26; 22:17).

DEUT. 18:1-14: THE LEVITICAL PRIESTS

The main concern of 18:1-8 is that the Levites, whether priests at the central place of worship or in the towns, be cared for by the offerings and sacrifices given by the rest of the populace. The Levites were a class of people totally dependent on Yahweh and the offerings given to Yahweh: "They shall have no inheritance among the other members of the community; the LORD is their inheritance" (18:2). The Levites were in perpetual exile. They relied on God alone for their well-being. They were a tangible reminder of Israel's dependence on God.[28]

---

28. A. H. J. Gunneweg, *Leviten und Priester,* FRLANT 89 (Göttingen: Vandenhoeck & Ruprecht, 1965), 128. According to Gunneweg, the ideal of the "poor" Levite is limited to forms of the tradition earlier than those in the present form of the text. On the larger and complex question of the Levites in the actual history of Israelite priesthood and religion, cf. A. Cody, *A History of Israelite Priesthood,* AnBib 35 (Rome: Pontifical Biblical Institute, 1969); and Rodney Duke, "The Portion of the Levite: Another

The laws concerning obligations to the Levites are followed by a series of prohibitions against worshiping other gods and using cultic practices associated with other nations for their gods. In keeping with the commandment to honor parents, limits are placed on parents. They cannot make "a son or daughter pass through fire," a practice of human child sacrifice apparently practiced by some surrounding religions (18:10). Nor can grown children seek to make contact with dead parents or ancestors in the context of a cult of the dead; honoring does not mean worshiping parents, even when they are deceased (18:11). Other attempts to invade or manipulate the world of the gods and spirits through divination, soothsayers, ghosts, or spirits are abhorrent; other nations do these things, but Israel is strictly forbidden from doing so (18:9-14). Once again, laws relating to the first commandment and not worshiping the gods of the other nations intrude into these laws concerning human leadership and authority.

The laws in 18:9-13 also function as a transition into the next section of leadership laws. The prohibited practices of divination, soothsaying, sorcery, or consulting dead spirits are all means that presume to know the will of the deity or the course of the future. But if Israel is prohibited from using these methods and if Moses is soon to die, how will the people know God's will? Judges litigate. Kings govern. Levitical priests sacrifice. But who speaks the word of God to the community?

DEUT. 18:15-22: A PROPHET LIKE MOSES

Judges, kings, and priests all have relatively secure and institutionalized bases of power and authority. Deuteronomy's scheme of leadership and distribution of power includes one other group, a wild card who often arises from the margins and is beholden to no one but God. *"The LORD your God* will raise up for you a prophet" (18:15).

Although the prophet is "raised up" by God, the prophet is still chosen "from among your own people" (18:15). The prophet is no superhero from afar but "one of us." The Hebrew emphatically highlights this dimension by placing it first in the sequence of the sentence, literally reading, "A prophet *from among you, from your brethren,* like me the LORD your God will raise up for you" (18:15). Like Moses, this prophet will not have superhuman strength. Recall the first chapter

---

Reading of Deuteronomy 18:6-8," *JBL* 106 (1987): 193–201. Cf. also McConville, *Law and Theology in Deuteronomy,* 151.

of Deuteronomy, which highlights the humanness of Moses and his inability to cope with judging all the people (1:9-18).

The future prophet, says Moses, will be "like me" (18:15). The next verses (18:16-19) probe what it means for a future prophet to be like Moses. Moses refers back to the crucial chapter of Deuteronomy 5, which we have seen to be a summary of the whole book of Deuteronomy. There Moses recalls what happened at Mount Horeb (Sinai) when the Decalogue was given (5:22-27; cf. Exod. 20:18-21). The people of Israel shrink back in terror because of what they see and hear, and they say to Moses: "If I hear the voice of the LORD my God any more, or ever again see this great fire, I will die" (Deut. 18:16). Thus, Moses is commissioned to stand in for the people, to "take the heat" on their behalf, and to mediate between God and the people. The clear implication is unspoken but inescapable: the prophet like Moses will die. If the prophet is one "from among your own people," the prophet's fate will be no different from anyone else who hears the voice of God or sees the fire: death. I again touch upon the theme of the final chapter of Deuteronomy, the death of Moses, and its role in the theological structure and movement of the book as a whole.

The remainder of the passage, Deut. 18:20-22, deals with the problem inherent in charismatic prophecy. How does one tell a true prophet like Moses from a false prophet claiming to speak a word from God? The criteria are set forth, but they leave room for ambiguity. First, "any prophet who speaks in the name of other gods" is false and "that prophet shall die" (18:20). Speaking a word by the name of any god other than "the LORD your God who brought you out of the land of Egypt, out of the house of slavery" leads to death. As we saw in Deuteronomy 6-11, the names of other gods may include the gods of militarism, self-sufficient materialism, and self-righteous moralism along with the other idols of Canaan and the surrounding nations (Baal, Anat, Marduk, etc.).

But that safeguard is not enough. Yahweh knows that some would-be prophets will presume "to speak in my name a word that I have not commanded the prophet to speak" (18:20). This too will lead to death. Yet the people may say, "How can we recognize a word that the LORD has not spoken?" (18:21). The definitive guideline is that the word is false if "the thing does not take place or prove true" (18:22). Unfortunately, this guideline is not always self-evident in the immediate circumstance; the hearer must simply wait and see whether the prophet's words come true. Jeremiah 28 provides a classic case of the encounter between two prophets, Jeremiah and Hananiah, who speak contradictory messages in the name of Yahweh. Jeremiah's true word is confirmed when his prophecy comes true and Hananiah's does not. In the meantime, however, even Jeremiah is not always sure who is speaking the true word of Yahweh (Jer. 28:5-9).

There is one more potential problem. What if a prophet predicts something that comes true while speaking in the name of another god? Earlier, Deut. 13:1-3 made clear that the guideline of the first commandment, "you shall have no other gods," would override any other criterion, even if a prophet's predictive success rate was a hundred percent. Deuteronomy 18:20 confirms this point: "any prophet who speaks in the name of other gods . . . shall die." Once again limits are placed on the exercise of authority. Prophets who speak in the name of the divine are to be honored but not worshiped. Their words must be tested. The reality is that sometimes such tests of truth will be ambiguous and may require the hearer to wait and see, remaining open to the new truth that may be revealed through the prophets. Even with the prophets as guides, the Deuteronomic community of faith is not removed from the ambiguities and struggles of real human existence in a broken world. The false prophet will die. But ironically so will the true prophet. The prophet, whether true or false, is finally also human—one like us, like Moses, one who will die outside the promised land.

SUMMARY: DEUTERONOMY 12–18
AND THE DEATH OF MOSES

As we have noted, two dimensions emerge in Deuteronomy's exploration of themes that are associated with Moses' death outside the promised land. On one hand, Moses' death functions as a cipher for the human failure to arrive at some paradisaical promised land where moral and epistemological foundations are secure, justice and righteousness are unambiguously achieved, boundaries are absolutely demarcated, and authority is singular and centered. But Moses' death also has a second and more positive dimension in Deuteronomy. Moses' death functions as a model of faithful dying to self-interest for the sake of others within the ambiguities and struggles of life before God. Deuteronomy concludes the narrative of Moses' death with a note that celebrates Moses' life which had been given in powerful service for the sake of Israel and of Israel's God (Deut. 32:10-12).

The interplay of these dual themes associated with Moses' death—the realism of human limitations and boundaries and the positive model of God working through Moses' self-giving and dying—resurface throughout the statutes and ordinances in chapters 12–18 in various ways:

- The presence of God "at the place the LORD your God will choose"—the limitation and provisional character of humanly created "foundations" for locating the presence of God and yet the affirmation that God will be present and active in specific places as God chooses (chap. 12)
- Discerning the voice of God amid competing human voices of falsehood—the limitation and falsehoods of human voices claiming to speak for the gods and yet the need to discern the true voice of God through human mediation (chap. 13)
- The necessity of boundaries of holiness against worshiping the dead and other gods and against eating animals who cross over certain boundaries of creation. Israel is set apart as holy and yet exists in the midst of unholy powers that threaten its purity and life (chap. 14)
- The sabbath call to give offerings with joy and regularity to God and to those in need, the need to set slaves free and yet the realistic recognition that "there will never cease to be some in need in the land," which underscores both the limits of human abilities to eradicate poverty and the possibilities for achieving some proximate justice (Deut. 14:22—16:17)
- The decentralization and limits of all human authorities in light of the first commandment's prohibition of worshiping other gods before Yahweh and yet the need for human judges, rulers, priests and prophets to serve the human community (Deut. 16:18—18:22)
- The limits of Moses as a prophet and of his words mediated through the book of Deuteronomy indicated by the need for God to speak through future "prophets like Moses" who will also die outside the promised land (Deut. 18:15-22)

Moses explicitly draws himself into these laws only in Deut. 18:15-22. The statutes and ordinances, however, explore many facets that relate both to the limitations of human action and to the positive blessings that God achieves through human agency, both of which are part of Deuteronomy's reflection on the death of Moses at the boundary of the land of promise.

CHAPTER 6

"These Are the Statutes
and the Ordinances" —
Deuteronomy 19–28: Expansions of
the Ten Commandments, Part Two

"You have heard that it was said to those of ancient time, 'You shall not
murder . . .' but I say to you that if you are angry with a brother or
sister, you will be liable to judgment."
—Matt. 5:21-22

Deuteronomy continues to interpret the Ten Commandments
through Part 2 of the section entitled "statutes and ordinances" in
Deuteronomy 19–28. These laws expand the last six of the Ten Commandments from Deuteronomy 5, which include the prohibitions
against killing, adultery, stealing, false witness, coveting, and desiring.
These last six of the Ten Commandments are grammatically joined
together as a group in Deuteronomy 5 through the recurring Hebrew
conjunction *waw* (translated "neither"; cf. Deut. 5:17-21). They are
also set apart from the previous five commandments by their terseness
and their thematic focus on relationships with one's neighbor. As we
shall see, the statutes and ordinances in Deuteronomy 19-26 which
expand these latter six commandments likewise focus more on relationships with other humans and the sociopolitical facets of human life.
This group of statutes and ordinances is grammatically and themati-
cally intertwined in other ways as well. The chapter ends with a look
at Deuteronomy 27–28, which provides a concluding frame to the
statutes and ordinances with important theological consequences for
understanding the role of the laws in Deuteronomy.

DEUTERONOMY 19:1 – 22:8: KILLING
(FIFTH COMMANDMENT) – LIFE AND DEATH

The commandment against killing in Deut. 5:17 stands out from the
preceding commandments by its simple and terse form "You shall not
murder" or alternatively, "You shall not kill" (in Hebrew, simply

lō' tirṣāḥ).[1] The block of statutes and ordinances in 19:1 – 22:8 explicate this short commandment through a group of statutes that are the "longest," "most complex," and "climactic" section in chapters 12-26.[2] These laws related to the commandment against killing may be divided into four sections:

A. Deut. 19:1-21: The protection of innocent life – cities of refuge, boundary markers, witness laws
B. Deut. 20:1-20: Limits on killing in warfare
C. Deut. 21:1-23: Possibilities and limits in the clash between life and death
D. Deut. 22:1-8: Positive obligations to enhance life

Study of this section begins with a few observations about the commandment prohibiting murder and its related statutes and ordinances.

1. The statutes and ordinances in Deut. 19:1 – 22:8 are bound together under a common topical concern; they all deal with matters of life and death. The areas covered include murder and the judicial system, war, untraced homicides, a dying father and questions of inheritance, the death penalty and rebellious children, a criminal hanging from a tree, saving endangered animals, and preventive, life-saving measures.

Key words also serve to bring cohesion to these statutes and ordinances. The relatively rare Hebrew word for "murder, kill" that is used in the commandment itself (*rṣḥ,* Deut. 5:17) occurs in the opening section of this block of statutes and ordinances in 19:3, 4, 6. Words for "death" and "dying" (Hebrew *mwt*) recur throughout this section (19:5, 6, 11, 12; 20:5, 6, 7; 21:21, 22). The word for "blood" or "bloodguilt" appears at several points: 19:6, 10, 12, 13; 21:7, 8, 9; 22:8. Interestingly, the word translated "tree" or "wood" is found in several of the

---

1. The meaning of the Hebrew *rṣḥ* is not fully captured in English by either "kill" or "murder." The verb concerns a form of illegal violence that threatens the life of the community. Cf. J. J. Stamm and M. E. Andrew, *The Ten Commandments in Recent Research,* SBT 2/2 (Naperville, Ill.: Allenson, 1967), 98–99. Other studies have noted a connection of the verb with blood vengeance that was subsequently broadened in its use in the biblical tradition. Childs summarizes: "The verb *rāsāḥ* at first had an objective meaning describing a type of illegal slaying which called forth blood vengeance. Increasingly the verb came to designate those acts of violence against persons which arose from personal feelings of hatred and malice. The commandment forbids such acts of violence and rejects the right of anyone to take the law into one's own hands out of a feeling of personal injury" (*Old Testament Theology in a Canonical Context,* 76).
2. Kaufman, "Structure," 135, 137. Comparing the relative number of verses assigned to each of the Ten Commandments within chaps. 12–28, the fifth commandment has by far the most verses assigned to it (19:1 – 22:8 – 72 verses).

laws, used both for that which causes death (19:5; 20:20; 21:22-23) and that which gives life (20:19; 22:6).[3]

2. The statutes and ordinances in Deuteronomy 19-21 begin to shift the focus of the laws from the religious to the more earth-bound social, political, and economic dimensions of human communities. Chapters 16-18 introduced the judges, priests, and other political authorities under the commandment on parents and authorities. Chapters 19-21 detail the laws governing the functions of these judges, priests, elders, and other leaders.[4] This shift is appropriate in the light of the passage that immediately precedes this section of statutes and ordinances, the passage about the coming of a new prophet like Moses after Moses' death. New leaders will be raised up to take Moses' place. We recall the opening scene in Deuteronomy when Moses acknowledged his finitude and limits as a leader and so shared power with others (1:9-18).

3. The overarching theme of these diverse laws is the conflict between two forces: the priority of life-giving compassion versus the necessary but ambiguous limits of reality and death. The tug is between protecting the innocent so that "you may live long" (Deut. 22:7) and showing no pity, "life for life, eye for eye, tooth for tooth" (19:21). The laws circle around ambiguous boundaries, mixtures, and extreme cases involving difficult issues of life and death. The scales tip decidedly in favor of mercy, compassion, and humaneness in these matters (19:1-10, 15; 20:10-15, 19-20; 21:10-14, 15-17; 22:1-4, 6-8). Yet the laws uphold the need for some limits, some discipline, some legally irredeemable situations where the law may lead only to tragedy and death (19:11-13, 18-21; 20:16-18; 21:18-21).

4. The statutes and ordinances on killing in Deuteronomy 19-22 extend the meaning of the commandment in three other important directions. First, killing is not just face-to-face murder. Killing can be more systemic and involve the removal of the economic base of a community or of one's neighbor. Moving a neighbor's property boundary and thereby taking someone else's land as one's own falls under the killing commandment (19:14). Such an act undermines the careful distribution of land among the families and tribes of Israel.

---

3. Other key words that bind together smaller subsections of diverse laws include "territory/boundary" (19:3, 8, 14), "son" or "child" (21:15, 16, 17, 18, 20; 22:6, 7), "road/path" (19:3, 6, 9; 22:4, 6), "abomination" (20:18; 22:5), "purge the evil/guilt" (19:13, 19; 21:9, 22), "bloodguilt/innocent blood" (19:10, 13; 21:8, 9; 22:8). Cf. also Kaufman, "Structure," 135–37; and Rofé, "Arrangement," 610–11. A thorough and insightful study of the interconnections and redactional shaping of this section of laws is Georg Braulik, "Zur Abfolge der Gesetze in Deuteronomium 16,18–21,23," 63–92.
4. "Elders"—19:12; 21:2, 3, 4, 6, 19, 20; "priests"—19:17; 20:2; 21:5; "judges"—19:17, 18; 21:2; "officials"—20:5, 8, 9; "commanders"—20:9.

Second, these laws include the killing not only of humans but also of nature. This ecological concern for the care of animals and vegetative life is present in several laws (21:19-20; 22:1-4, 6-7). The nonhuman parts of creation must be sustained so that they can renew themselves and continue to provide food, labor, life, and even forgiveness (21:1-9) for people and communities.

Third, the commandment "you shall not kill" is extended to imply its positive counterpart: "you shall preserve life and work proactively to prevent death." This feature is most evident in the concluding section of these laws.

5. The group of statutes and ordinances in Deut. 19:1 – 22:8 is the first group to contain transitional units or laws that either anticipate the next commandment and its related laws in subsequent chapters or harken back to preceding chapters and their laws. Thus, 22:5, a law against transvestism, falls within the boundaries of the laws having to do with killing but anticipates the laws on sexuality and adultery that come next in 22:9 – 23:18. Similarly, 23:15-16 fall within the laws on sexuality but anticipate the upcoming laws on stealing in 23:19 – 24:7. Another transitional unit in 24:1-5 stands among the laws on stealing but refers to the preceding section of laws on adultery and sexuality.[5]

What is the literary effect of such overlapping transitional units of laws among the various sections having to do with killing, adultery, stealing, bearing false witness, and coveting? One literary effect is to enhance the sense of ambiguity and struggle to discern clear boundaries that I mentioned previously. Form in this way mirrors content. The broken boundaries between some topical units reflect the sometimes ambiguous struggle between right and wrong in matters of human relationships and actions.

The transitional units of laws also underscore the interconnection and interpenetration of these commandments and laws with one another. The statutes and ordinances related to the commandment against killing encompass facets of many of the other commandments,

---

5. Other commentators (e.g., Georg Braulik, "Die Abfolge der Gesetze in Deuteronomium 12-26 und der Decalog," in *Das Deuteronomium, Entstehung, Gestalt und Botschaft,* ed. Norbert Lohfink [Leuven: Leuven Univ. Press, 1985], 260) have discerned these transitional sections of overlapping laws. In my judgment, Braulik has unnecessarily expanded the transitional units to include two larger blocks: 22:1-12 and 23:16 – 24:5. This feature of transitional blocks of material is found in other ancient Near Eastern collections of laws. The Code of Hammurabi includes such transitional units, which seem to intrude in a group of laws dealing with a different topic. But the seemingly intrusive laws serve to anticipate a topic of a group of laws that immediately follows. Cf. Petschow, "Zur Systematik und Gesetzestechnik im Codex Hammurabi," 146–72.

including stealing, bearing false witness, adultery, and coveting. Just as the commandment against other gods is intertwined with all the other commandments, so the commandment against killing is intertwined with the other prohibitions relating to obligations to the neighbor.

DEUT. 19:1-21: PROTECTING INNOCENT LIFE — CITIES OF REFUGE, BOUNDARY MARKERS, AND WITNESS LAWS

The first law in Deut. 19:1-7 makes provisions for establishing three cities of refuge within the boundaries of the promised land once the people have settled there. In the discussion of 4:41-43 in chapter 2, I noted the establishment of three cities of refuge in the territory on the east side of the Jordan River, which is outside the promised land of Canaan. Cities of refuge are a partial solution to a gray area of law, the unintentional killing of one person by another. The three cities are sanctuaries of safety but also places of exile far from home. If God at some future time enlarges the territory of the Israelites "as he swore to your ancestors" (19:8), "then," says the law, "you shall add three more cities" (19:9; cf. Gen. 15:18). The law displays an openness to the future, to new situations, to new promises, and to new contexts.

The next law moves from designated boundaries set around cities of refuge to designated boundaries set around plots of ancestral land that belong to each family or clan (19:14).[6] When Israel entered the promised land, it was to divide the land according to tribes and clans in order to ensure that every family had a piece of ground from which to draw its livelihood (cf. Num. 33:53-54). To move the boundary markers of that ancestral land was to diminish the life of one's neighbor. Another reason this law may be placed among the laws about murder and war is that boundary disputes over land were often the prime cause of conflict, murder, and war. Moreover, in the ancient Near East covenants and treaties typically had at their core the prohibition of moving boundary markers.[7] The prohibition is also part of the wisdom tradition (Prov. 22:28; 23:10). The seriousness of the law is highlighted by its repetition in one of the curses for disobedience in Deut. 27:17 "Cursed be anyone who moves a neighbor's boundary marker."

---

6. The repetition of the word *gĕbûl* meaning both "territory" and "boundary" in the city of refuge law in 19:3, 8 and in the boundary marker law in 19:14 functions to bind the two laws together.
7. Cf. Kaufman, "Structure," 137; and Weinfeld, *Deuteronomy and the Deuteronomic School,* 73–74. An example is the sixth chapter of the Instruction of Amen-em-Opet, *ANET,* 422.

The next law concerns requirements for witnesses to sustain any criminal charge against a person. The requirements protect the innocent from unfounded accusations by a malicious individual. If a witness testifies falsely, that person is to receive the same punishment that the accused would have been given if found guilty. The so-called *lex talionis,* "life for life, eye for eye, tooth for tooth," is applied here to discourage false witnesses and thereby protect the wrongly accused.

DEUT. 20:1-20: LIMITS ON KILLING IN WARFARE

Perhaps one of the most difficult issues in regard to the commandment against murder is the rampant killing that occurs in the Old Testament, some of which God orders in the holy war conquest of the Canaanites (e.g., Deut. 20:16-17; cf. Joshua and Judges). Contemporary readers often find the biblical descriptions of God as a divine warrior troubling (Deut. 32:41-43). The issue of war and peace in the Old Testament opens up a host of problems that I cannot address here. But in general, it is important to recognize that the military conquest of Canaan was a once-for-all, time-bound event consigned to the past in the plan of God. God never told the Israelites later in their history to embark on another holy war. Indeed, the vision of the future to which God is working is portrayed as a future of peace, proclaimed most powerfully by the prophets as a time when "I will abolish the bow, the sword, and war from the land" (Hos. 2:18). In the "latter days" (NRSV "days to come"),

> they shall beat their swords into plowshares,
>   and their spears into pruning hooks;
> nation shall not lift up sword against nation,
>   neither shall they learn war any more. (Isa. 2:4)

But in Deuteronomy as Moses stands at the edge of the promised land, the goal of peace among the nations remains elusive. From Deuteronomy's perspective, the conquest is in the immediate future and is part of the fractured reality within which God and God's people work. Thus Israel will go to war and kill, but it will do so under specific restrictions and limits (Deuteronomy 20).[8]

The first limitations placed on the practice of warfare is a set of exclusions for certain warriors: those who have built a new house,

---

8. An extensive critical discussion of these laws of warfare as an example of "intra-biblical legal exegesis" is provided by Alexander Rofé, "The Laws of Warfare in the Book of Deuteronomy: Their Origins, Intent and Positivity," *JSOT* 32 (1985): 23–44.

planted a new vineyard, become engaged to be married, or those who are "afraid and disheartened" (20:5-8). Limitations on warfare also involved dealing charitably with enemies, at least those from towns "that are very far from you" and not located in the promised land (Deut. 20:15). For any towns or people located within the promised land itself, however, "you must not let anything that breathes remain alive" (Deut. 20:16). We encounter once again the ideology of holy war. The reason is a theological one: "so that they may not *teach* you to do all the abhorrent things that they do for their gods, and you thus sin against the LORD your God" (20:18). It is, in other words, a catechetical battle. The teaching of idolatry and other gods is pitted against teaching the love of Yahweh alone.

As the conquest is played out in the books of Joshua and Judges, Israel does not carry out this last instruction to eliminate all the peoples of the land of Canaan. Indeed, Israel finds itself trapped and forced to disobey the law. With their life in her hands, Rahab the Canaanite prostitute forces Israelite spies into agreeing to allow her and her family to live when the Israelites conquer Jericho. Rahab ends up proclaiming and "teaching" the Israelite spies about faith in Yahweh in eloquent testimony to Deuteronomy's theology (Josh. 2:8-14)! Yet the Israelites will have to disobey the war law of Deuteronomy 20 as they allow Rahab and her family to live. Similarly, the Gibeonites, who are native to the land of Canaan, trick the Israelites into thinking they are from a far country (Joshua 9). The Gibeonites accept terms of peace in a treaty and agree to forced labor. But the Israelites inadvertently again disobey the law of Deuteronomy 20 as they allow the native Gibeonites to live in their midst. The result in Judges 1-2 is that the native peoples of Canaan are not eliminated, and God decides to let the other nations remain "because this people have transgressed my covenant that I commanded their ancestors" and "in order to test Israel, whether or not they would take care to walk in the way of the LORD" (Judg. 2:20-22).

Israel had been trapped into disobeying the law of warfare in Deuteronomy 20. Although the people of God had tried to obey the law carefully, they encountered situations that they did not foresee and for which the law could not adequately prepare them. Thus, God made an adjustment in the divine plan. God allowed the native peoples to remain in the promised land as a teaching device, to test Israel's faithfulness. The promised land would not be a pure and perfect land. Akin to the paradise of the Garden of Eden (Gen. 3:22-24), the promised land after the conquest of Joshua and Judges would always remain in some way a heritage lost, an unrealized promise, a future hope.[9]

Moreover, after the partially fulfilled conquest of Canaan, the law of warfare in Deuteronomy 20 would become in many ways obsolete and irrelevant. For now a new way would have to emerge by which Israel would do battle and cope with the lure of other gods by nations and peoples who lived within Israel itself. Other peoples and other religions would remain in their midst. Israel would have to find a way to teach its children to fear and love God. The people of God could not assume that its land would be totally free of temptations to worship other gods. The promised land would be a place of struggle, of ambiguity, of imperfection, of hardship, a place not unlike the wilderness through which Israel had traveled before. God's people would come to see that there would be no Garden of Eden, no paradise even in this life, even in the promised land. But when God's people laid down their weapons of war, God would place in their hands something else and teach them another way to live in the world. As we shall see, that other way is the way of Deuteronomy, teaching the "book of the *torah* of Moses" (cf. the discussion of Deuteronomy 33 in chap. 8).

The law of warfare continues at the end of chapter 20 with an important and suggestive law about the killing of trees in war (20:19). The sensitivity toward the interdependence of people and nature here shapes even the conduct of war, an activity notorious for its unrestrained pillaging of the environment. The laws place limits on the practice of war. As one study of the war laws in Deuteronomy concludes, "these laws bespoke a humanitarian idealism that sought to hold in check military abandon, bestiality, destructiveness and cruelty."[10]

DEUT. 21:1-23: POSSIBILITIES AND LIMITS
IN THE CLASH BETWEEN LIFE AND DEATH

The statutes and ordinances related to the commandment against killing force the reader into a whole series of ambiguities and limits in dealing with the boundary issues of life and death. We have seen that already in laws related to the judicial system (chap. 19) and in laws dealing with war (chap. 20). The same theme arises in a collection of

---

9. Cf. Gerhard Hauch, "Texts and Contexts: A Literary Reading of the Conquest Narrative (Joshua 1–11)," (Ph.D. diss., Princeton Theological Seminary, 1991); and Christa Schafer-Lichtenberger, "Das gibeonitische Bündnis im Lichte deuteronomischer Kriegsgebote: Zum Verhältnis von Tradition und Interpretation in Jos 9," *BN* 34 (1986): 58–81.
10. Rofé, "Laws of Warfare," 37.

six seemingly unrelated laws in chapter 21. Studies by Calum Carmichael and by Gordon Wenham and J. G. McConville have attempted to discern the coherence of this varied group of laws.[11]

Wenham and McConville have noted a chiastic structure in which the individual laws mirror one another (Diagram 3):[12]

Diagram 3

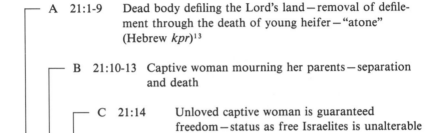

    A   21:1-9   Dead body defiling the Lord's land — removal of defilement through the death of young heifer — "atone" (Hebrew *kpr*)[13]

      B   21:10-13   Captive woman mourning her parents — separation and death

        C   21:14   Unloved captive woman is guaranteed freedom — status as free Israelites is unalterable

        C' 21:15-17   Unloved firstborn son is guaranteed his inheritance — status as firstborn son is unalterable

      B' 21:18-21   Rebellious son executed by parents — separation and death

    A' 21:22-23   Dead body defiling the Lord's land — removal of defilement through burial (Hebrew *gbr*)

However, these laws in Deuteronomy 21 reverberate in interesting ways with Deuteronomy's own portrayals of the relationships of God, Moses, and Israel. Following the chiastic structure of the chapter, some examples include the following:

---

11. Carmichael, "Common Element," 129–42; and Wenham and McConville, "Drafting Techniques," 248–51.
12. Wenham and McConville, "Drafting Techniques," 251.
13. David P. Wright ("Deuteronomy 21:1-9 as a Rite of Elimination," *CBQ* 49 [1987]: 387–403) surveys the various ways in which this ritual slaughter of an unworked heifer at an uncultivated, flowing wadi has been understood. Wright understands the rite as "a reenactment of the homicide in order to eliminate bloodguilt from the community." The pollution of the untraced murder is relocated to an uncultivated area, and the bloodguilt is carried away by the flowing stream from the land to the distant sea. A redactional study of the text is Paul-E. Dion, "Deutéronome 21,1-9: Miroir du dévelopement légal et religieux d'Israël," *SR* 11 (1982): 13–22.

1. The outer frame: A—21:1-9 and A'—21:22-23
   a. 21:1-9—The atoning death of the young heifer—The death of the young heifer in place of the murderer "atones" (Hebrew *kpr*) for the community's guilt. Similarly, Moses takes the sin of the community upon himself in his death (1:37; 3:26; 4:21). The verb *atone* (*kpr*) occurs only twice in Deuteronomy, here in 21:8 and in the Song of Moses where God promises "to cleanse (*kpr*) the land for his people" (Deut. 32:43).
   b. 21:22-23—The burial of the man hung on a tree—The verb *bury* (Hebrew *gbr*) is used here (21:23) and in two other places in Deuteronomy: the burial of Aaron (10:6) and God's burial of Moses on Mount Pisgah (34:1).
2. The inner frame: B—21:10-13 and B'—21:18-21
   a. 21:10-13—Captive woman mourning her parents—The verb *desire/fall in love with* (Hebrew *ḥšq*) is used for an Israelite's love for a captive foreign woman, which leads him to free her and marry her (21:10-13). In Deuteronomy's other two uses of the verb, it is used for God's "desire/love" for a captive Israel in Egypt, which leads God to free Israel and establish a covenant with its people.
   b. 21:18-21—Rebellious son given up to execution by parents— The image of the rebellious and unrepentant son given up by parents to judgment and death (21:18-21) echoes with the image of God as parent who gives up the rebellious Israel to judgment and death (31:27; 32:6, 10, 13-15, 18, 20, 35).
3. The chiastic center: C—21:14 and C'—21:15-17
   Two laws form the center of the chiasm: the law which guarantees the formerly captive woman her freedom (21:14) and the law which guarantees the firstborn son his inheritance (21:15-17). The shared premise of the two central laws is that a promised commitment of freedom or inheritance takes priority over all other considerations. The status of freed Israelite granted to a foreign captive woman through marriage to an Israelite man cannot be taken away (21:14). The status of a firstborn son and his inheritance cannot be altered (21:15-17). Similarly, God will ultimately honor the promise and commitment made to Israel through its ancestors to be their God and to give "the land that the LORD has sworn to their ancestors to give them" (31:7; cf. 9:27; 29:13). God "will not forget the covenant with your ancestors that he swore to them" (Deut. 4:31).

This particular group of laws within Deuteronomy has been the springboard for a number of interesting interpretations in the ongoing life of the biblical tradition. For example, the Jewish rabbinic tradition affirmed the validity of the law of the rebellious son. But the rabbis in the Mishnah placed so many restrictions that had to be met to convict a son of rebellion that the penalty was probably never actually carried out.[14] The New Testament appropriated the claim that "anyone hung on a tree is under God's curse" in its interpretation of the death of Jesus on the cross. The classic text is Gal. 3:13, where Paul quotes Deut. 21:23 "Christ redeemed us from the curse of the law by becoming a curse for us—for it is written, 'Cursed is everyone who hangs on a tree.'"[15]

This collection of laws in Deuteronomy 21 witnesses to the dialectical dimensions of relationships between humans and relationships between God and God's people. On one level, the laws concern mundane social situations and anomalies in the life of a family or community. Isolated from their present context in the book of Deuteronomy, the laws would have no other function. On another level, however, as they are now set within the present form of the book, these laws reverberate with other parts of Deuteronomy. Within this wider setting, the laws in chapter 21 are "nationalized" and "theologized" to reflect upon the ways of God with the people of Israel. The interplay of laws with images of God's relationship to Israel expands the meaning of the commandment against killing into a profound exploration of the tragedy and triumph of human life lived under both the wrath and the love of God.

DEUT. 22:1-8: POSITIVE OBLIGATIONS TO ENHANCE THE NEIGHBOR'S LIFE

The commandment "you shall not kill" entails by extension a positive commitment to enhance and protect life. Thus, Israelites are to care for and return a neighbor's stray or fallen animal (21:1-4), protect mother birds so they can go on producing young (21:6-7), and build a parapet or guard rail on the roof of a house to prevent someone from falling off the edge and being killed (22:8).

Finally, the law in Deut. 22:5 is a transitional prohibition that anticipates the upcoming group of laws related to the commandment against adultery in 22:9—23:18. The theme of these laws relating to adultery and sexuality involves the prohibition of improper mixtures and the concern to maintain the holiness and purity of the people

---

14. *Sanhedrin* 8:1ff. in *The Mishnah,* trans. Herbert Danby (Oxford: Oxford Univ. Press, 1933), 394–95. Cf. Phillip R. Callaway, "Deut. 21:18-21: Proverbial Wisdom and Law," *JBL* 103 (1984): 341–52.
15. Max Wilcox ("Upon the Tree—Deut. 21:22-23 in the New Testament," *JBL* 96 [1977]: 85–99) seeks to link the Deuteronomy texts with the use of the near-sacrifice of Isaac in Genesis 22 as a motif of early Jewish-Christian exegesis.

against the forces of impurity, uncleanness, and improper mixtures. Thus, 22:5 prohibits the mixing of male and female garments or transvestism as "abhorrent to the LORD your God." The law is tied into the preceding laws by repeating the pair — "donkey-garment" — in 22:3 and again in 22:4-5. I say more about the role of prohibited mixtures when I deal with the commandment on adultery in the next section.

DEUT. 22:9 – 23:18: ADULTERY (SIXTH COMMANDMENT) –
GOD, SEX, AND FOREIGNERS

The next section of laws interprets the commandment against adultery. The laws attempt to draw clear lines of proper relationship and conduct in order to avoid improper mixtures on three levels: the improper mixture of men and women in sexual relationships, the improper mixture of Israelites and foreigners in the place of worship, and the improper mixture of unclean conduct or substances and the holy presence of God in the holy war camp.

Many in our day will object to elements in these laws. Sexuality is regulated within a system or network of patrilineal authority that gives predominant control of a woman's sexuality to either her husband or her father. The relationship with foreigners is regulated within a parochial system of exclusion against outsiders. The concern for the purity of the holy war camp in terms of how soldiers relieve themselves seems crude and primitive. The laws are in many ways culture-bound and must be interpreted within the realities of the ancient Near Eastern environment and culture in which they arose. We will see, however, that these patriarchal and exclusionary laws in a sense begin to deconstruct even within this section of laws. The clear boundaries of control and separation begin to waver and blur through the introduction of particular exceptions and limitations that fracture the boundaries and cause cracks to appear at the seams of the respective systems.

The following is an outline of the statutes and ordinances related to the adultery commandment:

22:5: Proper boundaries between women's and men's clothing [transitional unit from previous section]
22:9-12: Proper boundaries in nature — seeds, animals, cloth
22:13-30: Proper boundaries in sexual relations within families
23:1-8: Proper boundaries in membership in the cultic assembly
23:9-14: Proper boundaries of conduct in the holy war camp
[23:15-16: transitional unit for next section of laws related to stealing — freedom for escaped slaves]

23:17-18: Proper boundaries between prostitution wages and vows paid to God

24:1-4: Proper boundaries in divorce and remarriage [transitional unit in the next section of laws but related back to the laws on adultery]

As in previous collections of laws in Deuteronomy, recurring words and themes overlap among these various sections of the laws associated with adultery. Words related to clothes, cloth, cloak, and skirt occur in 22:5, 11, 12, 17, and 30. The related concepts of holiness, cleanness, abhorrence, purging evil, and the maintenance of proper boundaries between things that should be separated and not mixed run throughout the laws. Themes involving sex and gender are prominent and connect with the commandment against adultery.[16]

DEUT. 22:5, 9-12: MARKING BOUNDARIES—
MEN, WOMEN, AND NATURE

The transitional unit in 22:5 prohibiting transvestism as "abhorrent to the LORD" sounds already the major theme of the laws related to adultery. The prohibition against wearing clothes associated with the opposite sex is concerned to demarcate particular boundaries between the sexes. Indeed, the entire section of sexual laws in Deuteronomy 22 presupposes a fairly rigid patriarchal network of gender-defined relationships wherein the husband and father typically exercise authority in relation to women and their sexuality.[17] Men are addressed in the laws, not women. Men are typically the actors and subjects of the verbs in these laws. Men and male elders carry out the judgments and punish-

---

16. Cf. Stephen A. Kaufman, "The Structure of the Deuteronomic Law," *Maarav* 1/2 (1979): 138–39. Georg Braulik ("Die Abfolge der Gesetze in Deuteronomium 12–26 und der Decalog," in *Das Deuteronomium, Entstehung, Gestalt und Botschaft,* ed. Norbert Lohfink [Leuven: Leuven Univ. Press, 1985], 252–72) treats the whole of 23:15−24:5 as a transitional unit from laws relating to adultery and sexuality to laws relating to stealing and possessions. That position is defensible, but it means severely reducing the actual section of laws concerned with stealing proper to only two verses: 24:6-7. Braulik counts all the rest as transitional material. I view the laws concerned with stealing as including all of 23:19−24:7, with the exception of 24:1-4 (a transitional unit looking backward to the adultery laws).

17. Some commentators have over optimistically interpreted Deuteronomy as advocating equality between men and women in conscious opposition to the predominantly patriarchal culture of the ancient Near East. But Carolyn Pressler (*The View of Women in the Deuteronomic Family Laws* [Berlin: W. de Gruyter, 1993]) argues that the family laws of Deuteronomy are thoroughly patriarchal in character, presupposing the authority of husbands and fathers over women. This patriarchal orientation is tempered somewhat by Deuteronomy's additional concern for the welfare of dependent individuals within the community, including the widow and other dependent women.

ments (22:17-18, 21). Payment for improper sexual conduct with a woman is paid not to the woman herself but to her father (22:19, 29). Transvestism is abhorrent "to the LORD." Some ancient Near Eastern evidence suggests that such transvestism was often associated with the worship of foreign gods, both in ancient Mesopotamia and in the later Greco-Roman religions of Asia Minor.[18] The Deuteronomic prohibition of transvestism, which is unique among biblical laws, may reflect Deuteronomy's characteristic emphasis on the worship of Yahweh alone and the avoidance of any practices related to the cultic activities of the gods of other nations. The same word *abhorrence* is used elsewhere in Deuteronomy to describe forbidden forms of worship of other nations (18:9-13).

The laws forbidding some mixtures in nature (22:9-12) continue this theme of ensuring clear boundaries of separation. A vineyard is not to be mixed with a second kind of seed. An ox and an ass should not plow together. Wool and linen were not to be mixed and woven into the same garment. The series of negative commands then moves into a positive injunction: "You shall make tassels on the four corners of the cloak with which you cover yourself" (22:12). What do these laws have to do with prohibiting adultery? Apart from the shared theme of forbidden mixtures, some commentators have argued that these mixtures all have sexual overtones. The references to "planting," "plowing" and clothes may point in subtle ways to improper sexual activity.[19]

Others have suggested the forbidden mixtures are simply reflections of a broader theological concern to establish proper boundaries between those things in creation that are separate and distinct. Creation in Genesis 1 involved divine acts of separation (light from dark, dry land from water, plants and animals, each "according to their kind," etc.). Mixing what has been separated threatens to revert creation back to chaos.[20] From this perspective, the forbidden mixtures display an understanding of the world comparable to the purity and dietary laws of Deuteronomy 14 under the rubric of the commandment about the use of the divine name. The forbidden mixtures may also allude to

---

18. W. H. Ph. Römer, "Randbemerkungen zur Travestie von Deut. 22,5," in *Travels in the World of the Old Testament*, FS M. A. Beek, ed. M. S. H. G. Heerma van Voss et al. (Assen: Van Gorcum, 1974), 217–22; and S. R. Driver, *Deuteronomy*, ICC, 3d ed. (Edinburgh: T. & T. Clark, 1902), 25–51.

19. Calum Carmichael ("Forbidden Mixtures," *VT* 32 [1982]: 394–415) draws connections between these laws prohibiting particular mixtures and stories about Israelites engaging in illicit sexual activity with Canaanites in Genesis 34; 38; and 49:5-12. There may be some sexual overtones, but the connections Carmichael draws with the Genesis narratives often seem stretched and overly generalized.

20. C. Houtman, "Another Look at Forbidden Mixtures," *VT* 34 (1984): 226–28.

prohibitions of intermingling with foreigners, particularly Canaanites. The vineyard can be an image of Israel (Jer. 12:10; Isa. 5:7), and planting a second seed may allude to intermarriage with foreigners, which Deuteronomy 7 explicitly condemns. The ox is an image used of Israel (Deut. 33:17), and the donkey may represent Canaanites or other foreigners.[21] Whatever their precise meaning, these laws serve as introductions to the wider theme of forbidden mixtures at the level of nature that find analogues in the realms of social relationships and cultic activity. The community struggles to maintain proper boundaries and avoid dangerous mixtures.

The two concluding laws about clothing in 22:11-12 both prohibit a mixture (wool and linen) and command the wearing of tassels on the four corners of one's cloak. This law is likely an earlier form of the law in Num. 15:37-41, which instructs that one wear fringes on the garment as a reminder of God's commandments so that "you will not follow the lust of your own heart and your own eyes." The fringes or tassels are to have one blue thread or cord, likely a dyed *woolen* thread in the midst of the typical, undyed *linen* cloth used for clothing.[22] Thus, if one reads Deuteronomy 22 in the light of Numbers 15, the two laws in 22:11-12 forbid mixtures of wool and linen on one hand, yet on the other hand they make an exception. They provide for tassels on the four corners of one's cloak, which would be white linen with a blue wool thread. A mixture is prohibited, but an exception is allowed.

DEUT. 22:13-30: ADULTERY: PATRIARCHY AND ITS LIMITS

The laws concerning sexual relations in 22:13-20 follow a fairly systematic structure that presents six cases of illicit sexual relations between a man and a woman: (1) a husband's false accusation of his wife's lack of virginity at marriage, (2) a husband's true accusation of his wife's lack of virginity at marriage, (3) a man's adultery with a woman married to another man, (4) a man's illicit sexual encounter, in a city, with a virgin engaged to marry another man, (5) a man's illicit sexual encounter, in the open country, with a virgin engaged to marry another man, (6) a man's illicit sexual encounter with a virgin not yet engaged to marry another man.

I have already noted the thoroughly patriarchal character of these laws, with men as the primary actors. Fathers and husbands are

---

21. Carmichael, "Forbidden Mixtures," 406-7. Carmichael notes that in the story of the rape of the Israelite woman Dinah in Genesis 34, the foreigners are led by "Hamor" the Hivite. "Hamor" is the same word used in Hebrew for "donkey" in Deut. 22:10. While intriguing, the intentionality of the connection between the two is not self-evident.
22. Jacob Milgrom, "Of Hems and Tassels," *BARev* 9 (1983): 61-65.

primary plaintiffs and defendants. Fathers are compensated for harm done to their daughters. Women are seen as dependents under the authority of either husbands or fathers. Men and male elders are responsible for adjudicating the cases and carrying out the punishments. Yet this patriarchal system of male control of women and their sexuality has some limits as well. The mother joins the father in defending their daughter against false charges (22:15). The case in 22:13-19 sets some limits on a husband's authority over his wife. He must prove his accusations by showing evidence of his wife's lack of virginity. If his accusations are false, he must pay a fine "because he has slandered a virgin of Israel" (22:19). Moreover, the husband in this case can never divorce his wife, thus ensuring her status within the family. Both women and men may be executed for adultery outside the bonds of marriage, depending on the circumstances. If a man lies with an unengaged virgin, he must pay a fine to her father and never divorce the woman.

The laws clearly remain within a patriarchal network of relationships, with women in a subordinate role. In this aspect, they share the wider ancient Near Eastern cultural pattern of patriarchy. The concluding prohibition of a man marrying his father's wife in 22:30 likewise centers on the harm to the male because the son thereby literally "uncovers his father's skirt." The shame is a matter between the son and the father, not the wife. Nonetheless, the laws also seek to maintain some limits to male authority and dominance. The laws strive to protect the dependent elements of the society, including women. From our vantage point, the laws are sorely inadequate in terms of gender equality. But within the thoroughly patriarchal culture represented by Deuteronomy and ancient Israel, cracks in the patriarchal system may signal a fracturing or limitation in the system of a male-dominated social structure.

DEUT. 23:1-8: US VS. THEM—THE STRUGGLE BETWEEN EXCLUSIVITY AND INCLUSIVITY IN CULTIC MEMBERSHIP

Just as the adultery laws may be troubling to our contemporary sensibilities, so too the exclusivistic tendency in the laws in 23:1-8 may also be unsettling. But again a closer look at these laws in their context in Deuteronomy may reveal some fissures in the exclusionary shell that seems so strongly to demarcate boundaries between insiders and outsiders.

The first law about membership in "the assembly of the LORD" involves males with mutilated testicles or penis. The root concern in this law is not clear. Was such mutilation characteristic of some cultic practices of other religions, a violation of the order of God's creation that blurred the boundaries between sexes, or a limitation of God-given procreative powers and thus grounds for inadmissibility? The meaning of the law remains obscure, but it was one criterion by which people were excluded from the worshiping community.

The second law excludes those "born of an illicit union," even to the tenth generation. The precise meaning of the law again is not clear. Does it refer to those born out of an incestuous relationship (Deut. 22:30) or out of an "illicit union" between an Israelite and a non-Israelite (Deut. 23:3-6; cf. 7:3)? At any rate, some exclusion of people born out of improper sexual relations is envisioned.

The next law prohibits cultic membership to Israel's two closest neighbors, the nations of Ammon and Moab, which lie on Israel's eastern border. Two reasons are given for the exclusion. They did not meet Israel with food and water on their journey from Egypt, and they hired the seer named Balaam to curse Israel. The first reason in the context of Deuteronomy's present form seems to apply only to Ammon since Moab did give food and water to Israel on its journey (Deut. 2:28-29). Chapter 2 says nothing about Ammon so the Ammonites presumably did not aid Israel. The second reason applies really only to Moab since it was the king of Moab who hired Balaam to do the cursing (Num. 22:4-6).

In the present form of Deuteronomy, the discussion of Balaam's attempt to curse Israel rises to some importance. Commentators often overlook the significance of the reference to Balaam. Balaam is explicitly identified as being "from Pethor of Mesopotamia" (literally "Pethor of Aram of the two rivers," referring to the Tigris and Euphrates rivers). The allusions to the exile in Babylon in the later redactional layers of Deuteronomy (Deut. 4:27; 30:4) reverberate here with the mention of "Aram of the two rivers," also known as Babylon. An important parenthetical comment interrupts the law in 23:5 and thus stands out from its context "Yet the LORD your God refused to heed Balaam; the LORD your God turned the curse into a blessing for you, because the LORD your God loved you." This summary of the meaning of the Balaam story connects with the structure of Deuteronomy in its final form. Deuteronomy's laws move toward their end in "curse," judgment, and death (chaps. 27–28), which become associated with the Babylonian exile (30:4). But God will turn the "curse" into a "blessing" (chaps. 30; 33), which will be God's final word and ultimate goal for Israel. The only basis for this miraculous reversal of curse into blessing is in the mystery of God's own mercy and compassion: "because the LORD your God loved you." The exclusion of those who have rejected Israel and its God becomes an opportunity to affirm the enduring faithfulness and love of God to God's people — "because God loved you."

But the exclusion of foreigners or outsiders is not an airtight lockout. The next law commands Israel to be open to "the Edomites, for they are your kin" (23:7). The Edomites are "the descendants of Esau," who was the twin brother of Jacob, the ancestor of the people of Israel (2:4; cf. Gen. 25:19-26). The boundaries between Israel and other nations are not absolute. The necessary fluidity in relationships between God's people and others demands some limitations to the boundaries between "us and them."

The next law allows the children of the Egyptians who enslaved the Israelites to join the assembly of the LORD after three generations (Deut. 23:7-8). The reason for this openness to Israel's former oppressor and enemy is "because you were an alien residing in their land" (23:7). Israel had lived in their land, and the reality was that Israel had intermingled with their people and their world. The walls of separation are fractured here and anticipate a later prophetic vision in which the "eunuch" and the "foreigner" are explicitly invited to come and worship in the house of Yahweh, "for my house shall be called a house of prayer for all peoples" (Isa. 56:1-8).

DEUT. 23:9-18: BOUNDARIES AMONG SOLDIERS, SLAVES, AND TEMPLE PROSTITUTES

The statutes and ordinances explicating the adultery commandment have dealt with the question of proper boundaries in nature, sexual relations, and foreigners in the LORD's assembly. The next section of laws in 23:9-18 deals with proper boundaries among three groups: soldiers in a military camp engaged in a holy war campaign that is about to occur in the conquest of Canaan, escaped slaves, and temple prostitutes. I begin with the laws of purity associated with the holy war military camp. Like the worshiping assembly, a holy war camp is a place of intense divine presence and holiness. Thus, it has special rules about matters of purity and cleanliness since any impurity will jeopardize the success of the holy war campaign (cf. Joshua 7). A "nocturnal emission" makes a soldier unclean. Uncovered excrement in the camp renders the camp unholy. In both cases provisions are made to preserve the purity of the camp through the passage of time, washing with water, or burial in the ground.

The next unit in this section, the escaped slave law in 23:15-16, functions primarily as an anticipatory transitional unit looking ahead to the laws related to the commandment against stealing. But as a transitional

unit, its subject overlaps with the theme of necessary social and theological boundaries balanced with an acknowledgment of the need often
to break through or diminish the significance of such boundaries. The
escaped slave law deals with a social boundary between slave and free.
Typical ancient Near Eastern law prohibited any fugitive slave from
attempting to escape and thereby to cross the social boundary from the
status of a slave to a free citizen.[23] Escaped slaves were to be returned
to their owners.

In the light of its experience of being freed as slaves from Egypt
(Deut. 15:15; 24:18, 22), however, Israel reversed the norms of its
cultural context and demanded that runaway slaves *not* be given back
to owners. Rather, the slaves "shall reside with you." Moreover,
Deuteronomy highlights the new freedom of an escaped slave with the
next phrase: They shall reside "in any place they choose in any one of
your towns" (23:16). Deuteronomy uses this phrase eighteen times. In
seventeen of those occurrences, the deity is the subject as Yahweh
chooses a place of worship for his name to dwell. Only here in 23:16
is the same phrase applied to someone other than God. Thus, the status
of the slave is elevated to a freedom comparable to God's and thus
follows the injunction "you shall not oppress them" (23:16). The social
boundary between slaves and free citizens is fractured in remembrance
of God's freeing of Israel from the slavery of Egypt.

The next unit in this section of laws concerns temple prostitutes,
both male and female (23:17-18). Temple prostitution was a clear violation not only of the adultery commandment but also the commandment against worshiping other gods since it was a practice associated
with idolatry (Hos. 4:12-14; 1 Kings 14:24; 2 Kings 23:7). The osten-
sible boundary is set between money earned in the conduct of temple
prostitution and money used to pay sacred vows to God. Here the
boundary is quite firm between what one might call "idolatrous money"
and money used for sacred purposes. The way money is earned during
the week cannot be divorced from the worship of God done on the
sabbath.

DEUT. 24:1-4: DIVORCE AND REMARRIAGE —
WILL HE RETURN TO HER?

One final law connected with adultery is embedded as a transitional
unit in the laws on stealing in Deut. 24:1-4. While the other transitional
units (22:5; 23:15) look forward to the following section, this unit
looks backward to the preceding collection of laws on adultery. The

23. Code of Hammurabi, §§15-20, *ANET,* 166-67.

law prohibits a man from remarrying a woman whom he had previously divorced if the woman in the interim had married a second man. This law is without parallel either in other biblical laws or in ancient Near Eastern law codes. The law has received much attention in the history of biblical interpretation, from early rabbinic and early church sources up to the present day, because it is one of the few biblical laws dealing directly with the subject of divorce.[24] The reason given for the intial divorce, that the husband "found something objectionable" about his wife, is vague; its meaning is uncertain. The burden of the law, however, is not to describe what constitutes legitimate grounds for divorce. Rather, the law prohibits the reestablishment of a marriage relationship that has already been broken once where a second marriage has occurred in the interim. The prophet Jeremiah quotes and applies this law to the broken relationship between God and Israel and the question of Israel's return (Jer. 3:1-2).

DEUTERONOMY 23:19−24:7: STEALING
(SEVENTH COMMANDMENT)−MONEY, FREEDOM, AND LIFE

The statutes and ordinances in 23:19−24:7 expand and interpret the commandment, "Neither shall you steal" (5:19). We have already looked briefly at the transitional law about the runaway slave in 23:15-16. This fugitive slave law leads into the other statutes and ordinances relating to a neighbor's property. This section contains a number of laws related to stealing and money: a prohibition against interest on loans to a poor neighbor (23:19-20), a command to keep vows and pledges made to God (23:21-23), limits on what travelers can take from a neighbor's crops (23:24-25), limits on what a community can demand from newlyweds (24:5), a prohibition of taking a millstone in pledge because one thereby steals a person's livelihood (24:6), and stealing the life of a fellow Israelite (24:7). These ordinances are topically united and joined to the stealing commandment by placing limits on what can be taken from others: from God, neighbor, or nature. If this amalgam of laws on stealing has any key word, it is Hebrew *nepeš,* which is used in three different contexts: (1) eating "your fill" (literally "according to your desire," 23:24), (2) taking "a life" in pledge (24:6), and (3) kidnapping "the life/person" (my translation) of another Israelite (24:7).

24. Cf. the commentaries. Other studies include R. Yaron, "The Restoration of Marriage," *JJS* 17 (1966): 1–11; G. Wenham, "The Restoration of Marriage Reconsidered," *JJS* 30 (1979): 36–40; R. Westbrook, "The Prohibition of Marriage in Deuteronomy 24:1-4," in *Studies in Bible,* ed. S. Japhet, ScrHier 31 (Jerusalem: Magnes, 1986), 385–405; and Pressler, "View of Women."

Stealing is diminishing the life and well-being (the *nepeš*) of the neighbor. The laws on stealing are also set off from their context and bracketed at their beginning and end by laws relating to slavery and stealing the freedom of a human being (23:15-16 and 24:7).

DEUTERONOMY 24:8 – 25:4: BEARING FALSE WITNESS (EIGHTH COMMANDMENT) – GOD AND THE OX

The commandment against "bearing false witness against your neighbor" protects the honor and good name of a person against false charges in the court. The next section of laws in Deut. 24:8 – 25:4 seeks to preserve the reputation, dignity, and respect of people within the community, whatever their status or condition within the society. The series of ten laws follows a traditionally defined gradation of levels of society and extends the reach of the commandment all the way from the leaders of the community to the criminals and even to the animals within the community. The laws guard the reputation and dignity of people in the following order: Moses and Levitical priests (24:8-9), any debtor (24:10-11), a poor debtor (24:12-13), poor laborers (24:14-15), children and parents (24:16), resident alien, orphan, and widow (24:17-22), criminal (25:1-3), and an ox (25:4).[25] In various ways, the commandment against false witness upholds the legitimate dignity of each of these groups, who often are not dignified or honored by the societies in which they live.

The first law in the series in 24:8 seems out of place with its reference to leprosy, Miriam, and obeying the Levitical priests. What does this have to do with false witness? The answer becomes clearer if one does as the text says: "Remember what the LORD your God did to Miriam on your journey out of Egypt" (24:9). The incident with Miriam is recorded in Numbers 12. There Aaron and Miriam spoke unjustifiably against Moses, who was the legitimate leader of God's people. They slandered Moses "because of the Cushite woman whom he had married." But it becomes clear that their real complaint was that they did not share the unique role of leadership that God had given to Moses (Num. 12:1-2, 5-8). Miriam suffered the skin disease of leprosy as punishment for bearing false witness against Moses.[26] She was exiled out of the camp for seven days. She was then healed and returned to the camp through the intercession of Moses for her.

---

25. Kaufman, "Structure," 141–42.
26. Ibid. The connection of this text with Numbers 12 and the commandment against false witness and gossip is noted already by the rabbis. Cf. Jacob Neusner, *Sifre to Deuteronomy: An Analytical Translation* (Atlanta: Scholars Press, 1987), 244–45.

The memory of the past shapes present conduct. Moses' leadership will be replaced by the leadership of the Levitical priests (Deut. 31:9-13). Thus, 24:8 enjoins the people to "carefully observe whatever the levitical priests instruct you" as a way of avoiding the leprosy and subsequent exile from the community that Miriam had suffered. Disobedience of the *torah* taught by the Levites will be counted as "bearing false witness," and the resulting punishment of disease and exile will be Israel's fate. Moses the person will die, but his office of leading and teaching will continue with the Levites in the Deuteronomic program.

The next series of laws strives to prohibit the many ways in which those who are wealthy or in power may strip those less fortunate of common human dignity and honor. Deuteronomy 24:10-11 instructs any creditor not to barge into the house of a borrower in order to secure a pledge. Verses 12-13 prohibit a creditor from literally "taking the shirt" off a poor person's back as collateral for a loan. One may take the garment as a pledge during the day, but each evening one must give it back "so that your neighbor may sleep in the cloak and bless you" (24:13). Such a blessing from a poor person "will be to your credit before the LORD your God."

If the poor have the power to move God to bless, they also have the power to move God to punish. The next law (Deut. 24:14-15) instructs employers to pay wages to poor and needy workers promptly and daily. The poor live day by day, and to withhold their wages even for one day may endanger their livelihood. If the employer withholds wages, the poor "might cry to the LORD against you, and you would incur guilt" (24:15; cf. 15:9). The cry of the poor is a powerful voice that moves God both to bless and to curse.

Deuteronomy 24:16 proclaims that family ties between parents and children should not translate into shared guilt for each other's sins. Parents should not be put to death for the crimes of their children, and children should not die for their parents' transgressions. This law is quoted and applied in the account of King Amaziah's restraint in letting the children of his father's murderers live (2 Kings 14:6). The law applies limits to the human community's reckonings of guilt and punishment in capital cases. The restriction is placed on human exercise of justice but not on God's exercise of justice (cf. Deut. 5:9). Under the umbrella of the false witness commandment, this law intends to guard the dignity and self-respect of other family members when one person in the family has committed a crime or other serious transgression.

The next cluster of statutes and ordinances (24:17-22) is surrounded by a reminder of Israel's identity: "Remember that you were a slave in Egypt and the LORD your God redeemed you from there" (24:18, 22).

Their identity as "freed slaves" leads to a concern for the dignity and care of those who continue to suffer: the poor, the widow, the alien, and the orphan. Thus, the laws framed by this remembrance of slavery prohibit taking a widow's garment as collateral, and they ensure justice for the resident alien and orphan (24:17). Some of the crop is to be left in the vineyards, fields, and orchards so that the poor and powerless may work in their own harvest in dignity and eat freely of their own labors (24:19-21).

The law in 25:1-3 describes a typical court case in which the guilty party is punished with forty lashes. But even a criminal's dignity and honor are to be preserved. No more than forty lashes will be allowed. If more would be given, then "your neighbor will be degraded in your sight" (25:3).

The last law connected with not bearing false witness against your neighbor seems odd at first blush. The statute reads simply, "you shall not muzzle an ox while it is treading out the grain" (25:4). The history of the interpretation of this law has been varied. Jewish interpretation has tended to take the law literally. But already in the New Testament the apostle Paul gave the law an allegorical interpretation to defend his right to material support as he worked as a missionary preacher:[27]

> Does not the law also say the same? For it is written in the law of Moses, "You shall not muzzle an ox while it is treading out the grain." Is it for oxen that God is concerned? Or does he not speak entirely for our sake? It was indeed written for our sake, for whoever plows should plow in hope and whoever threshes should thresh in hope of a share in the crop. If we have sown spiritual good among you, is it too much if we reap your material benefits? (1 Cor. 9:8-11)

"Is it for oxen that God is concerned?" For Paul, this rhetorical question obviously demands a negative answer; God is not concerned about oxen and thus the law must be allegorized. But the fact that the Deuteronomic statutes and ordinances often express concern and reverence for the life of nature and animals suggests a positive answer to Paul's question. Yes, it *is* for oxen that God is concerned! The progression of the laws on false witness affirms the dignity and honor of all people, from leaders to criminals. Deuteronomy extends that dignity and honor even to oxen and the sphere of all creation.

---

27. G. Lisowsky, "Dtn 25,4," in *Das ferne und nahe Wort,* FS L. Rost, ed. F. Maass, BZAW 105 (Berlin: Töpelmann, 1967), 144–52; and Neusner, *Sifre to Deuteronomy,* 2:244–45.

DEUTERONOMY 25:5-12: COVETING A NEIGHBOR'S WIFE
(NINTH COMMANDMENT)—RULES AND EXCEPTIONS

Toward the end of the Ten Commandments and the end of the statutes and ordinances related to them, the sections begin to shorten and a sense of winding down emerges from the text. The ninth commandment has only eight verses associated with it, consisting of two laws. The laws are joined by a common set of characters, a wife and two brothers. Both laws deal with dangerous boundaries between life and death associated with procreation and the maintenance of the family line.

The first law (25:5-10) involves an institutionalized exception to the commandment against coveting a neighbor's wife. When two brothers live together and one dies, the remaining brother has an obligation to marry the wife of the deceased brother in what is called a "levirate marriage." In such a case, the law against coveting another man's wife is suspended. The one brother indeed has an obligation to "covet" his dead brother's wife. The purpose of such a marriage is to ensure that children will be born. The children born out of this levirate union will carry the name of the deceased brother "so that his name may not be blotted out of Israel" (25:6). Israel had no concept of individual resurrection and eternal life until quite late in the Old Testament period (e.g., Dan. 12:2-3). The only means of preserving the memory of the departed was through children and grandchildren who would carry on the family name.

But what if the brother refuses to carry out the levirate marriage? The law in 25:7-10 prescribes a course of action by which the deceased brother's wife may come to the elders of the city to file a complaint and perform a ritual of public disgrace. She pulls off his sandal, spits in the face of the unrepentant brother, and declares, "This is what is done to the man who does not build up his brother's house." The overriding concern is to maintain the patrilineal line of future generations. In this case, the wife has the authority to attack her husband's brother through a ritualized curse.

The second law under coveting your neighbor's wife (25:11-12) is likewise ultimately concerned to maintain the procreative potential for the sake of future generations. The case describes an incident of two men wrestling with one another. In this case, the wife is prohibited from intervening in the fight against her husband's opponent by "reaching out and seizing his genitals" (25:11). There are limits to the extent to which a wife may go to protect her husband and his name.

In the preceding law, she could attack another man with a curse. In this law she is prohibited from an attack that might endanger the man's ability to procreate.[28] Again, the overriding concern in both cases is the preservation of life into future generations. Both laws deal with transgressing marital boundaries. In one case, such crossing of boundaries is allowed for the sake of preserving the name and life of the family line. In the other case, such a crossing of marital boundaries of intimacy and modesty is not allowed, but again it is for the sake of preserving the life of the family line. There are limits. But in some extreme cases (such as levirate marriage) traditional boundaries may need to be transgressed, laws broken, and customs changed for the sake of the life of future generations.

The provisional and ambiguous character of laws and boundaries is by now a common theme in the statutes and ordinances of Deuteronomy 12–26. Reality somehow continually defies easy categories, simple rules, or generalized commands that cover every contingency. The law by itself is unable to ensure blessing and life. The law of levirate marriage contradicts the usual strictures against marrying another man's wife, especially within the family. But the special case is allowed for widows in order to ensure life into future generations. Yet even this special legal exception cannot finally guarantee that the deceased brother's line will continue. His brother may refuse to do his duty and thus end the line. The stubborn brother will be punished with a curse, but the name of the dead brother will be blotted out forever. The law by itself finally cannot ensure that it will be obeyed or that life will be preserved.

DEUTERONOMY 25:13–26:15: DESIRING
(TENTH COMMANDMENT)–POWER, BUSINESS, AND BULLIES,

The tenth commandment in Deut. 5:21 reads, "Neither shall you *desire* your neighbor's house, or field, or male or female slave, or ox, or donkey, or anything that belongs to your neighbor." The verb translated "desire" (Hebrew *'wh*) is different from the verb in the other version of the tenth commandment, Exod. 20:17, which uses the verb often translated "covet" (Hebrew *ḥmd*). "Coveting" in Hebrew refers

---

28. Miriam Shrager ("A Unique Biblical Law," *DD* 15 [1986/87]: 190–94) cites examples of the common ancient Near Eastern view of male genitals as the source of human procreation. Thus, the woman in this law may not only be injuring the man but also threatening his posterity.

typically both to the desire to get what belongs to another *and* to the actions that lead to taking possession of what one coveted. The Hebrew verb used in Deut. 5:21 meaning "desire" refers to the will or desire alone, apart from actions to attain what is desired.[29] Thus, Deuteronomy's version of the tenth commandment more explicitly focuses on the inner emotion and will of desiring. This focus on the interior life of a person is in line with the central confession of the Shema: "You shall love the LORD your God with all your heart, and with all your soul, and with all your might" (6:5; cf. 30:2, 10). The intentions and attitudes that shape conduct are important ingredients in living faithfully and obediently.

All humans naturally have desires of one sort or another. Deuteronomy uses the verb translated "desire" in other texts as a positive encouragement to enjoy the basic gifts of food, shelter, and life that God has given (Deut. 12:15, 20, 21; 14:26; 18:6). But the statutes and ordinances in 25:13 — 26:15 aim the "desiring" commandment against those with power and wealth who may "desire" to take from those who are powerless and poor. Some may misconstrue the commandment against desiring as a ploy by the rich and well-to-do to keep the lower levels of society from demanding their fair share of the economic pie: "Don't desire more than you already have!" But the commandment is not aimed at the disadvantaged. It does not intend to cut off those who are poor or powerless from legitimate desires and demands for justice. Its true target is the advantaged people of a society who have more than enough and who have the power to get even more.

DEUT. 25:13-16: HONEST WEIGHTS AND MEASURES

Business in the ancient world depended on the exchange of goods and money based on honest weights and measures. The relative price of food, clothing, and other commodities was determined by its weight. This law prohibits not only the *use* of dishonest weights and measures but even their *possession,* which is counted as signifying an intention to use them. The law reveals the commandment's focus on the intention or attitude of the person as part of the process of ethical determination.

Dishonesty is a vice, and even more it is "abhorrent to the LORD your God" (25:16). We have seen the term *abhorrent* associated with concerns of purity (17:1; 22:5; 24:4) but much more frequently in connection with the worship of other gods (7:25; 18:9, 12; 20:18; 23:18; 27:15;

29. J. J. Stamm and M. E. Andrew, *The Ten Commandments in Recent Research,* SBT 2/2 (Naperville, Ill.: Allenson, 1967), 101-7.

32:16). Thus, the intention to take from another what does not rightfully belong to you involves not only wrongful desiring or coveting but also idolatry. The worship of the false god of materialism has replaced the true worship of Yahweh alone (7:25). The idolatrous and abhorrent character of dishonesty derives from the affirmation of Yahweh's character as "a faithful God, without deceit" (the same Hebrew word for "dishonesty" — 32:4). God is honest and faithful, and to act in any other way is to worship another god.

DEUT. 25:17-19: AMALEK — THE BULLY WHO DID NOT FEAR GOD

The law commands Israel to remember what Amalek did to Israel in the wilderness on their way out of Egypt. The older account in Exod. 17:8-16 relates how Amalek attacked Israel but was defeated by Joshua as Moses held up his hand holding the staff of God. The writer of Deuteronomy 25 has added important details to the account, details that clearly bring it under the theme of the tenth commandment and the prohibition of desiring what belongs to the poor and powerless. Deuteronomy 25:18 adds to the Exodus account that Amalek attacked Israel in wilderness "when you were faint and weary, and struck down all who lagged behind you." Amalek's crime is desiring and taking advantage of a people when they were weak, powerless, and unable to defend themselves.

An additional remarkable note is added. Amalek took advantage of a weakened Israel because "he did not fear God" (Deut. 25:18). The fear of God when applied to Israel refers to Israel's obedience and loyalty to Yahweh (4:10; 6:2, 13, 24; 31:12-13). But the fear of God can also apply to foreign nations as in the case of Amalek. In these cases, the fear of God is an appeal to human conscience, even among those who have no relationship to Yahweh. The "fear of God" is that human quality, an inner sense of conscience, which deters people "from harming somebody even though there be no fear of punishment."[30] Thus, Leviticus repeatedly links the fear of God with secret actions that take advantage of the powerless and cannot be controlled or punished by outward authorities: cursing the deaf or putting a stumbling block before the blind (19:14), not deferring to the old (19:32), cheating in business (25:17), demanding interest on loans to poor family members (25:36), or treating a slave harshly (25:43). Obedience in these cases depends on a sense of character and conscience, not external pressure or punishment.

---

30. Moshe Weinfeld, *Deuteronomy and the Deuteronomic School* (Oxford: Clarendon, 1972), 275.

Although Amalek acted against Israel when it was weak and power-less, God saw and remembered and now encourages Israel to remember as well. When the Israelites come into the promised land and are given rest from all their enemies, then "you shall blot out the remembrance of Amalek from under heaven; do not forget" (Deut. 25:19). This law is explicitly recalled by the prophet Samuel when Saul is chosen as king (1 Samuel 1–3). Saul defeats the Amalekites but lets the Amalekite king Agag live, contrary to Samuel's instructions. Eventually, Saul loses the kingship to David because of his failure (1 Sam. 28:16-19). King David finally succeeds in wiping out the Amalekites entirely (2 Sam 1:1). Because Amalek "desired" what belonged to Israel when it was weak, God would ensure that justice would one day be done.

DEUT. 26:1-15: A RITUAL OF STEWARDSHIP
AS AN ANTIDOTE TO WRONGFUL DESIRING

The ritual of presenting the first fruits and tithes in Deuteronomy 26 is often interpreted as a general conclusion to the whole of the statutes and ordinances in chapters 12–26. But 26:1-15 continue in the same vein as the preceding laws in the form of a statute or instruction. Only 26:16-19 provide a genuine conclusion to the laws of chapters 12–26, since there the prevailing mood of the sentences shift from imperatives to declarative statements. In what way then is the ritual of presenting offerings related to the tenth commandment against desiring a neigh-bor's property?

The ritual of the stewardship of one's harvest and the offering of the first fruits of that harvest is a positive and structured antidote for over-coming the wrongful desire prohibited in the tenth commandment. The ritualized action puts into practice the kind of faithful response shaped by the story of God's deliverance of the Israelite slaves out of Egypt. Habits begin as ritualized and intentional actions. Deuteronomy 26:1-15 is an expanded ritualized version of the provisions for offering first fruits and tithes in 14:22-29. The worshiper first gives the offering to God and then receives the offering back to eat and to share with Levites and aliens and so joyfully "celebrate with all the bounty that the LORD your God has given to you and to your house" (26:11). Remembering the gracious gifts of God provides an antidote to wrong-fully "desiring your neighbor's house." Desiring gives way to sharing and thus guards against breaking the tenth commandment.

Deuteronomy 26:12-15 specifies that every three years a tithe of the fruits of one's labors is to be offered to God and given to "the Levites, the aliens, the orphans, and the widows" (26:12; cf. 14:28-29). As worshipers present the offering, they are to confess their obedience to the commandments, their adherence to the laws of purity, and the affirmation that "I have not offered any of it to the dead" (26:14). The worshiper confesses allegiance to the living God, Yahweh, and renounces the worship of human ancestors who have died.

The last word of the worshiper is a plea for God to "look down from your holy habitation, from heaven, and bless your people Israel and the ground that you have given us" (26:15). This view of God's transcendence and dwelling in the heavens is balanced by the beginning of the chapter, which instructs the worshiper to go "to the place that the LORD your God will choose as a dwelling for his name" (26:2). The LORD's name is present in an earthly place, but the divine presence also reaches to the heavens where humans do not dwell. God is present and active among God's people, and yet the mystery of God eludes our full comprehension in any human or earthly place or construction.

DEUTERONOMY 26:16-19:
SEALING THE RELATIONSHIP "TODAY"

The words translated "this very day" and "today" are repeated here three times within four verses, thus returning to the central theme of Deut. 5:3. The words seal the relationship between God and the people. The words create the relationship through second person direct address: "Today you have obtained the LORD's agreement: to be your God; and for you to walk in his ways. . . . Today the LORD has obtained your agreement: to be his treasured people, as he promised you, and to keep his commandments" (26:17-18). Images of other words that seal relationships come to mind: the making of a contract, the signing of adoption papers, or the exchange of marriage vows. The relationship between God and the people of God that is enacted here binds God and the people to one another in a unique and exclusive way.

DEUTERONOMY 27: A PUBLISHING PARTY
AND A CURSE ON SECRET SINS

Now that Moses has orally proclaimed all the statutes and ordinances, "Moses and the elders of Israel" charge the people to erect at Mount Ebal a public billboard made of large stones covered with plaster. The people shall write on these stones "all the words of this *torah.*" They should also erect an altar, offer sacrifices, and then eat the sacrifices in a spirit of "rejoicing before the LORD your God" (Deut. 27:1-8). Israel is to enjoy a party to celebrate coming into the land and publishing the first written edition of the *torah.* The instructions for this ritual upon arrival in the promised land are carried out by the

Israelites in Josh. 8:30-35. There the stones are erected, the altar is built, and the *torah* is written and read before all Israel. Such stone monuments were often erected in the ancient world. One of the most famous examples is the stone monument containing the law code of Hammurabi, a notable king of ancient Babylon. The stone monument in Deuteronomy 27 with "all the words of this law" written on it fixes the law in stone, makes it known to all the people, and casts its long shadow over the land, the people, and all that they say and do.

The Levitical priests next join Moses in speaking to Israel words that echo the Shema of Deut. 6:5: "Keep silence and hear [*šěm'*], O Israel! This very day you have become the people of the LORD your God. Therefore obey [*šěm'*] the LORD your God" (27:9-10). The first word they hear is that the relationship is hereby established, the partnership is sealed. The expected response is to hear and do what God commands.

It is noteworthy that for the first time in the entire book Moses shares the podium with other leaders as he addresses the people: "the elders of Israel" (27:1) and "the levitical priests" (27:9). The shift is subtle but pivotal within the movement of the entire book. The sharing of the stage and leadership recalls the first narrative in Deuteronomy 1 about Moses' sharing of leadership with the seventy elders (1:9-18). Already then it was a kind of dying for Moses, a letting go, a recognition of human limits and boundaries beyond which Moses could not go. As Deuteronomy now marches ever closer to the story of Moses' death in chapter 34, Moses begins to step aside so that another generation may take over. But such leadership in the future will always be done under the guidance and correction of a *torah* written very clearly and displayed for all to see (27:8). As this *torah* moves toward a written form, Moses begins to die.

Moses instructs the people to divide the twelve tribes of Israel into two halves when they enter the promised land with six tribes standing on Mount Gerizim "for the blessing" and six tribes standing on Mount Ebal "for the curse" (27:11-13). The mention of the gathering at the mountains of Gerizim and Ebal echoes the same command that had preceded the statutes and ordinances in 11:29-30. The division of Mount Ebal with the curse and Mount Gerizim with the blessing thus frames the entire collection of laws in Deuteronomy 12–26. It is significant that the mountain on which the laws are to be written is Mount Ebal, the mountain of curse (27:4; cf. 27:13), and *not* Mount Gerizim, the mountain of blessing. As we shall see, the accent in Deuteronomy 28 is on the curse and judgment associated with transgressing the law more than the blessing associated with obedience.

At the assembly where the two alternatives of curse and blessing are represented, Moses says that "the Levites" shall speak "in a loud voice to all the Israelites" (27:14). The voice of the Levites grows louder as Moses' own voice moves a step closer to dying out. Moses is speaking *with* the Levites now, but he will soon die and leave the Levites to speak without him. The Levites on that day of entry into the land will declare a series of curses against twelve specific acts. In the discussion of Amalek and Deut. 25:18, I noted that Amalek "did not fear God" because the Amalekites secretly attacked the weak and powerless stragglers of Israel out in the wilderness. The same concern for preventing secret transgressions — those which the human community's judicial process cannot detect — is evident in the series of twelve curses in 27:15-26. The curses proclaim a divine judgment that will be set in motion when a prohibited action is done in secret.[31] In the case of secretive transgressions, God will replace the human in judging wrongdoing. Once again Moses is stepping aside, to make room not only for the elders and the Levites but also for God. The curses in effect acknowledge the limits of human processes and institutions in shaping ethical and just behavior within the community.

Thus, the Levites will declare first, "Cursed be anyone who makes an idol" and "sets it up in secret" (Deut. 27:15). The important first commandment against worshiping other gods again makes its presence felt as the first of the curses. Because the idol is secretly worshiped, only God can know and punish the idolatry. The people respond to this and the other curses by binding themselves to the curses with the word *Amen,* meaning "Yes, it shall be so." The other matters deal with wrongful, secret actions in matters of sexuality and family (dishonoring parents, sexual relations with a father's wife, a sister, a mother-in-law, or an animal), secretive actions that abuse the disadvantaged (the blind, the alien, the orphan, the widow), and secret actions done against a neighbor (moving a boundary marker, striking a neighbor, or taking a bribe to shed innocent blood). The final curse extends the reach of God's judgment against "anyone who does not uphold the words of this law" (27:26). The curses at the end of the statutes and ordinances recognize the limitations of human capacities to monitor

---

31. Elizabeth Bellefontaine ("The Curses of Deuteronomy 27: Their Relationship to the Prohibitives," in *No Famine in the Land: Studies in Honor of John L. McKenzie,* ed. James Flanagan and Anita Robinson (Missoula, Mont.: Scholars Press, 1975), 49–61) underlines the connection of the curses with actions specifically done in secret and thus not determinable or punishable within the judicial process: "With regard to the curse, only the scrutiny of the deity could assure the execution of justice for secret crimes" (p. 58).

and to mold human beings into people so that they do what is good, just, holy, and in accord with God's will. In the secret places of the heart, only God can judge.

DEUTERONOMY 28: THE LAW—SHORT ON BLESSING, LONG ON CURSE

Chapter 28 consists of less than one-fourth blessings "if you will only obey the LORD your God" and more than three-fourth curses "if you will not obey the LORD your God" (28:1, 15). The blessings for obedience extend over only fourteen verses while the curses for disobedience extend over fifty-four verses. The attachment of blessings and curses at the end of a document is common to various kinds of ancient Near Eastern documents. Examples include law codes that kings published for their nations (e.g., the Code of Hammurabi), or international covenants or treaties that bind two leaders into a mutual relationship. In both covenant documents and law codes (as here in Deuteronomy), the size of the curse section typically far exceeds the size of the blessing section of the document.[32] The blessings and curses as they appear in Deuteronomy 28 seem to be most similar to those attached to known ancient Near Eastern treaty or covenant documents rather than to law codes. Many of the vivid and lurid images and phrases used in Deuteronomy 28 have striking parallels in language and even sequence to curses and blessings used in Near Eastern treaties: drought, defeat, plague, illness, blindness, slavery, exile, locusts, the ruin of the city, and even cannibalism.[33]

An earlier form of the blessings and curses in Deuteronomy 28 may have originated out of the treaty or covenant tradition of the ancient Near East. But their placement in the present form of the book of Deuteronomy suggests that the blessings and curses cover the section titled "the commandment—the statutes and the ordinances" (6:1), consisting of chapters 6–28. Some scholars have argued that this central

---

32. Martin Noth, "'For All Who Rely on Works of the Law Are Under a Curse,'" in *The Laws in the Pentateuch and Other Studies,* trans. D. R. Ap-Thomas (Philadelphia: Fortress, 1967), 118–31, esp. 122–26. Cf. also Delbert Hillers, *Covenant: The History of a Biblical Idea* (Baltimore: Johns Hopkins Univ. Press, 1969), 38; and the fuller discussion in Dennis J. McCarthy, *Treaty and Covenant,* AnBib 21A; 2d ed. (Rome: Pontifical Biblical Institute, 1978), 173, who notes that the preponderance of curses over blessings is typical of Syrian and Assyrian treaties but not of Hittite treaties.

33. McCarthy, *Treaty and Covenant,* 172–74. Of all the sections of Deuteronomy, the set of curses in chap. 28 most closely resembles the covenants of the ancient Near East, especially the Neo-Assyrian treaties of the seventh century B.C.E. Cf. Moshe Weinfeld, "Traces of Assyrian Treaty Formulae in Deuteronomy," *Bib* 46 (1965): 417–27, and other literature cited there.

section of Deuteronomy is cast in a covenant form, but the correspondences are imprecise and the number of the stipulations in chapters 12–26 far exceed the number of stipulations usually found in Near Eastern treaties. Deuteronomy 6–28 may well have many affinities to covenants and may borrow many of its features (allegiance to one sovereign, stipulations, blessings, and curses). But the present form of Deuteronomy defines the genre or form of this section (chapters 6–28) as "the commandment—the statutes and the ordinances" (6:1; cf. 12:1). This is primarily legal material, and the blessings and curses in chapter 28 thus function as a specific conclusion to the collection of laws. While words for "law," "commandment," "statutes," and "ordinances" are prevalent throughout this concluding section (26:16, 17, 18; 27:1, 3, 8, 10, 26; 28:1, 9, 13, 15, 45, 58), the word for "covenant" (Hebrew *bĕrît*) is entirely absent.

Therefore, the brief section of blessings and the larger section of curses apply to the requirements of the commandment, statutes, and ordinances of chapters 6–28. As noted, the preponderance of curses is typical of comparable ancient Near Eastern material. But Dennis McCarthy notes how Deuteronomy 28 has transformed the mechanical or objective view of the blessings and curses as coming into effect automatically upon obedience or disobedience, an objective view characteristic of other ancient Near Eastern documents. Deuteronomy has turned the blessings and curses into something more emotive, persuasive, and internal rather than mechanical:

> In Dt this more objective point of view has been covered over by the desire to persuade. This the blessings and curses doubtless remain effective in themselves, but the full rhetorical expansion, the vivid picture of the promised good or evil, turns them into a means of convincing, or producing in the hearer or reader the will to obey because he is moved and persuaded. . . . The desire to produce an internal consent, a conviction which will move one to obedience, has been given an exceptionally important place.[34]

The blessings and curses appeal, cajole, encourage, and mostly threaten with powerful and often horrendous language designed to explode complacency and awaken urgency and obedience through the most shocking of images (e.g., 28:54–57).

Four features of the blessings and curses in Deuteronomy 28 deserve mention. First, both the blessings and curses display the same interdependence of divine, human, and natural worlds or spheres that I have noted throughout the statutes and ordinances in chapters 12–26. On the one hand, obedience leads to blessing in the relationship with

---

34. McCarthy, *Treaty and Covenant,* 187.

God, with other nations and peoples, and also with nature in terms of fertility and agricultural prosperity. On the other hand, the breakdown in relationships between God and people (disobedience) mushrooms into ecological disaster (drought, diseased crops), the revenge of nature (28:26, 42), political defeat and slavery at the hands of other people, and the loss of personal health, family, and security. The images for the curse that follows disobedience is a spiraling collage of personal, natural, social, political, and theological chaos. The theological, social, dietary, and natural boundaries that the statutes and ordinances sought to preserve will be utterly undone. Free Israelites will become slaves. People will eat their children. Adultery will be rampant. Foreigners will marry Israel's sons and daughters. Resident aliens will lend to Israelites, but Israelites will not lend to foreigners. The images of disease, darkness, locusts, and the death of children all recall the plagues that came upon the Egyptians at the time of the exodus, but this time it is Israel who is threatened. The portraits of disaster constitute an undoing of the promised conquest of the land (chap. 8) and a return to the slavery of Egypt (28:68).

A second feature of the blessing and curse list is the alternation between the agency of God in carrying out the blessings and curses and an agency that is more impersonal, a kind of fixed order of correspondence between blessing and obedience, curse and disobedience. For example, the formulations in 28:3-6 say nothing of Yahweh as the agent of the blessing, but 28:7-13 make Yahweh the direct agent of the verbs of blessing. Correspondingly, the curses in 28:16-19, 30-34, 38-44 are impersonal, but the curses in 28:20-29, 35-37 emphasize direct divine agency. In 28:45-68, God's punishing activity is done through the agency of a nation whom "the LORD will send against you" (28:48-49). God's agency is not again explicitly mentioned until 28:58-68, where the text again links God with the punishment of a rebellious Israel.

A third feature of the list is a remarkable correspondence between the act of disobedience and the punishment that God imposes. Israel's worship of the other gods and idols of the nations (27:15) will itself become the punishment that God will impose on an idolatrous Israel (28:36). Israel's eager idolatry will become God's enforced idolatry (28:64). Because Israel did not "serve the LORD your God," therefore "you shall serve your enemies whom the LORD will send against you" (28:47-48). If God's people become slaves to lawlessness and act as if they lived in pre-Horeb days in Egypt when they had no law, then "the LORD will bring you back in ships to Egypt . . . and there you shall offer yourselves for sale to your enemies" (28:68).

The fourth and perhaps most important feature of the blessings and curses is the key grammatical shift that takes place in the enumeration of the curses in 28:45-48. In the preceding list in 28:1-44, the curses and blessings remain open possibilities and entirely dependent on Israel's apparently free decision to obey or to disobey God. The conditional clause that begins 28:15 rules over the entire section of curses in 28:15-44: "*If* you will not obey the LORD your God." But in 28:45-48, the text shifts abruptly from this conditional mode into a declarative and narrative mode. The syntactical structure changes dramatically from 28:15, which is an open-ended conditional clause—"But *if* you will not obey . . . then all these curses shall come upon you"—to a declared state of fact that will happen in the narrated future. The conditional clause ("if you will not obey") now becomes a causal or explanatory clause in 28:45—"All these curses shall come upon you . . . *because* you did not obey." The curse shifts from a conditional possibility to a narrated future actuality.[35]

Deuteronomy has transformed the blessing and curse list from a list of *possible* consequences (blessing or curse) to a declaration of *assured* future events, events leading inevitably to curse, judgment, and exile (28:45-68). Whether or not these verses have been added at some later time to conform to events of Israel's historical experience of exile, they function in the present form of Deuteronomy as narrative paradigms of what Israel's future experience will be. The commandments, statutes, and ordinances lead not only to the *possibility* of curse and death (as in the Near Eastern examples) but also to the *inevitability* of that end. The laws are limited, finite, and unable to protect the community from eventual disaster, disintegration, and death. The laws are designed by God to bring blessing, but God's people will experience them as agents of curse and judgment.

The section titled "the commandment—the statutes and the ordinances" (6:1) began with the call for obedience to the laws that followed "so that it may go well with you" (6:3). But our study of the statutes and ordinances revealed how difficult it was for God's people to have both the will ("you have been rebellious against the LORD as long as he has known you"—9:24) and the ability to follow laws often freighted with deep ambiguity, unresolvable paradox, and blurred boundaries. The struggle to follow God's statutes and ordinances was necessary and crucial to the ongoing life and health of the community. But eventually that human struggle for obedience and fidelity to God seems fated to end in curse, judgment, and death. The book of Deuteronomy could

35. Ibid., 178.

end here with the list of blessings and overwhelming curses, as did many of the ancient Near Eastern law codes and treaty documents. But Deuteronomy takes the treaty form and fashions something entirely new that embraces the pain of exile and curse, moves through it, and overcomes it. Deuteronomy then sends the reader back again into the ambiguities and shifting sands of life seeking obedience in the ordinary realms of family, economics, politics, justice, and worship. This radical new turn — so radical that one may call it a revolution — occurs in Deuteronomy 29-32. These chapters are often dismissed as secondary additions to the "core" of Deuteronomy in chapters 12-26. But in Deuteronomy's present form, these chapters constitute a decisive turning point and fulcrum for the book as a whole.

SUMMARY: DEUTERONOMY 19-28
AND THE DEATH OF MOSES

The second half of the statutes and ordinances in Deuteronomy 19-28 reverberate with the dual themes associated with Moses' death outside the promised land: the realistic limits and failures that prevent humans from entering an ideal promised land and the positive model of self-giving for the sake of others that Moses' death also exemplifies. The limits and ambiguities of human laws and actions emerge in the laws on killing. The cities of refuge are an imperfect balance between exile and refuge for innocent and unintentional killers. The laws of holy war and the conquest of the promised land could not protect Israel from disobeying the law so that the promised land of Canaan would not become an ideal paradise but a place of continuing struggle with foreign gods. The set of laws in chapter 21 wrestle with the clash between life and death. The death and burial of a criminal hanged on a tree recalls the death and burial of Moses because of his own sin (Deut. 32:48-52). The death of the rebellious son poses the extreme dilemma of parents giving up their child to death, a metaphor used later in chapter 32 for the relationship of God and Israel.

The statutes and ordinances associated with the adultery commandment begin with a series of forbidden mixtures, one of which provides for an exception (22:11-12). The laws concerning sexual relations assume a patriarchal system and yet limits provide for the protection of women. Rules for membership of the worshiping community exclude certain foreigners, and yet exceptions are made for Egyptians, Edomites, and others. Under the law on coveting a neighbor's wife, an exception (levirate marriage) is made. But even the legal exception cannot guarantee the ongoing life of the next generation if a brother refuses to obey (25:3-10). The limits of the law preclude its ability to resolve all exceptions and ambiguities in shaping human behavior and life.

The theme of Moses' death as a metaphor for the limits and failure of human action continues in the concluding frame to the statutes and ordinances in Deuteronomy 27–28. Moses increasingly shares leadership with the elders and levitical priests whose voices become louder as Moses' voice diminishes. This sharing of leadership recalls the opening narrative of Deut. 1:9-18. The statutes and ordinances are written on Mount Ebal, the mountain of curse, and not on Gerizim, the mountain of blessing. Human mechanisms of laws cannot deal with secret sins and so the curses on secret transgressions in 27:15-26 replace human administration of justice with God' justice. Finally, and most significantly, the limits of humanly mediated law and the inevitable failure of human obedience are graphically underlined in the long list of curses in chapter 28. The curses for disobedience of the laws move grammatically from hypothetical conditionality ("*if* you will not obey . . . then all these curses") to declarative future inevitability ("All these curses shall come upon you . . . *because* you did not obey"). The statutes and ordinances of the Horeb covenant end in curse, judgment, and exile for Israel, even as Moses' life ends in death outside the promised land.

The second and more positive dimension of Moses' death as a model of self-giving and compassion also finds corollaries throughout this second part of the statutes and ordinances. The laws connected with the killing commandment stress the priority of life-giving compassion and mercy. Boundary markers protect family land and economic well-being. Ecological compassion is exercised even in war. The law enjoins Israelites to help a neighbor's fallen or lost animal, to protect mother birds, and to enact measures that prevent the death of others. The atoning death of the young heifer (21:1-9) resembles in theme and vocabulary the interpretation of Moses' death outside the land as vicarious atonement for Israel (Deut. 1:37; 3:26; 4:21). The correlation of Moses' self-giving compassion and God's gracious compassion (which we will explore in Deuteronomy 29–32) emerges in a series of parallels with the overriding commitment to past promises, whether in regard to the foreign captive woman in Deut. 21:10-14 or the right of the firstborn son in Deut. 21:15-17.

The laws associated with the adultery commandment include an important reference to the story in Numbers 22–24 where the prophet Balaam was hired to curse Israel. Deuteronomy 23:5 notes, "The LORD your God turned the curse into a blessing for you, because the LORD your God loved you." As we will see by the end of Deuteronomy, God promises again to turn the curse of Moses' death and of Israel's exile into a blessing when the LORD will again "have compassion on his servants" (Deut. 32:36). The means by which this dramatic shift from the curses in which the Horeb covenant ends (Deuteronomy 28) and the blessings that come in chapter 33 will be the subject of our next chapter as we explore the Moab covenant of Deuteronomy 29–32.

CHAPTER 7

"These Are the Words
of the Covenant" —
Deuteronomy 29–32: The New
Covenant for the Future

"Indeed the LORD will . . .
    have compassion on his servants,
when he sees that their power is gone,
    neither bond nor free remaining."

—Deut. 32:36

"See now that I, even I, am he;
    there is no god beside me.
I kill and I make alive;
    I wound and I heal;
and no one can deliver from my hand."

—Deut. 32:39

The structure of the book of Deuteronomy has moved from the story of God's faithfulness in the past (chaps. 1–4) to the commandments, statutes, and ordinances to guide human action in the present and near future (chaps. 6–28). The movement from past story to present law ended in dramatic images of curse, judgment, and death in chapter 28. Human obedience of the statutes and ordinances leads to some measure of blessing and good life (28:1-14). But the boundaries and situations of ethics and laws are fraught with ambiguity, often in flux, and in need of constant reinterpretation and renegotiation. Sole trust in imperatives, threats, and laws cannot ultimately save the community from the encroaching powers, both internal and external, that bring the community's eventual destruction and death (28:15-68).

I argued earlier that Deuteronomy 5 provided a road map for the structure of the entire book of Deuteronomy as it moved from past story (5:6) to present commandments (5:7-21) to future mechanisms for mediating the word of God (5:22-31) and finally to God's ultimate goal of life and blessing for the people of God (5:32-33). The new covenant section of chapters 29–32 corresponds to 5:22-31, which makes provisions for the continuation of the Mosaic mediation of God's word into the future. Like 5:22-31, chapters 29-32 look to the future and the ways God will speak and act among God's people in succeeding generations.

What will happen to God's people in the future? Will the divine promise of blessing and life be forfeited or nullified? Is there any hope in the midst of the gods and powers of militarism, materialism, and moralism (Deuteronomy 7-10) that seem to wield such awesome power over people and communities, leading to curse and death? In answer to such pressing questions about the future, chapters 29-32 announce a whole new way of being in the world. Through daring discourse and powerful poetry, these chapters proclaim a new covenant. It is a new relationship based not as much on *human* abilities and faithfulness as on the promise of *God's* faithfulness and *God's* active transformation of people and communities.

The best illustration of the newness of the covenant in Deuteronomy 29-32 is a distinctive phrase that occurs only twice in all of Deuteronomy and rarely elsewhere in the Old Testament. Deuteronomy 10:16 casts this distinctive phrase in the imperative: "Circumcise, then, the foreskin of your heart, and do not be stubborn any longer." Circumcising the foreskin was a physical mark of belonging to the covenant community of Yahweh, a "sign of the covenant" (Gen. 17:11; cf. Josh. 5:1-9). Deuteronomy 10:16 exhorts the people to struggle to make their covenantal circumcision a matter of their heart, their inner will, intention, and thought.

In the new covenant section in 30:6, the same phrase is used as a clear echo of chapter 10. The command is dramatically transformed, however, as it is joined with an echo of the Shema in 6:5, which commands, "You shall love the LORD your God with all your heart, and with all your soul, and with all your might." The commands to circumcise the heart and love the LORD undergo a profound transformation. The *command* has become a *promise:* "Moreover, the LORD your God *will circumcise* your heart and the heart of your descendants, so that you *will love* the LORD your God with all your heart and with all your soul, in order that you may live." Commanded *human* action has now become a promised *divine* gift.

This shift from commandment to promise signals an overturning of the normal pattern of national relationships and alliances in the world and culture of Deuteronomy's origins. In the ancient Near Eastern treaty form that Deuteronomy both borrows and reshapes, the relationship begins on the basis of the good things that the more powerful ruler (the suzerain) has done for the less powerful ruler (the vassal).

This recital of past gracious acts is called the historical prologue. In return, the lesser king is expected to reciprocate and show gratitude with acts of obedience to laws laid down by the more powerful ruler, the so-called stipulations. Blessings are then promised for obedience, and harsh curses are promised for disobedience.

The typical structure of the ancient Near Eastern treaty has the following elements:

1. Preamble
2. Historical prologue — the beneficial actions that the suzerain has done for the vassal
3. Stipulations — obligations of the vassal to the suzerain
4. Invocation of witnesses
5. Blessings and curses — consequences of obedience or disobedience

The previous sections of Deuteronomy correspond in a rough way to this treaty pattern with a historical prologue of God's faithfulness in chapters 1–4; a catalog of stipulations, statutes, and ordinances in 6–26; and a conclusion with blessings and curses in 27–28. But chapters 29–32, which are explicitly described as a "covenant" (29:1), fracture the old Near Eastern treaty form and fashion a new kind of covenant. In this "theologized" covenant of Moab, the people (the "vassals") inevitably fail to keep the covenant, hence bringing the curses into effect. But the covenant relationship does not end there. God (the "suzerain") transforms the curse into blessing, the command into promise, and the stipulation into gift. God's love transcends the quid pro quo of imperial powers and exchange. God forgives and loves even when the people do not love in return. More than that, God creates a love and empowers an obedience within the hearts of the people and community that humans on their own cannot attain.

But God's people are not thus relieved of moral responsibility. The covenant at Horeb based on law remains in place. The new covenant at Moab supplements Horeb; it is made "in addition to the covenant that he had made with them at Horeb" (29:1). The Horeb laws (chaps. 6–28) remain important and necessary; the struggle to obey and re-interpret them for new times and places continues. But whatever partial and imperfect obedience emerges is understood under the new covenant of Moab not as a human achievement but as a gift from God. Just as an awareness of the divine giftedness of the land and conquest precludes devotion to militarism and materialism, so too the awareness of the divine giftedness of human obedience precludes self-righteous moralism. Apart from God's work within individuals and communities, it remains the case that they "have been rebellious against the LORD as long as he has known" them (9:24). Obedience is God's ongoing work in and through individuals and communities.

But what are the means of God's transforming work, this transformation that no human person or community alone is able to accomplish? What could be powerful enough to overcome the gods and idolatries that enslave people and nations so mightily? The answer to these questions emerges as we trace the structure and movement of chapters 29–32.

THREE VERSIONS OF THE NEW COVENANT OF MOAB

The superscription in Deut. 29:1 functions to bind together all of chapters 29–32 under the rubric "These are the words of the covenant."[1] This new covenant of Moab is presented in three parallel versions within chapters 29–32.

WORSHIP	WORD	SONG
chapters 29–30 the covenant liturgy of Moab—a ritual of covenant making	chapter 31 the covenant leadership and text of Moab— Joshua and *torah*	chapter 32 the covenant poetry of Moab—the Song of Moses

The oldest layer of the three parts of Deuteronomy 29–32 is likely the poetic Song of Moses in chapter 32, although it may have been inserted at a relatively late time in the composition of the book. Similar ancient poems like the Song of the Sea in Exodus 15 or the Song of Deborah in Judges 5 were supplemented with later prose reinterpretations that now precede them in the text (Exodus 14 and Judges 4, respectively). In the same way, the Song of Moses in Deuteronomy 32 has been

---

1. The function of the superscription in 29:1 (Hebrew 28:69) to unite all of Deuteronomy 29–32 is argued effectively from a redaction-critical perspective by Norbert Lohfink, "Der Bundesschluss im Land Moab: Redaktionsgeschichtliches zu Dt 28,69–32,47," in *Studien zum Deuteronomium und zur deuteronomistischen Literatur,* ed. G. Dartzenberg and N. Lohfink, vol. 1 (Stuttgart: Katholisches Bibelwerk, 1990), 53–82. Alexander Rofé ("The Covenant in the Land of Moab [Dt 28,69–30,20], Historio-Literary, Comparative and Form-Critical Considerations," in *Das Deuteronomium: Entstehung, Gestalt und Botschaft,* ed. Norbert Lohfink, BETL 68 [Leuven: Leuven Univ. Press, 1985], 310–20) argues that the covenant of Moab extends only through chaps. 29 and 30, which ends, as in other Near Eastern covenants, with blessings and curses. But Rofé ignores the function of the superscriptions throughout the book of Deuteronomy to mark off major sections of the book. The next superscription does not appear until 33:1, "This is the blessing," so that the superscription in 29:1 (Hebrew 28:69) covers all of chaps. 29–32. Moreover, the appeal to the Near Eastern covenant form that concludes with blessings and curses fails to take into account Deuteronomy's fracturing of the ancient Near Eastern covenant form. The Moab covenant moves beyond the simple alternative of blessing and curse.

supplemented and restated in two prose additions that precede it: chapters 29–30 (the covenant liturgy of Moab) and chapter 31 (the covenant leadership and text of Moab).

These three parallel versions of the Moab covenant — the covenant liturgy of chapters 29–30, the covenant leadership and text of chapter 31, and the covenant song of chapter 32 — share a threefold movement: from (1) the affirmation of God's past faithfulness to (2) the present reality of human limits and death, and finally to (3) the future activity of God, who alone has the power to overcome human limits and rebellion through divine justice and compassion. This threefold movement from past to present to future reflects a structure similar to the "Small Catechism" of Deuteronomy 5 as well as to the entire book of Deuteronomy as it moves from past story (chaps. 1–4) to present law (chaps. 6–28) to future covenant (chaps. 29–32).

This threefold movement is first illustrated in chapters 29–30, which begin by affirming God's past faithfulness (29:2-8). The chapters then proclaim the limits of human knowledge (29:4, 29), the limits of human obedience (29:18-19), and the ultimate limits of human life and power as curse and exile crowd in upon God's people (29:18-28). But mysteriously (29:29), God will "restore your fortunes and have compassion on you" even "if you are exiled to the ends of the world" (30:3, 4). God's unbounded compassion breaks the barriers of finite time and space so that God is present in every place we call "this place" (29:7; 30:11-14) and in every day we call "this day" (29:4, 10, 12, 13, 14, 15; 30:11, 15, 16, 18, 19).

Chapter 31 likewise displays this threefold movement from past to present to future. It begins with a reminder of God's past blessings as a foundation for trusting God in the future (31:1-6). It then moves to the limits and impending death of the individual Moses (31:14-15), whose death prefigures the rebellion and death of the whole community of God's people (31:16-21, 27-29). In response to human limits and death, God provides concrete mechanisms for carrying forward the faith and traditions of Moses to new generations. Those mechanisms include the transfer of leadership by God from Moses to Joshua (31:7-8, 14-15, 23), the writing down of the book of the *torah* of Moses for future generations (31:9-13, 24-29), and a song that will serve as a witness against the people (31:19, 22, 30).

The Song of Moses in chapter 32 also moves from the confession of God's gracious acts of the past (32:3-14) to the people's attempt to break free from the bonds of obedience and faith in God and the resulting experience of the limits and curses of human life (32:15-35). But when Yahweh "sees that their power is gone," when they have come up against their ultimate limits, then God will have compassion on them and will win the victory on behalf of God's people (32:36-43).

One other striking feature that all three versions of the Moab covenant share comes out of the ancient Near Eastern treaty or covenant tradition. It is the involvement of the wider creation, particularly in the invocation of the witnesses to the covenant making. In Near Eastern covenants, the list of witnesses often includes various gods, but it may also include "heaven and earth." Each of the three forms of the Moab covenant in Deuteronomy 29–32, appeals to "heaven and earth" as witness to the covenant-making process (30:19; 31:28; 32:1). We have noted throughout the laws of chapters 6–28 the constant intertwining of relationships of God, humans, and creation. Once again in this new covenant context, creation ("heaven and earth") plays a role as witness. Creation also plays a role in carrying out the judgment of God (29:23; 32:22-24) as well as the blessing of God (30:9; 32:11-14, 43) on the people. God, humans, and nonhuman creation form an interlocking network of relationships; the well-being of humans depends on a balanced relationship with both God and nature.

DEUTERONOMY 29–30: THE LITURGICAL FORM

Although the three versions of the Moab covenant share a basic theme or movement, each of the three versions makes a unique contribution to understanding the new covenant at Moab. Deuteronomy 29–30 begin by presenting the liturgical form of the Moab covenant. Some scholars believe that an actual Israelite covenant-making ceremony underlies the present text, with some later editorial insertions dating from the Babylonian exile (especially Deut. 29:21 – 30:10).[2] In its present form, the whole of chapters 29–30 serves as a covenant-making liturgy spoken by Moses to all Israel on the edge of the promised land (29:2). The full structure includes the following elements:

1. Recital of God's past actions (29:1-8) – God's saving actions in Egypt, the wilderness, and the preliminary conquests east of the Jordan
2. Proclamation of the covenant making (29:9-15) – inclusive list of parties involved (leaders, elders, officials, men, children, women,

2. Lohfink, "Bundesschluss," 66–68. Jon Levenson ("Who Inserted the Book of the Torah?" *HTR* 68 [1975]: 203–21) argues that Deut. 29:21-28, all of chap. 30, and some verses in chap. 31 were written later during the Babylonian exile. The ancient Song of Moses in chap. 32 was also inserted by this exilic redactor or writer. In addition, this exilic editor composed 4:1-40, since its vocabulary and movement of thought have parallels to chaps. 29–30. Dennis J. McCarthy (*Treaty and Covenant*, AnBib 21A, 2d ed. [Rome: Pontifical Biblical Institute, 1978], 202–5) also perceives chaps. 4 and 29–30 as forming a frame around the Deuteronomic code of chaps. 5–28.

aliens — "you who stand here with us today" and "those who are not here with us today")

3. Sermonic warning (29:16-20) — "it may be that there is among you a root sprouting poisonous and bitter growth. . . . All the curses written in this book will descend on them"

4. The curse of exile and the blessing of return (29:21 – 30:10) — "The LORD uprooted them from their land in anger, fury, and great wrath, and cast them into another land" (29:28); key transition point — "The secret things belong to the LORD our God, but the revealed things belong to us and to our children forever" (29:29); the LORD "will bring you back . . . will circumcise your heart . . . so that you will love the LORD. . . . Then you shall again obey the LORD" (30:4, 6, 8)

5. Sermonic encouragement (30:11-14) — "this commandment . . . is not too hard for you, nor is it too far away. . . . The word is very near to you; it is in your mouth and in your heart for you to observe" (30:11-14)

6. Blessing and curse, heaven and earth as witnesses, and final encouragement (30:15-20) — "I have set before you life and death, blessings and curses. Choose life."

The central issue throughout this covenant-making liturgy is exclusive devotion to Yahweh in line with the first of the Ten Commandments and the Shema of Deut. 6:4-5. The worship of other gods leads to curse and death for God's people (29:17-18, 26-27; 30:2, 6, 10, 16, 20). But *God's* action will restore obedience and trust to the people. As for the people's ability to obey God, Moses proclaims that "to this day the LORD has not given you a mind to understand, or eyes to see, or ears to hear" (29:4). Yet at the same time Moses exhorts the people to obedience and faithfulness. A delicate dialectic exists in this liturgy between the promise of *God's* creation of obedience (30:6-9) and the exhortation and command to the *people* to be obedient (30:10-20). The promise without expectations of obedience is cheap grace. The call to obedience without the promise of God to create faith and obedience becomes an exercise in browbeating and legalism. Somehow the liturgical promise of God and the persuasive call to obedience in worship combine to become active speech that generates and empowers. The dialectic of promise and obedience is resolved only in the mystery of God's active presence in and among the community at worship. How it happens is a "secret"; that it happens is "revealed" (29:29).

One of the hallmarks of this liturgy of covenant making is the powerful speech of direct and contemporizing address. Moses' words are second person direct address, "you."[3] The words create the relationship as Moses speaks for God: "I am making this covenant . . . with you . . . today" (29:14). This is the kind of powerful language in which liturgy and proclamation properly engage: "I love you." "I baptize you." "I circumcise you." "I condemn you." "I forgive you." "I bless you." "I make this covenant with you."

Exhortation, explanation, recital of God's past acts, commands, illustration, and rhetoric may all play a role in liturgy and proclamation. But they do not replace or substitute for the central action of liturgy done in the Moab covenant mode: the action of God through human speech to address and transform the hearts of people and communities. This direct and powerful word creates and sustains the relationship. It is for "you." It is for "today." It is for "this place." It is not a lofty abstract word up in the heavens somewhere (30:12). It is not some exotic theological explanation from "beyond the sea" (30:13). "The word is very near to you; it is in your mouth and in your heart for you to observe" (30:14).

DEUTERONOMY 31: THE HUMAN AND TEXTUAL FORM

The liturgical form of the Moab covenant consisted of the direct address of Moses speaking in the name of God to the people. But what will happen when Moses dies? Who will speak the words of direct address in the name of God? What will those words be, and how will future generations know what and where and when to speak them? This is the unique problem of Deuteronomy 31 and its form of the Moab covenant.

Norbert Lohfink has argued that Deuteronomy 31 displays a carefully crafted literary structure, and I have adapted it to outline this section (see diagram 4).[4]

The imminent death of Moses forms a crisis for the community of faith. Deuteronomy 31 notes repeatedly the nearness of Moses' death: "I am now one hundred twenty years old. I am no longer able to get about, and the LORD has told me, 'You shall not cross over this Jordan'" (31:2). "Your time to die is near" (31:14). "Soon you will lie down with your ancestors" (31:16). Moses knows that Israel's rebelliousness will only increase "after my death" (31:27, 29). In the face of Moses' death, three important themes are carefully interwoven in

---

3. As often throughout Deuteronomy, the "you" in these chapters alternates between a singular or individual "you" (marked in the Hebrew—e.g., 29:10-12) and a corporate or plural "you" (29:13-16).
4. Lohfink, "Bundesschluss," 74–77.

Diagram 4

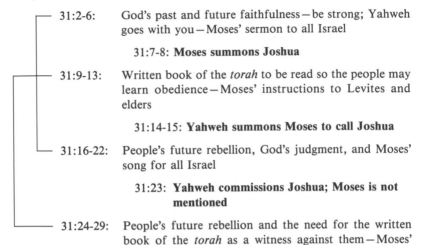

31:2-6:   God's past and future faithfulness—be strong; Yahweh goes with you—Moses' sermon to all Israel

31:7-8: **Moses summons Joshua**

31:9-13:   Written book of the *torah* to be read so the people may learn obedience—Moses' instructions to Levites and elders

31:14-15: **Yahweh summons Moses to call Joshua**

31:16-22:   People's future rebellion, God's judgment, and Moses' song for all Israel

31:23: **Yahweh commissions Joshua; Moses is not mentioned**

31:24-29:   People's future rebellion and the need for the written book of the *torah* as a witness against them—Moses' instructions to the Levites

chapter 31: the need for a foundational song or catechetical anthem, the need for continuing human leadership, and the need for a normative text to serve as guide. Moses will be replaced not with just another human leader, but by a combination of a human leader, a text, and a song. These three needs are made urgent by the recognition that the people will become even more rebellious after Moses' death. Thus, the text as well as the song that follows in Deuteronomy 32 will function "as a witness against" them (31:19, 21, 26).

The first theme, the transfer of leadership from Moses to Joshua, is accomplished in an artful literary progression of three short texts that are in boldface in diagram 4.[5] In Deut. 31:7-8, Moses summons Joshua and assures him of God's presence: "It is the LORD who goes before you. He will be with you." God is discussed but not actually present in this first exchange. In the second short text, 31:14-15, the LORD summons Moses to call Joshua to the tent of meeting where God appears veiled in a pillar of cloud. Here God, Moses, and Joshua are all present. Finally, in the third short text, 31:23, the LORD commissions Joshua ("you shall bring the Israelites into the land . . . I will be with you"), but no mention is made of Moses. Thus, the texts move

---

5. Ibid., 74–75. Cf. also Norbert Lohfink, "Die deuteronomistische Darstellung des Übergangs der Führung Israels von Moses auf Josue: Ein Beitrag zur alttestamentlichen Theologie des Amtes," in *Studien zum Deuteronomium und zur deuteronomistischen Literatur,* 1:83–97.

from Moses commanding Joshua to God commanding Moses and Joshua to God commanding Joshua alone. Moses literarily moves off the stage. He has reached the end of his power, his leadership, and soon his life. The inevitability of death and mortality limits all human claims to authority and power. Thus, Deuteronomy 31 reiterates the first commandment theme that warns against trusting in humanly crafted idolatries. It encourages the love and trust of one God alone, Yahweh, who holds ultimate power and thus will not fail or forsake (31:6, 8, 16, 18, 20). At the same time, a human leader is required to lead the next generation; the text and its traditions require ongoing human study, interpretation, proclamation, and action. The word of God requires embodiment in real human words and lives, an embodiment that renews the word for every new generation and time.

The second major theme of chapter 31, the transfer of Moses' oral word to a written text, is narrated in two passages: 31:9-13 and 31:24-29. In verses 9-13, Moses hands over the written *torah* to "the priests, the sons of Levi" and "to all the elders of Israel." As with the transfer of leadership to Joshua, the transfer of the written *torah* is a kind of dying for Moses. His role as the mouthpiece of God gives way to a book. Moses instructs the Levites and elders to read the *torah* before all Israel every seven years during the Feast of Booths. The text is for all people: men, women, children, and aliens residing within in the community (31:12). The primary reason for this regular time of reading of the *torah* is "so that their children, who have not known it, may hear and learn to fear the LORD your God" (31:13). Thus, this first passage about the transfer from oral to written *torah* focuses on the element of time and generations. The periodic reading of the *torah* transcends and overcomes the limits of human time and mortality so that the *torah* may be made new for each generation.

In the second text concerning the written *torah* in 31:24-29, Moses commands the Levites who carried the ark of the covenant to "take this book of the law and put it beside the ark of the covenant" (31:26). In the present context of the passage, one must identify this book of the *torah* as the book of Deuteronomy itself. The ark of the covenant already contained a uniquely authoritative text. The two stone tablets on which God had written the Ten Commandments were placed "in" the ark (10:1-5). The command to place the book of the *torah* of Moses "beside" the ark of the covenant rather than "in" it (31:26) signals both the authority of the book of Deuteronomy but also its derivative and secondary character in relation to the Decalogue itself.[6]

6. Terence Fretheim, "The Ark in Deuteronomy," *CBQ* 30 (1968): 5. Samuel Amsler

More importantly, however, putting the *torah* beside the mobile ark of the covenant, which the Levites carried, underlines the ability of the written *torah* to travel and thus to transcend physical limitations of space as well as time. Moses could not cross over into the promised land, but the ark and the Levites will cross over the boundary. The portable ark that carried the Decalogue and the *torah* could move with the people wherever they were and wherever "the LORD your God will choose as a dwelling for his name" (Deut. 12:11). Moreover, copies of this *torah* could be made and read and studied so that geography could not limit who or where the *torah* was studied (17:18). Thus, the writing of the Mosaic *torah* did not freeze the tradition into a dead letter. Instead, the writing of the text freed it to become a dynamic witness by which God's word could tangibly transcend boundaries of time, generations, and space. Moreover, the provisions for its continued reading, studying, and interpreting by human priests, elders, and all people ensured that its words would be constantly reinterpreted and reapplied to new situations and times.

The transfer from oral to written *torah* is particularly urgent because Moses knows that "after my death you will surely act corruptly, turning aside from the way that I have commanded you" (31:29). People will forget the story, the commandments, and the covenant. The text is "a witness against you" (31:26), an objective center that holds to the truth even as the people's subjective and errant inclinations tend to drag them off center, away from the truth and from God.

The third major theme of Deuteronomy 31, the introduction of the song that follows in chapter 32, serves to tie the Song of Moses clearly into the covenant of Moab. Like the written *torah,* the song functions as "a witness for me against the Israelites" (31:19). God knows even now before they enter the land that the people will turn to other gods, despise Yahweh, and break the covenant (31:20, 22). When the troubles and curses come upon them because of their rebellion, then the song "will confront them as a witness" (31:21). In the midst of crisis and disaster, the song will have power to move and transform the people.

The text introducing the song in 31:16-22 is paired in the structure of chapter 31 with the opening verses, which function as a short sermon of encouragement and assurance spoken by Moses to "all Israel" (31:1-6). The other sections of chapter 31 involve instructions and

---

("Loi Orale et Loi Écrite dans le Deutéronome," in *Das Deuteronomium: Entstehung, Gestalt und Botschaft,* 51–54) notes the progression within Deuteronomy from God's *writing* on the stone tablets to Moses' *oral proclamation* to Moses' *writing* of the *torah* to its subsequent and regular *oral proclamation* in every succeeding generation.

guidance to various leaders of the people: Moses, Joshua, the Levites, and the elders. But the sermon in verses 1-6 and the song discussed in verses 16-22 are aimed at "all Israel." God instructs Moses to "write this song, and teach it to the Israelites; put it in their mouths" (31:19).

Songs and music appeal to the human imagination because they integrate the intellects, the deep emotions, and the wills of those who sing. The imagery of song and poetry in Deuteronomy 32 is dramatic, evocative, and powerful. The song is a fitting complement to the prosaic liturgy of covenant making in chapters 29-30 and the administrative provisions for covenant leadership and text in chapter 31. The song's poetry moves and transforms in ways that mere discourse, command, or prose cannot do as well.

The Song of Moses is designed to be sung "when many terrible troubles come upon" the people (31:21). It is designed to recall a wilderness past when God faithfully led the people in response to a future time of rebellion, disorder, and hopelessness. According to Harold Fisch, in that future time of chaos, the Song of Moses

> will then act as a mnemonic, an aid to memory, because during the intervening period it will have lived unforgotten in the mouth of the reader or hearer, ready to come to mind when the troubles arrive. Poetry is thus a kind of time bomb; it awaits its hour and then springs forward into harsh remembrance. . . . The poem will come as a warning, even a kind of punishment, to a people that has broken the covenant. It will live in their minds and mouths, bringing them back, whether they like it or not, to the harsh memory of the desert sojourn. Once learned it will not easily be forgotten. The words will stick, they will be importunate, they will not let us alone.[7]

Once learned, the Song of Moses becomes indelibly imprinted on human hearts, moving with God's people into the future across boundaries of time, space, and culture.

A short summary of the song is given already in 31:16-20. God's faithfulness ("when I have brought them into the land flowing with milk and honey"; cf. 32:13-14) will be answered by the people's rejection of Yahweh, and their disobeying the first commandment ("they will turn to other gods and serve them, despising me and breaking my covenant"; cf. 32:16-18). God will punish the people ("my anger will be kindled. . . . I will forsake them and hide my face from them . . . many terrible troubles will come upon them"; cf. 32:19-26). The summary of the song in chapter 31 ends with the threat of judgment upon

7. Harold Fisch, *Poetry with a Purpose: Biblical Poetics and Interpretation* (Bloomington and Indianapolis: Indiana Univ. Press, 1988), 51.

the people. As we shall see, however, the Song of Moses itself moves one crucial step further. The song of the new covenant of Moab in chapter 32 does not end with judgment or curse. God's last word in the new covenant poem is a word of compassion and of a hopeful future. It is God alone who ensures that hope.

DEUTERONOMY 32:1-47: THE POETIC FORM

An ancient Jewish sage once observed that the Song of Moses in Deuteronomy 32 "contains all the Torah's principles."[8] Another scholar has called the song a "compendium of the prophetic theology."[9] The Song of Moses in chapter 32 presents a summary of Deuteronomy's version of the book of the *torah*. At the end of the book, Deuteronomy names both "the book of the *torah*" and the "song" as "a witness" (31:21, 26). They are reliable summaries and stable witnesses to the truth, to reality—to how things really are in the relationships of God, humans, and the world.

Scholars have long debated the origins and dating of this exemplar of Hebrew poetry, characterized by a rhythmic parallelism of lines, one line echoing and expanding on the line preceding. Many scholars in the earlier part of this century dated the poem to a period late in Israel's history, sometime during or after the Babylonian exile (587 B.C.E.). This position continues to have its supporters, but others see the poem as a creation from much earlier in Israel's history, perhaps in the early monarchy (11th–9th century B.C.E.).[10] In my judgment, the poem could

---

8. Shem-tob b. Joseph Falaqera, "Book of the Seeker," cited in James Kugel, *The Idea of Biblical Poetry: Parallelism and Its History* (New Haven: Yale Univ. Press, 1981), 186.
9. Carl Heinrich Cornill, *Introduction to the Canonical Books of the Old Testament*, trans. G. H. Box (London: Williams and Norgate, 1907), 123.
10. Attempts to date the poem have often centered on identifying the enemy of Israel mentioned in 32:19-29. The candidates for the enemy include the Philistines from the eleventh century, the Arameans from the mid-ninth century, the Assyrians in the eighth century, or the Babylonians in the sixth century B.C.E. Representatives of various positions include Otto Eissfeldt, *Das Lied Moses: Deuteronomium 32.1-43* (Berlin: Akademie, 1958); and George Mendenhall, "Samuel's Broken *Rib:* Deuteronomy 32," in *No Famine in the Land: Studies in Honor of John L. McKenzie,* ed. James Flanagan and Anita Robinson (Missoula, Mont.: Scholars Press, 1975), 63–74—eleventh century B.C.E. (1 Samuel 4–7); G. Ernest Wright, "The Lawsuit of God: A Form-Critical Study of Deuteronomy 32," in *Israel's Prophetic Heritage,* FS James Muilenburg, ed. B. W. Anderson and Walter Harrelson (New York: Harper, 1962), 26–67—ninth century B.C.E.; Sten Hidal, "Some Reflections on Deuteronomy 32," *ASTI* 11 (1977/78): 15–21; Jos Luyten, "Primeval and Eschatological Overtones in the Song of Moses (Dt 32,1-43)," in *Das Deuteronomium, Entstehung, Gestalt und Botschaft,* 341–47; D. A. Robertson,

have fit and may have functioned in several historical situations in ancient Israel, ultimately including the exile in Babylon. That some more ancient form of the poem was reshaped and edited over the course of this history to bring it to its present form seems the most likely scenario.

On the question of its form, the Song of Moses has been called a covenant lawsuit with God as prosecutor and Israel as the defendant accused of breaking the covenant.[11] Images and language are certainly borrowed from judicial or court proceedings: words like *witness, just, upright, vengeance, recompense, vindicate,* and *repay,* along with the extended case demonstrating God's faithfulness and Israel's breach of covenant loyalty. But just as we needed to pay attention to Deuteronomy's self-designation of the form of the whole book as *torah,* so too we need to pay attention to Deuteronomy's self-designation of the form of chapter 32: it is clearly a "song" (*šîrâ*—31:30; 32:44) that functions as an ongoing "witness" transmitted through teaching (31:22; 32:2). It is, in other words, a catechetical song that seeks to bring the past to remembrance in order to interpret and reshape the present and future for a new generation: "Remember the days of old . . . ask your father, and he will inform you; your elders, and they will tell you" (32:7). Its present form is that of a *torah* song that is to be taught and sung generation after generation. As we shall see, the present form of the song both indicts and gives hope in a way that a covenant lawsuit form could not do.

Much can be said and much has been written about the poetic structure, language, and imagery of this carefully crafted Song of Moses.[12] But I wish to emphasize four dimensions of the poem important to a theological interpretation of Deuteronomy: (1) the imagery used for

---

Linguistic Evidence in Dating Early Hebrew Poetry, SBLDS 3 (Missoula, Mont.: Scholars Press, 1972), 154–55 — sixth century B.C.E.

11. So Wright, "Lawsuit of God."

12. A few examples include Patrick Skehan, "The Structure of the Song of Moses in Deuteronomy (Deut. 32:1-43)," *CBQ* (1951): 153–63; Jos Luyten, "Primeval and Eschatological Overtones," 341–47; Stephen Geller, "The Dynamics of Parallel Verse: A Poetic Analysis of Deut. 32:6-12," *HTR* 75 (1982): 35–56; C. J. Labuschagne, "The Song of Moses: Its Framework and Structure," in *De Fructu Oris Sui: Essays in Honor of Adrianus van Selms,* ed. I. H. Eybers et al. (Leiden: Brill, 1971), 85–98. A stimulating study of the imagery and literary interplay of the Song of Moses in the light of other biblical texts is Harold Fisch, "The Song of Moses, Pastoral in Reverse," in *Poetry with a Purpose,* 55–79. Several of the verses in the poem (e.g., vv. 5, 26, 31) are notoriously difficult to translate since they contain words that occur only here in the Hebrew Bible. Other verses contain variant readings found in other Hebrew manuscripts or versions that appear more original than the traditional Masoretic text (e.g., vv. 8, 10, 13, 15, 19, 43).

God, (2) the affirmations about the activity of God in relation to other nations, (3) the view of nature, and (4) the dramatic structure and movement of the poetic drama within the song as a whole.

First, the *imagery used for God* is striking, suggestive, and varied. Images for Yahweh in this poem arise from the realms of nature, families, and warfare. Some images are borrowed from Israel's ancient Near Eastern context but are significantly reshaped. The most frequent image from nature used for Yahweh is the "Rock," which occurs five times (vv. 4, 15, 18, 30, 31). Yahweh as "Rock" is set in contrast to other gods also called "rocks" (vv. 31, 37) "their rock is not like our Rock" (v. 31). The association of a rock or mountain with the deity is part of the common stock of ancient Near Eastern religion, including the Canaanite religion of Israel's predecessors in the land. The image affirms the strength, refuge, and stability provided by the deity. But the Song of Moses redefines and expands the associations of the Rock to include Yahweh's perfection, justice, faithfulness, and uprightness (32:4).[13] The metaphor of Israel's God as the Rock is also given an ironic twist. Elsewhere in the Old Testament and in the ancient Near Eastern uses of the image, God as the Rock is usually portrayed as a strong refuge and fortress against disaster for God's people (Ps. 31:3; 62:7; Isa. 17:10). But here in the Song of Moses, the Rock no longer only shelters but also threatens Israel with judgment (32:23-25). Israel had sought refuge in other "rocks," other gods, and so experienced the judgment of Israel's one true Rock, Yahweh (32:15-18, 37). Yahweh as Israel's Rock would ultimately vindicate and have compassion on the people (32:36).

Another image of God derived from nature is that of the mother or father eagle who cares for its young, spreads out its protective wings, and carries the young eagles aloft in its claws (32:11). The solitary eagle on the heights with its young becomes the image of Yahweh alone who guides, feeds, and nurses the people: "the LORD alone guided him; no foreign god was with him" (32:12). What is striking about the use of the "eagle" for God is that the "eagle" (same Hebrew word) is explicitly named as the first in the list of "unclean" birds in 14:12. In a later section I consider the significance of God's crossing over the boundaries of purity from "clean" to "unclean."

Moving from the realm of nature to human families, Deuteronomy

---

13. On the use of a rock imagery for God elsewhere in the Bible and in the ancient Near East as background to its distinctive use of Deuteronomy, see Michael Knowles, "The Rock, His Work Is Perfect: Unusual Imagery for God in Deuteronomy XXXII," *VT* 39 (1989): 307–22.

32 interchanges images of father and mother for Yahweh. Israel is several times called the "children" or "sons and daughters" of God (32:5, 19, 20, 43). Yahweh is called "your father, who created you, who made you and established you" (32:6). The parental imagery of mother and father stands behind much of the description of God's caring, guarding, feeding, and nursing the children of Israel (32:10, 13-14). Verse 18 portrays Yahweh as the mother who gave birth to Israel: "You were unmindful of the Rock that bore you; you forgot the God who gave you birth." Images for Yahweh here move fluidly between male and female metaphors. Such fluidity in the use of male and female imagery was typical of ancient Near Eastern depictions of deity, even when a given Near Eastern god was understood as distinctly male or female.[14] The uniqueness of Yahweh is that Yahweh is neither male nor female; Deuteronomy affirms a oneness in God that transcends the division of sexuality into male and female (4:15-16). Yet male and female metaphors are used because they illuminate particular characteristics of God. The interchange of such gender-specific metaphors, however, suggests no one image captures or exhausts the understanding of God.

For many, the most troubling image of God in this song is that of the vengeful and bloodied divine warrior:

> For I lift up my hand to heaven,
> and swear: As I live forever,
> when I whet my flashing sword,
> and my hand takes hold on judgment;
> I will take vengeance on my adversaries,
> and will repay those who hate me.
> I will make my arrows drunk with blood,
> and my sword shall devour flesh —
> with the blood of the slain and the captives,
> from the long-haired enemy. (32:40-42)

Is not such imagery for God simply a license for violence, hatred, and warfare? Does it not encourage any powerful nation or group to go to war and claim God is fighting on its side, even though its cause may be less than just? Such questions are important, but one can answer them only in the context of the larger chapter itself.

The divine warrior image for Yahweh affirms God's involvement in and ultimate power over the destiny of the nations and peoples of the world. God does fight for some causes in the world and against others.

---

14. Trygve Mettinger, *In Search of God: The Meaning and Message of the Everlasting Names,* trans. Frederick Cryer (Philadelphia: Fortress, 1987), 206.

The preceding parts of the poem help one discern how that is the case. When God's people were weak and powerless, then it was that God cared for them in the wilderness and blessed them with the gifts of the promised land (32:10-14). But when Israel "scoffed at the Rock of his salvation," then God promised to go to war and to "heap disasters upon them, spend my arrows against them" (32:15, 23). God sent another nation against Israel as an agent of God's wrath (32:21). But this other nation in turn misunderstood its mission and arrogantly saw its power as self-achieved: "Our hand is triumphant; it was not the LORD who did all this" (32:27). Thus Yahweh, the divine warrior, declares, "the day of their calamity is at hand, their doom comes swiftly" (32:35). At the same time, Yahweh turns again in compassion toward Israel "when he sees that their power is gone" (32:36).

The pattern of the intervention of the divine warrior emerges clearly and consistently. On the one hand, when God's people are weak and powerless, God turns to them with compassion and fights on their behalf against those who oppress. On the other hand, when God's people or any people become powerful, self-assertive, and forget their dependence on God, then the divine warrior fights against them. Yahweh's battle against oppression is real but hidden in the cycles of politics and competing national interests that inevitably overturn the powerful and oppressive empires of the world. The inevitability of the downfall of arrogant, imperial powers is part of God's plan and design: "Is not this laid up in store with me, sealed up in my treasuries?" (32:34). God's sovereignty over all rival powers and gods will in the end prevail. As Israel surveyed its long history in the context of the surrounding imperial powers, the image of the divine warrior made comprehensible the rise and seemingly inevitable fall of mighty empires like Egypt, Assyria, and Babylon.

Like the image of the Rock, the divine warrior image was a common stock of Canaanite and Near Eastern depictions of gods. The typical Near Eastern warrior god fought for and protected the people or nation to whom the warrior god was attached. But the God of the Song of Moses was not always on Israel's side. Yahweh did defend and fight *for* Israel and against its enemies. But Yahweh was also free to fight *against* Israel when the people of Israel rebelled and forgot the God who gave them birth (32:18). Thus, Israel's utilization of the divine warrior imagery affirms Yahweh's freedom to discipline as well as to protect Israel.

Is the human community then encouraged to join in violently overthrowing those whom they see as oppressive? Are the oppressed allowed to use violence on their behalf to resist tyranny? In the larger context

of Deuteronomy, the answer to such questions remains open and ambiguous. On the one hand, Deuteronomy knows well the potent and
deadly idolatries of militarism and self-righteous moralism that can
delude and mislead a people to point fingers at the oppressions of
others while ignoring their own complicity in oppression, idolatry, and
rebellion against God (chaps. 7–10). On the other hand, the Song of
Moses knows the realities of the world and God's sometimes necessary
working within the imperfect nexus of power politics, violence, and
warfare. As I note in the conclusion to this chapter, however, Deuteronomy urges God's people to rely primarily on a more nonviolent
strategy for overcoming the threatening powers of this world.

Indeed, the dominant result of the divine war imagery in the Song
of Moses is ultimately one of human nonviolence, of active trust in
God, and of submitting feelings of hatred and retaliation to God, the
divine warrior. Alluding to Deut. 32:35, Walter Brueggemann comments on those psalms that ask God to take vengeance on the peti-
tioner's enemies (e.g., Psalm 109):

> When God is able to say, "Vengeance is mine" (Deut. 32:35; Rom.
> 12:19), it implies, "not yours." The submitting partner is no longer
> free to take vengeance—may not and need not. So the submission
> is an unburdening and freeing from pettiness and paralysis for praise
> and thanksgiving. . . . It releases us and promises that soon or late,
> in God's wisdom, the retaliation will be more sure and more pro-
> found than we could imagine.[15]

The divine warrior image does not lead inexorably to a license for
human violence against others. It may have the opposite effect. Because
real human desires for violent revenge may be relinquished to a divine
warrior, humans are freed to act in nonviolent but effective strategies
for resisting and putting to death the powers and gods who resist God's
will and oppress the powerless.

Thus, the collection of metaphors for God in the Song of Moses—
Rock, eagle, father, mother, spouse, and divine warrior—combine to
form a rich tapestry of imagery for Yahweh. It is a tapestry that weaves
new patterns out of old cloth, a new covenant out of old forms.

The second dimension comprises some important *affirmations about
the activity of God in relation to other nations.* People in the ancient
Near East commonly thought that each nation had its assigned gods.
Deuteronomy 32:8 takes up and adapts this view, declaring that "the

---

15. Walter Brueggemann, *The Message of the Psalms: A Theological Commentary*
(Minneapolis: Augsburg, 1984), 86.

Most High" (Hebrew 'elyôn, who is identified here as Yahweh) assigned other gods to all the other nations, saving Israel as Yahweh's own people:

> When the Most High apportioned the nations,
>   when he divided humankind,
> he fixed the boundaries of the peoples
>   according to the number of the gods;[16]
> the LORD's own portion was his people,
>   Jacob his allotted share.

Juxtaposed to this seemingly "pluralistic" or "universalistic" text is a more "exclusivistic" statement made later in the same song:

> See now that I, even I, am he;
>   there is no god beside me. (32:39)

As we saw earlier, Deuteronomy 4 holds together the same juxtaposition of recognizing the pluralism of religions among other nations (4:19) and a more exclusive view of Yahweh as the only true God in the entire world (4:39). What do we make of these apparently contradictory views of the relationship between Yahweh and other religions? Do other nations and peoples legitimately have their own gods or religions that one should honor and affirm? Or is Yahweh the only true God for all people everywhere? The issue is important in our time, and a full answer would certainly entail a much broader study of biblical, theological, and missiological resources than I can give here. But the Song of Moses does make a contribution to the discussion. The song holds together two paradoxical affirmations about Yahweh, the God of Israel. On the one hand, Yahweh is one and without equal among other gods and powers: "There is no god beside me" (32:39). On the other hand, other gods do exist and seem to be apportioned to other nations (32:8).

The Song of Moses does not overcome the paradox with any glib resolution. But its affirmations do seem to exclude at least two options in the debate over the relationship of the worship of Yahweh and the worship of other gods in other religions of the world. The Song of Moses excludes any easy universalism that blithely affirms that all gods and religions are equally valid and legitimate. Such a relativistic univer-

---

16. Probably because of this concern that the original text suggested the existence of other gods, the Hebrew Masoretic tradition provides a variant reading of Deut. 32:8: The LORD "fixed the boundaries of the nations according to the number of the *Israelites.*" But the early Qumran manuscript, the Greek Septuagint, and the Targums attest what is likely a more original reading: The LORD "fixed the boundaries of the nations according to the number of the *gods*" (so the NRSV).

salism ignores Deuteronomy's sharp critique of some gods, especially those associated with militarism, materialism, or self-righteous moralism. Deuteronomy assumes that all humans and communities have gods that they trust, particular allegiances that they worship. Discernment is necessary in critiquing which gods and loyalties are more appropriate than others.

At the same time, Deuteronomy does not permit a narrow exclusivism or the total denial of the legitimacy of other religions and gods for other peoples. Yahweh, says the song, has assigned other gods to other nations. Worshipers of Yahweh may be open to a dialogue with other religions, aware that they may encounter there a people with whom Yahweh has dealings and to whom Yahweh is in some way connected. Finally, however, as in some of the issues raised by the statutes and ordinances and as in the realities of life itself, ambiguities remain, contexts differ, struggle is required, and a final answer may not always be readily at hand.[17]

A second affirmation about God's activity in relation to other nations concerns the way in which God's judgment is enacted against Israel. Yahweh responds to Israel's rebellion: "I will hide my face from them, I will see what their end will be" (32:20). Yahweh in a sense withdraws the protective shield of the divine face or blessing. The hiding of the divine face makes Israel susceptible to the forces of chaos and destruction at the hands of another nation, which becomes the agent of divine punishment (32:21). The punishment is precisely commensurate with the sin that Israel commits, as Yahweh proclaims:

> They made me jealous with with what is no god,
>   provoked me with their idols.
> So I will make them jealous with what is no people,
>   provoke them with a foolish nation. (32:21)

The people of God receive exactly the judgment they deserve. But the just punishment of God is hidden, mediated through the events of world politics, real nations, and natural forces (32:24-25).

---

17. This tension between the allowance for many gods in Deut. 32:8-9 and the affirmation of only one God, Yahweh, in 32:39 has often been explained as the result of historical development within Israelite Yahwism from an early polytheism to later monolatry or henotheism (worship of one God but acknowledgment of the existence of other gods) and then a move toward monotheism. Cf. the argument and literature cited in Saul Olyan, *Asherah and the Cult of Yahweh in Israel,* SBLMS 34 (Atlanta: Scholars Press, 1988), 71-73. Some evolution in the history of Israel's understanding of its God is a plausible assumption. But the tension within the text of Deuteronomy 32 is not thereby resolved, for the two claims have been retained in the present form of the text, neither one totally cancelling out the other.

A third dimension of the Song of Moses is *the view of nature within the song*. In his study of Deuteronomy 32, Harold Fisch notes how the song begins as if it is going to be a "pastoral" poem, a poem about the blessings and wondrous cycles of nature. Deuteronomy 31 instructs that the song be sung in "the land flowing with milk and honey" (31:20). The first lines of the poem call on the heavens and earth to listen to the song's teaching, which will fall like life-giving rain and morning dew upon the grass. But, writes Fisch, we shall not "be granted the delights of the pastoral with its shepherds and happy milkmaids — we shall be given something more like an antipastoral."[18]

Fisch is right. In the course of the Song of Moses, the images of nature shift from the source of harmonious blessing to the agent of deadly curse. The land of milk and honey turns into "a desert land . . . a howling wilderness waste" (32:10). The divine eagle who gently cares for its young (32:11) becomes "the teeth of beasts" and "venom of things crawling in the dust" (32:24). Yahweh's gift of the sumptuous "fat of lambs and rams" (32:14) is turned by the people into fat sacrificed to other gods (32:37-38). A people "fat, bloated, and gorged" on the produce of the land (32:15) become people suffering "wasting hunger" and "burning consumption" (32:24). Canaan's "fine wine from the blood of grapes" (32:14) turns into "grapes of poison" and "the poison of serpents, the cruel venom of asps" (32:32-33). The cool and refreshing rain and dew that begin the poem (32:2) give way to the fiery anger of God that "burns to the depths of Sheol; devours the earth and its increase, and sets on fire the foundations of the mountains" (32:22).

In short, the song moves from a "pastoral" introduction of soothing images of nature to an "antipastoral" portrayal of chaotic and destructive forces of nature unleashed on a rebellious people. Fisch's study of Deuteronomy 32 notes an array of literary echoes between the song's imagery and imagery found in the creation story of Genesis 1-3, the flood story of Genesis 6-10, the Sodom and Gomorrah episode in Genesis 18-19, and the prophetic vision of Isaiah 1.[19] In each case, the forces of nature turn into instruments of God's judgment.

But the Song of Moses makes one last, crucial turn in regard to its image of nature. Yahweh will again turn and fight for Israel, defeating its enemies and restoring God's people to its land. The heavens that were witnesses *against* Israel (31:28) will sound the voice of praise *for* God's people:

---

18. Fisch, *Poetry with a Purpose,* 55.
19. Ibid., 68-77.

Praise, O heavens, his people,
　worship him, all you gods!
For he will avenge the blood of his children,
　and take vengeance on his adversaries;
he will repay those who hate him,
　and cleanse the land for his people. (32:43)

The heavens along with the earth or land will in the end stand ready to welcome and bless the people of Israel once more. Nature will again be a blessing, not a curse.

One final element in the interpretation of the Song of Moses is *the dramatic structure and movement of the poem as a whole.* In particular, one needs to follow the actors in this poetic drama and trace the changes in the subjects of the action as the poem unfolds. Who takes center stage and occupies the spotlight? Who is moved off the stage to die as the main actor, only to join the audience to applaud and praise the lone remaining protagonist in the drama? The preceding discussion already mentioned the four main characters in this hymnic drama: Yahweh, Israel, an unnamed other nation, and the forces of nature.

The *formal introduction* (32:1-3) begins with a call to the heavens and the earth to listen, an expression of hope that the teaching of the poem may transform and give new life like rain on dry grass. This summons is followed by a word of praise to Yahweh: "For I will proclaim the name of the LORD; ascribe greatness to our God!" The poem tells us at the outset that the main actor in this drama is God. The movement of the poem bears that out, as we shall see.

The next portion of the poem, an *introduction of the theme* (32:4-6), contrasts the justice and faithfulness of God with the foolishness and rebellion of God's people. The protagonist is God; the primary antagonist is the people of God.

Deuteronomy 32:7-14 rehearse *the story of Yahweh's past faithfulness.* In this section, Yahweh is the subject of nearly all the verbs, which emphasize the blessings and care that Yahweh has given to Israel: created, made, established, sustained, shielded, cared, guarded, took up, bore, guided, set atop the heights, fed, and nursed them. God's people have been entirely dependent on the providential care of God.

The subject of the action changes dramatically in the next section (32:15-18), which is an *indictment of God's people.* Here Israel is the primary subject of verbs describing apostasy and rejection of Yahweh: ate their fill, grew fat, bloated, gorged, kicked, abandoned God, scoffed, made God jealous, sacrificed to new deities, were unmindful, forgot.

In 32:19-25 the subject of the action changes once more from Israel to Yahweh. Yahweh's actions again take center stage in an *account of God's judgment on Israel:* saw, was jealous, spurned his sons and daughters, hid his face, will make them jealous, provoke them, kindles a fire, burns, devours, sets on fire, heaps disasters upon them, and sends arrows and the teeth of beasts against them. In this scene, Yahweh directs the actions of two other, lesser subjects: an unnamed other nation called "no people . . . a foolish nation" whose sword shall bereave and terrorize (32:21, 25), and various forces of nature ("fire," "pestilence," "beasts," "things crawling in the dust") that will bring destruction (32:22-24).

The next section of the song, 32:26-42, is *a divine speech announcing judgment on the other nation and vindication of God's people.* In the previous section, God had sent a nation against Israel. God confesses: "I thought to scatter them [Israel] and blot out the memory of them from humankind." What stopped God from giving up on the people completely was not Israel's great number, military strength, accumulation of wealth, or moral superiority (chaps. 7–10). The reason God will not abandon Israel is because the enemy nation who destroyed Israel might misunderstand its role as God's agent of judgment and say, "Our hand is triumphant; it was not the LORD who did all this" (32:27). Just as Israel was condemned for arrogantly scoffing at Yahweh and trying to take center stage by seeking to determine its own gods and destiny, so too the "other nation" is condemned for a similar arrogance, seeking to take over what belongs to Yahweh alone. God pushes the other nation off center stage. God condemns the other nation as void of sense, without understanding, unwise, not discerning, and foolish. The only reason the other nation could defeat the Israelites was because "the LORD had given them up" (32:30). Thus, "the day of their calamity is at hand, their doom comes swiftly" (32:35).

The other nation's doom will mean the vindication of God's people; Yahweh will "have compassion on his servants when he sees that their power is gone, neither bond nor free remaining" (32:36). God will have compassion on the humbled ones, the powerless, those who discern that they have no choice but to turn to God for help. Second Kings 14:26-27 provides a historical illustration of God's vindication of Israel when it was powerless: "For the LORD saw that the distress of Israel was very bitter; there was no one left, bond or free, and no one to help Israel. But the LORD had not said that he would blot out the name of

Israel from under heaven, so he saved them by the hand of Jeroboam son of Joash." It was not the exemplary repentance or obedience of King Jeroboam or the people of Israel that moved God to save the people. Indeed, King Jeroboam "did what was evil in the sight of the LORD" and "caused Israel to sin" (2 Kings 14:24). Simply the distress and powerlessness of Israel caused God to act. Similarly, in the poem in Deuteronomy 32, nothing has changed in the character of God's people except that they have lost their power and have no choice but to turn to Yahweh.

Yahweh scoffs at the gods of the other nation: "Where are their gods, the rock in which they took refuge? . . . Let them rise up and help you, let them be your protection!" (32:37-38). This ridicule of other gods leads into the central point of the Song of Moses. God stands in the dazzling spotlight at center stage and proclaims to Israel and to the world:

> See now that I, even I, am he;
>   there is no god beside me.
> I kill and I make alive;
>   I wound and I heal;
>   and no one can deliver from my hand. (32:39)

The Song of Moses here takes the first commandment, "You shall have no other gods before me," and fashions it into poetry. Yahweh is the one who kills, and Yahweh is the one who makes alive. There is no other. The words put to death all others who claim to occupy the place and role of God. The words give life to all who place trust in Yahweh, witnessing to the reality of their dependence on God alone.

The Song of Moses concludes in 32:43 with a resounding *call to praise and a promise of vindication for God's people.* A disciplined and humble people of God are called up on stage to share the spotlight with Yahweh as the heavens and other nations or gods cheer the grand finale. Those who hate Yahweh will be repaid, but the people of Yahweh will receive back their land cleansed and ready for Israel's return. The final word for God's people is a word of promise, a word of hope, even as God's people leave this drama limping, humbled, aware of the real limits of human power, human life, and human communities. Forced to face the fact of their mortality, God's people are yet able to live hopefully by entrusting their future to Yahweh.

The concluding framework to the Song of Moses in 32:44-47 reminds the listener of the extreme urgency of the words just heard: "This is no trifling matter for you, but rather your very life." The song remains "a witness against you" (32:46) every time Israel is tempted to "be like God" (Gen. 3:5), to deny human limits, to refuse the vocation of being "servants" and "children" of God (Deut. 32:6, 20, 36).

DEUTERONOMY 32:48-52: MOSES—A SIN REMEMBERED, DEATH FORETOLD

The new covenant of Moab in Deuteronomy 29–32 concludes with a command by God to Moses to ascend Mount Nebo, which is at the boundary of the promised land: "you shall die there on the mountain that you ascend and shall be gathered to your kin, as your brother Aaron died on Mount Hor and was gathered to his kin" (32:50). Earlier in Deuteronomy, the reason given for Moses' death outside the promised land was because of the people's sin (1:37; 3:23-29; 4:21). But in this brief text, which many scholars argue is a later addition by a Priestly editor, the reason for Moses' and Aaron's death outside the land is the same: "because both of you broke faith with me among the Israelites at the waters of Meribath-kadesh in the wilderness of Zin, by failing to maintain my holiness among the Israelites" (32:51). Numbers 20:10-13 and 27:12-14 recount the story. The exact nature of Moses' sin in that text is unclear, but that some sin has been committed is clear.

This text is sometimes simply dismissed as a later insertion by a Priestly editor that one should not consider in the interpretation of Deuteronomy. But that view would dissolve the necessary dialectic between Moses as *both* living and dying for the sake of others *and* living and dying as the inevitable condition of his human mortality, limitation, and sin. It is precisely this dialectic that permeates the whole book of Deuteronomy. There is an uneasy and unsettled interplay between the total giving of oneself to God and neighbor and the inevitable limits, boundaries, and ambiguities that constrict and complicate our human lives and communities.

We struggle to obey, but even the best of us, even Moses, fails. We will never return to the idyllic Garden of Eden in this life. We will never fully enter the promised land: "You may view the land from a distance, you shall not enter it" (32:52). In his upcoming death, Moses becomes an embodiment of the song that he has just sung. Moses will stand with Yahweh in one last shining moment at the end of Deuteronomy and then Moses will die. Even the great Moses must bow down before the affirmation of Yahweh: "There is no god beside me: I kill and I make alive." God "kills" Moses and "makes alive" a new generation of God's people to journey toward the promised land. Such is the fate of all humans; there is simply no other way.

REFLECTIONS AT THE BORDER: THE OLD COVENANT
OF HOREB AND THE NEW COVENANT OF MOAB

The new covenant of Deuteronomy 29–32 is given "in addition to" the covenant of Horeb (29:1). The Moab covenant does not replace the commandments, statutes, and ordinances of Horeb but supplements them and places them in a broader and deeper understanding of the relationship between God and the people of God. The similarities between Horeb and Moab include a common commitment to the people's ongoing struggle to be obedient to God's will. That call to obedience is obvious throughout chapters 6–28 (the Horeb laws), but the Moab covenant also urges the people to struggle toward obedience of God (30:11-20; 31:9-13; 32:46). The commandments, statutes, and ordinances remain the goal toward which God's people are directed. Other similarities between Horeb (chaps. 6–28) and Moab (chaps. 29–32) include a shared emphasis on the first commandment;[20] attention to the role of nature and the interrelationships of God, Israel, other nations, and the natural world; and a shared pessimism about the ability of God's people to obey the commandments and laws of Horeb.[21]

But the Horeb laws and the Moab covenant have significant differences. The Horeb commandments and laws focus naturally on human actions. The laws were directed to God's people for them to obey. The rhetorical devices crafted to motivate obedience were varied: direct divine command, appeals to one's own self-interest, reasonable implications from Israel's past story (slavery in Egypt), and actions designed to avoid what were seen as self-evident "abominations." Throughout the laws, the *human actor* was the primary subject of the imperative verbs. In contrast, as already noted, in each of the three parts of the Moab covenant—the liturgy of chapters 29–30, the covenant leadership and book of chapter 31, and the covenant song of chapter 32—*Yahweh* and not the people emerges as the prime subject of the verbs. Yahweh will circumcise the heart so that the people will love Yahweh and obey the commandments (30:6-8). In chapter 31, Moses begins to fade out of sight as the faithfulness of Yahweh is repeatedly

---

20. In the Horeb laws, the first commandment is highlighted in Deuteronomy 6–11, but it reappears several times throughout the statutes and ordinances of chaps. 12–28. The Moab covenant highlights the first of the Ten Commandments in 29:17; 30:6, 10, 20; 31:16, 18; 32:15-18, 37-39.

21. The Horeb section speaks of Israel's constant rebellion since its birth (Deut. 9:7, 24), culminating in the section of assured future curses at the end of chap. 28 (28:45-68). At several points, the Moab covenant notes the predilection of God's people toward disobedience with an increased expectation of rebellion after Moses' death (31:16-22, 27-29; 32:15-18).

affirmed (31:3, 4, 6, 8, 20, 23). The Song of Moses in chapter 32 clearly places Yahweh in the spotlight as the main protagonist in the unfolding drama played out among the people of Israel, other nations, and the world of nature.

The conclusions of the two parts of Deuteronomy are also different. The Horeb laws end with a small dose of blessing but an almost overwhelming piling up of curses, which move from conditional potentiality (28:15-44) to an actualized future reality (28:45-68). In contrast, the Moab covenant ends with a word of hope and promise. The Horeb curses of 28:63 proclaim that the LORD takes delight in "bringing you to ruin and destruction." But Moab turns this curse into a promise: the LORD will again "take delight in prospering you" (30:9).

GOD, THE LAW, AND THE NEW COVENANT: THEOLOGICAL REFLECTIONS ON DEUTERONOMY 29-32

The Moab covenant, the provisions for leadership and for the book of the *torah,* and the Song of Moses in chapters 29–32 have sometimes been treated as minor and largely unrelated appendices to the core law code of Deuteronomy in chapters 6–28. I would argue, however, that the Moab covenant has an integral relation to the Horeb laws of chapters 6–28 and forms a climactic extension and reinterpretation of the Horeb commandments. The literary juxtaposition of the Horeb and Moab covenants in the present form of Deuteronomy creates a theological movement and interplay on the issues of God, the law, and the introduction of a new covenant into the relationship of God and God's people.

One of the primary preoccupations of the Horeb statutes and ordinances was the need to set boundaries and establish order in the midst of chaotic powers. Humans had to struggle to set lines of division between life and death, male and female, clean and unclean, heaven and earth, native and foreign. But the Yahweh of the Moab covenant is a God who breaks through and overcomes such boundaries. These legal boundaries may be provisionally necessary for human existence but ultimately relative from a divine perspective. The Song of Moses gives several examples. Yahweh ultimately rules over all creation without any boundaries: "There is no god beside me" (32:39). Yahweh is God of both life and death: "I kill and I make alive" (32:39).

Yahweh's image is both male father (32:6) and female mother (32:18; cf. 22:5). Images of purity and cleanness (the just, upright, faithful, and perfect Yahweh — 32:4) combine with the image of an unclean bird, an eagle (32:11; cf. 14:12), in the portrayal of Yahweh's character. The separate realms of heaven and earth are called together with one voice to praise the greatness of God (32:1, 43). Yahweh is the only one able to overcome the distinctions between native and foreign nations (12:29-32; 23:1-8) since it was Yahweh who originally "apportioned the nations" and "divided humankind" (32:8). Mysteriously, it is Yahweh alone who transcends the boundaries between the gods of the other nations and the God of Israel; Yahweh was the one who in the beginning "fixed the boundaries of the peoples according to the number of the gods" (32:8). Yahweh is described in images derived from Canaanite gods and mythology (Rock, Divine Warrior).

Finally, Yahweh is the one who holds together a system of retribution and reward as well as the alternative mystery of ungrounded divine mercy and compassion. In the Moab covenant, Yahweh is a God who fractures and transcends all humanly created boundaries and restrictions. Ironically, however, Yahweh is free enough to become "self-enslaved" by working in and through the life and times of earthbound, sinful, and historical people, communities, and events in order to give life and hope to God's chosen people. Even though God's people have been and always will be rebellious and sinful (31:16-22, 27-29), God remains devoted to them and works for their blessing and vindication (32:36, 43).

THE NEW COVENANTS OF MOAB AND JEREMIAH

The book of Jeremiah contains a well-known promise of a new covenant between Yahweh and Yahweh's people. The new covenant of Jeremiah is promised to the Israelites for future days. It will not be like the covenant of Horeb, "a covenant that they broke, though I was their husband, says the LORD" (Jer. 31:32). In this new covenant, Yahweh promises,

> But this is the covenant that I will make with the house of Israel after those days, says the LORD: I will put my law within them, and I will write it on their hearts; and I will be their God, and they shall be my people. No longer shall they teach one another, or say to each other, "Know the LORD," for they shall all know me, from the least of them to the greatest, says the LORD; for I will forgive their iniquity, and remember their sin no more. (Jer. 31:33-34)

Is this new covenant of Jeremiah the same as the new covenant of Moab in Deuteronomy 29–32? They have similarities. Both new covenants are presented as alternatives to the Horeb covenant or laws (cf. Deut. 29:1). Both are inclusive of the whole community: "from the least of them to the greatest" (Jer. 31:34) and "the leaders . . . your elders, and your officials, all the men of Israel, your children, your women, and the aliens who are in your camp" (Deut. 29:10-11). Both new covenants stress Yahweh's direct working within the hearts of God's people (cf. Deut. 30:6-8).[22]

But in the end key differences distinguish the Moab covenant from Jeremiah's new covenant. Deuteronomy's new covenant is intended as a present reality for "today," while Jeremiah's covenant is for a distant future time "after those days." The vocabulary of forgiveness is central to Jeremiah but not as prominent in the Deuteronomic covenant. In the Moab covenant, God "will circumcise your heart . . . so that you will love the LORD" and observe "all his commandments that I am commanding you today" (Deut. 30:6-8). The content of the commandments remain written in the Mosaic book to the *torah,* but God works within the heart to empower and motivate the *will* to observe the scriptural *torah.* By contrast, in Jeremiah's covenant a written book of *torah* is not required because God will write the contents of the law directly on the hearts. Therefore, Jeremiah promises that both the *will* and the *knowledge* of the law will be in the hearts of each follower of God.

This point leads to the most important distinction between the covenants of Deuteronomy and Jeremiah. The primary means by which Deuteronomy seeks to move people toward faith in God and obedience to God's will is through one person teaching the *torah* to another person (Deut. 4:1, 5, 10, 14; 5:31; 6:1, 6-7; 11:19; 31:19, 22). As Deuteronomy understands it, the *torah* is a catechism or foundational teaching document that is to be written down and taught from generation to generation (31:9-13, 24-29). In contrast, the new covenant of Jeremiah dispenses entirely with the office of teaching: no books, no teachers, no learning *torah.* Jeremiah's vision is for the most part an unrealized ideal in the religious communities with which we are acquainted. The promise of Jeremiah's new covenant is clearly for a distant time and reality that we do not yet know; it is for a time "after those days."

---

22. Scholars differ on the close identification of the new covenant of Moab in Deuteronomy 29–32 with the new covenant of Jeremiah 31. A. Cholewinski ("Zur theologischen Deutung des Moabbundes," *Bib* 66 [1985]: 96–111) and E. W. Nicholson (*Preaching to the Exiles: A Study of the Prose Tradition in the Book of Jeremiah* [Oxford: Basil Blackwell, 1970] are examples of those who tend to stress the continuities between the two covenant passages. H. D. Potter ("The New Covenant in Jeremiah 31:31-34," *VT* 33 [1983]: 347–57) joins a number of other scholars whom he cites in stressing the discontinuity between Jeremiah's new covenant and the covenant of Moab. While displaying some resemblances, the covenant of Jeremiah 31 and that of Moab (Deuteronomy 29–32) are in the end quite distinctive.

The new covenant of Moab, however, is a practical strategy for "today." It works in and through known realities and methods: written texts, human teachers, actualizing liturgies, poetic songs, persuasive appeals, and the real-life praxis of relationships, families, communities, politics, and economics where faith, ethics, and character are shaped and developed. The distinctive "newness" of the Moab covenant in relation to the Horeb statutes and ordinances is the shift from the primacy of *human* action, which is commanded (the Horeb laws), to the primacy of *God's* judging and saving action, which is mediated through liturgy, song, and text (the Moab covenant).

The Horeb laws command an ideal that *ought* to be but never really *can* be through human actions or power alone. The Moab covenant does not so much command an ideal as tell the truth about what is real. It announces the inevitable reality of human rebellion and the even stronger reality of God's faithfulness in spite of that rebellion. The reality of God's faithfulness cannot be humanly explained or captured in any system, ideology, or program; it is part of the "secret things" revealed and actualized through the direct discourse of proclamation, scripture, and song (Deut. 29:29). The Moab covenant turns the commands against which humans rebel into future promises toward which God is working. The commandments become an announcement of the goal toward which God struggles in the everyday lives of individuals and communities (30:6-8, 11-14). The struggle for humans to obey the commands remains, but the spotlight has shifted from human striving to divine action. God is finally the one who puts to death the rebel and struggles to make alive the obedient follower of God (31:6-8; 32:36, 39). By contrast, Jeremiah's new covenant is for a distant future time without the need for scripture or teachers, a time we do not yet fully know but only hope for. In the meantime, the strategy of the Moab covenant remains a viable, realistic, and hopeful alternative.

The discussion of old and new covenants (or testaments) necessarily raises the issue of the relationship of Jewish and Christian traditions to the covenants of Horeb, Moab, and Jeremiah. The Hebrew Bible clearly includes other covenant traditions. Examples include God's covenant with Noah (Genesis 9), with Abraham (Genesis 15), and with King David (2 Samuel 7). But the covenants of Horeb, Moab, and Jeremiah are distinctive in that they all fall within the same Deuteronomic stream of tradition. Within this one tradition, it is possible simultaneously to hold together three different covenants. The Moab covenant of divine faithfulness is made "in addition to" the Horeb covenant of human obedience. Moab does not cancel Horeb but rather supplements it in a definitive way. The new covenant of Jeremiah likewise does not invalidate the Horeb covenant. The people broke the covenant but its laws remain in force, and God will write them on the hearts of God's people in some distant future time.

In terms of catechizing strategy, Jews and Christians stand on equal footing in this scheme of three covenants. Neither tradition can claim that it has experienced the complete fulfillment of Jeremiah's vision of the new covenant. Both Jews and Christians rely on God's activity mediated through the down-to-earth instruments of written scripture, human teachers and preachers, and fallible human communities who confess and receive forgiveness for their inevitable shortcomings and failures in regard to the law. The actualization of Jeremiah's new covenant, which will not require such mundane mediation of the divine, remains a distant and future hope for Christians as well as Jews.[23]

Classic expressions of the Jewish and Christian traditions have not attained the fulfillment of *Jeremiah's* new covenant. On the other hand, Jews and Christians would understand themselves as communities in some way related to the *Horeb* covenant, struggling to be obedient to God's commands. Yet they would understand themselves also to be something more. Along the lines of the *Moab* covenant, most Jewish and Christian communities of faith would see themselves as arenas of God's active presence in and through the community's shared story, actualizing liturgy, human leaders and teachers, normative scripture, and poetic song. One should not minimize the very real differences that exist both within and between the Jewish and Christian traditions. But in terms of present reality, neither community should claim to have moved beyond the other in the three-covenant scheme of the Deuteronomic tradition. Self-righteous moralism, the claim to ethical superiority, is an idolatry that Deuteronomy will not tolerate (chaps. 9–10). We all remain Moab covenanters, on the boundary yearning for the promised land but not yet there. Like Moses, we will likely die before ever actually setting foot in the land of promise. We will get glimpses of the land from time to time. But we still finally have to trust God to carry forward our community and world in their journey toward "the land flowing with milk and honey."

---

23. Some sections of the New Testament, of course, refer to Jeremiah's promise of a new covenant as associated with the coming of Jesus as the promised Messiah. Hebrews 8–9 develop the theme at length. Jesus' words at the Lord's Supper allude to the "new covenant" in Luke 22:20. But these and other words of Scripture were written down into a New Testament and taught within the Christian community. This suggests that the full *actualization* of Jeremiah's promise of a new covenant has not yet been fulfilled ("no longer shall they teach one another"). Christians still teach one another.

SUMMARY: DEUTERONOMY 29-32
AND THE DEATH OF MOSES

The introduction of the Moab covenant in Deuteronomy 29-32 marks a decisive turning point in the structure and flow of the entire book of Deuteronomy. Moses' death as an expression of the limits and failures of human obedience and power form a major element in this critical juncture in Deuteronomy's theology. It is here that Deuteronomy explicitly links Moses' death with his own personal failure and disobedience at the waters of Meribath-kadesh (Deut. 32:48-52). The three parallel versions of the Moab covenant — liturgy (chaps. 29-30), leadership/text (chap. 31) and poetry (chap. 32) — all stress human limits and the failure of human obedience.

Chapters 29-30 speak of the people's failure to abide by the Horeb covenant's laws and the subsequent exile that will come upon Israel, an exile that will be overcome only through God's compassion. Chapter 31 turns its attention from the whole people to concerns raised by the individual death of Moses (31:14-15), a death that prefigures the future failure and death of the community (31:16-21, 27-29). The ministry of Moses is limited in time and space by his humanity. Thus, Moses is replaced by new leadership (Joshua, Levites, elders), a written book of the *torah* (Deuteronomy itself), and a written song to serve as "a witness" and teaching strategy "after my [that is, Moses'] death" (31:27, 29). The Song of Moses in chapter 32 returns again to the failures and obedience of the whole people (32:15-35) whom God would judge but finally vindicate and save (32:36).

Another motif associated with the theme of Mosaic and human limitations is featured in the Song of Moses. The song emphasizes the active involvement of the wider nonhuman creation along with other nations apart from Israel in the plan of God. Israel's people exist within and are subject to a nexus of powerful relationships with nature and other nations that transcend individual human and national boundaries. God works through this interdependent network of relationships to accomplish God's ultimate will for the salvation of God's people (32:36, 43). God's people live not as masters but as participants within this web of powerful natural, political, and theological forces that affect and shape Israel's destiny.

The human limitation to hold together and comprehend the full mystery of God's ways with Israel and the world is expressed as well in the unresolved and dialectical coexistence of the Horeb and Moab covenants. The Horeb covenant's emphasis on *human* obedience ("you shall have no other gods") stands side by side with ("in addition to" — 29:1) the Moab covenant's emphasis on the saving activity of *God* ("The LORD will vindicate his people . . . when he sees that their power is gone"). Human responsibility for obedience is held together with God's creation of obedience within the people (30:6). The two simultaneous covenants — the law of Horeb and the mercy of Moab — involve a theological dynamic that cannot be fully captured or reduced into a single logical formulation. Deuteronomy says as much when it affirms, "The secret things belong to the LORD our God, but the revealed things belong to us . . . to observe all the words of this *torah*" (29:29).

When we turn to consider the second major understanding of Moses' death as self-giving compassion for the sake of the people, an interesting shift occurs in Deuteronomy. The strong spotlight on *Moses'* self-giving death outside the land and intercession for the people (Deut. 1:37; 3:26; 4:21; 9:19-21, 25-29; 10:10) begins to fade into the background in the Moab covenant. Moses' function is taken over by the action of *God's* mercy and compassion. God will work not in and through a single individual (Moses) but in and through the liturgy of a worshiping community, a text, a song, other human leaders, nations, and all creation. Moses' death atoned for the rebellion of the old wilderness generation and allowed a new generation to enter the land of Canaan (Deut. 1:37). But now as Moses dies and the future begins to invade the present, God works in new ways to create new relationships and new possibilities for God's people.

CHAPTER 8

"This Is the Blessing" —
Deuteronomy 33–34:
God's Blessing, Moses' Death

"The LORD your God turned the curse into a blessing for you, because the LORD your God loved you."

—Deut. 23:5

He is on the track of Canaan all his life; it is incredible that he should see the land only when on the verge of death. This dying vision of it can only be intended to illustrate how incomplete a moment is human life, incomplete because a life like this could last forever and still be nothing but a moment. Moses fails to enter Canaan not because his life was too short but because it is a human life.

—Franz Kafka[1]

The book of Deuteronomy ends with Moses' prayer of blessing for the community of Israel (chap. 33) and the death and burial of Moses outside the promised land (chap. 34). At the end of his days, Moses is portrayed as letting go of his leadership, his power, and his life. He hands it over to God and a new generation to carry on with the story of God's people. These concluding chapters form an appropriate inclusio with the opening chapter of Deuteronomy around the theme of the inevitable rise and fall of human power and the need ultimately to trust God as Israel encounters the future. In Deuteronomy 1, Moses had given up his exclusive leadership and shared power with others, just as he does in Deuteronomy 34. Moses had recounted the spy story when an earlier generation of Israelites had refused to trust God's power and promise (1:19-45). The old generation had thus died outside the land, a death that Moses now shares at the end of Deuteronomy. But God had promised that a new generation would enter the land of promise (cf. 1:34-40). Thus, the beginning and end of Deuteronomy join

1. Franz Kafka, *Diaries 1914–1923,* ed. Max Brod, trans. Martin Greenberg and Hannah Arendt (New York: Schocken, 1965), 195-96.

together in affirming the limits of human capacities and powers, the need for human community, and the ultimate faithfulness of God, who transcends the limits of space, time, and human death to carry forward the story of God's people.

DEUTERONOMY 33: MOSES' PRAYER FOR GOD'S BLESSING

The act of prayer is a confession of human limitations. Intercessory prayer requests God to work in and through humans and creation to accomplish what humans alone cannot do. Moses has done all that he can do, and he must finally lay down his life and trust God to carry on with the future and to fulfill the powerful words of blessing that he speaks. Thus, Moses "the man of God" turned to God in prayer and "blessed the Israelites before his death" (Deut. 33:1).

Moses' blessing of the twelve tribes of Israel consists of an introductory and concluding framework (33:2-3, 5 and 33:26-29, respectively), which surrounds a catalog of specific blessings for each of the twelve tribes of Israel (33:6-25). The framework in verses 2-3, 5 and 26-29 was likely an older independent psalm of praise that celebrated the kingship and victory of God. Much of the framework's imagery seems to derive from Canaanite divine warrior language: the "shining forth" of the god from Seir or Sinai (v. 2), the heavenly army of "holy ones" (vv. 2-3), and the god who "rides through the heavens" (v. 26).[2] The psalm celebrating the victory of the divine warrior has been taken over, applied to Yahweh, and edited with the addition of verse 4 (see below) and the insertion of individual blessings of the Israelite tribes (vv. 6-25). Many of the tribal blessings may themselves be quite ancient in origin. This editing of the Divine Warrior hymn has redirected its meaning from a poem about the power of military might to a poem about the power of teaching the *torah* as a nonviolent but aggressive strategy to continue the blessing of the people of God from one generation to the next.

The *introduction in 33:2-5* portrays Yahweh's march with a divine army from the holy mountain. The mountain is given three different names: Sinai, Seir, and Paran. The mention of Mount Sinai immediately links this scene with that recorded in Exodus 19–20; Deuteronomy elsewhere always calls this mount Horeb. In its present context in the Pentateuch, this Divine Warrior march is thus associated not so

---

2. Patrick D. Miller, Jr., *The Divine Warrior in Early Israel,* HSM 5 (Cambridge: Harvard Univ. Press, 1973), 77–78. Similar imagery is found in Judg. 5:4-5; Ps. 68:7-8; 104:3; Hab. 3:3-4.

much with a military victory but with a giving of the *torah* at Mount Sinai or Horeb. Most scholars agree that 33:4 has been secondarily added to the introduction, but it serves to strengthen the association of the Divine Warrior image with the giving of the *torah* at Mount Horeb: "Moses charged us with the *torah.*" The *torah,* a term designating the catechism of Deuteronomy and later extended to the whole Pentateuch, becomes the weapon of the Divine Warrior. The violent militarism of the Canaanite gods is transformed into the powerful teaching of Yahweh through *torah.*

The last verse of the introduction (33:5) may have one of two meanings. The celebration of the rise of "a king in Jeshurun [an alternate name for Israel]" may refer either to the sovereign power of Yahweh as monarch or to the rise of a human king in Israel. In either case, Deuteronomy upholds the ultimate supremacy of Yahweh over all powers. Although the king may be a legitimate institutional channel of God's authority and care of the community, the human king of Israel remained subject to Yahweh as a student and servant of the book of the *torah* (17:18-20).

The *tribal blessings of 33:6-25* echo other biblical scenes where a dying parent pronounces final blessings upon his children (Genesis 27; 48–49). The Song of Moses had ended with a general promise about the vindication of God's people (Deut. 32:36, 43). The blessings in this next chapter give concrete expression and form to this vindication, providing specific and individual blessings to each of the tribes. The blessings given here involve down-to-earth realities in the life of the community: survival, family, security, land, fertility, vocation, government, economics, worship, and the teaching of *torah.* The blessings mirror the subject matter of the statutes and ordinances of chapters 12–28 and entrust them not to human obedience alone but to the work of God in and through ordinary communities of people, families, governments, politics, and economics. The last word of Moses and the Moab covenant is not a little blessing and much curse as in the Horeb material (chap. 28). Rather, chapter 33 declares that full blessing is God's final will for God's people.

The list of blessings begins with the tribe of Reuben (33:6). Reuben is the firstborn of the sons of Jacob and thus at the head of the list of tribes here and in most other tribal lists (Gen. 49:1-3; Num. 1:5).[3] The

---

3. The sequence of the Israelite tribes in Deuteronomy 33 is unique when compared to the various other lists of the twelve tribes of Israel (Genesis 49; Numbers 1 and 26; etc.). The order of tribes here seems to follow a roughly geographical pattern combined with other reasons for priority. Reuben from east of the Jordan is the firstborn and thus named first. Next is Judah, the tribe that ascended to supremacy through Jerusalem and

dwindling number and strength within the tribe of Reuben is foreseen. Reuben here may function as a forerunner of Israel as a whole in exile. Reuben lies on the east side of the Jordan, not technically in the land of Canaan. Reuben's "numbers are few," perhaps mirroring the exiles' sense of powerlessness and loss of numbers. Moses' prayer that "Reuben live, and not die out" is a prayer that the exiles may well have applied to Israel as a whole. Part of God's blessing is simply the survival of the people in the face of overwhelming disaster and death.

The blessing of Judah appears to reflect a time in Israel's history when Judah was isolated from the rest of the community of Israelite tribes. The prayer asks that Yahweh bring Judah back to God's people and strengthen him against his adversaries (Deut. 33:7). God's blessing here strengthens the uniting bonds of the community of Israel. Each tribe builds up and strengthens the whole people (Psalm 133).

The blessing of Levi is the most important and distinctive of all the tribal blessings. Throughout Deuteronomy, the Levites are set apart and dedicated to a unique calling as sacrificial priests (18:1-8; 33:10), as preachers (27:9-26), carriers of the tradition (31:24-25), and teachers of *torah* (33:10). The Levites are that part of the community of Israel who have no inheritance except the LORD, who are not tied to land and economic interests, who live solely in dependence on the community as a witness to Israel's sole dependence on Yahweh. The calling of the Levites even extends to the renunciation of family and kinship ties (33:9). The Levites teach and guide the community, whether in the ancient form of oracles through the Thummim and Urim (cf. Exod. 28:30; Lev. 8:8) or through the "word," the "covenant," the "ordinances" or the "*torah*" contained in the Mosaic book of the *torah*. Part of the blessing of the community is a group dedicated to interpreting God's will and proclaiming, teaching, and offering sacrifices for the sake of the community.

The last verse of the Levi blessing, Deut. 33:11, has violent and militaristic overtones. The image of the violent defeat of enemies is

---

the Davidic line. The priestly tribe of Levi has a prominent role in Deuteronomy as priests and teachers of *torah* and thus is named third. Benjamin and Joseph as the beloved sons of Jacob's favorite wife Rachel (Gen. 29:31; 30:22-24; 35:116-26) are named next. The extravagant blessing given to Joseph (and thereby Ephraim and Manasseh — Deut. 33:17) may reflect the origins of the Deuteronomic tradition in northern Israel, where the Joseph or Ephraimite tribe was often dominant. The sequence of the rest of the tribes seems to follow a counterclockwise geographical ordering of tribes as they settled in the land of Canaan. Simeon has dropped out of the list completely. For a discussion of the relationships of the various twelve-tribe lists in the Pentateuch, see my *The Death of the Old and the Birth of the New*, BJS 71 (Chico, Calif.: Scholars Press, 1985), 55–70.

sometimes perceived as incongruous in relation to the preceding images of Levi as nonviolent priests and teachers. Thus, some have argued that verse 11 is misplaced and ought to be attached to the blessing of Judah (v. 7).[4] But the transformation from the power of militarism to the power of teaching *torah* is part of the development of the biblical traditions associated with the tribe of Levi. In an earlier setting very similar to the blessing of Moses just before his death, the ancestor Jacob "blessed" Levi by denouncing the Levites for their "weapons of violence" (Gen. 49:5-7):

> Cursed be their anger, for it is fierce,
>   and their wrath, for it is cruel!
> I will divide them in Jacob,
>   and scatter them in Israel. (Gen. 49:7)

The Levites were known for their capacity for militaristic violence and revenge in earlier pentateuchal traditions (cf. Gen. 34:25-31). But in the blessing of Moses in Deuteronomy, the Levites are called to channel their militaristic energy into preaching, sacrificing, and teaching *torah.* The language of militarism and adversaries is retained. But the one who "crushes the loins of his adversaries" is shifted from Levi to the LORD (Deut. 33:11). Moreover, the arena is radically changed: the war rages on now not so much on the battlefield as in the classroom and religious assembly. The weapons are no longer chariots and spears but *torah* and the words of God.

A similar transfer from militaristic languages to the language of teaching and obeying *torah* is evident in the use of the formula "Be strong and courageous" as it occurs in Deuteronomy 31 and Joshua 1. The phrase has its origins in ancient Near Eastern and biblical exhortations in preparation for warfare. This militaristic context is evident when Moses encourages the Israelites in Deut. 31:4-6 concerning the upcoming military conquest of Canaan: "Be strong and bold; have no fear or dread of them." Michael Fishbane observes that this same militaristic formula

> is repeated a second time by YHWH to Joshua at the onset of the conquest (Josh. 1:5-6, 9). On this second occurrence, however, an entirely new dimension is added: for encased within the old military exhortation formula (in vv. 6, 9) is a piece of aggadic theologizing where Joshua is told to "be strong and of good courage" *in obeying the Torah,* since only in this manner will he succeed in his great

---

4. An example is A. D. H. Mayes, *Deuteronomy,* NCBC (reprint, Grand Rapids: Eerdmans, 1981), 404.

adventure (vv. 7-8). . . . Thus, the language of a military order has
been reformulated as an injunction to obey the Torah.[5]

As with the blessing of the Levites in Deut. 33:8-11 and the introductory
frame in 33:2-5, the language of violent militarism has been transformed
into the nonviolent but powerful medium of worship, teaching, and obeying *torah*. The blessing of God includes those in the community who
seek to be fully devoted to the interpretation and teaching of the tradition in the context of the worship life of the community.

The blessing of Benjamin, the youngest and most beloved of Jacob's
twelve sons, surrounds the tribe with Yahweh's love so that it "rests in
safety . . . all day long" (33:12). Blessing is the ability to let go, lean
back, and rest in the security of divine care.

The lavish blessing of Joseph (33:13-17) is the most extravagant of
all the tribes. The blessing overflows with pictures of fruitful land,
fertility, descendants, power, and prosperity. The gifts of nature, "the
choice gifts of the earth and its fullness," are featured in the Joseph
blessing. As in every other part of Deuteronomy, the world of nature
and creation form a crucial element of the interrelations of God,
humans, and nature. Blessing includes all the gifts of creation.

The blessings of Zebulun and Issachar (33:18-19) seem to reflect their
respective vocations with Zebulun as a seafaring tribe ("in your going
out . . . they suck the affluence of the seas" and Issachar as land-based
farmers ("in your tents . . . they suck . . . the hidden treasures of the
sand"). Part of God's blessing is the daily work of commerce, farming,
and production.

The blessing of Gad reflects a time when Gad was a leader among
the tribes. Government and leadership has its privileges but also its
heavy responsibilities of justice and obedience to God (33:21). The
meaning of the blessing of Dan is obscure, perhaps referring to Dan
as the northernmost outpost of Israel and its function in the military
defense of the land. Naphtali and Asher are blessed with prosperity,
favor, and security.

All in all, the blessings of the tribes of Israel in Deuteronomy 33
make quite specific requests about how the vindication and compassion
of Yahweh promised in chapter 32 should be worked out in the life of
the Israelite community. The blessing constitutes Moses' last will and
testament to Israel before his death.

The blessing of Moses ends with the concluding framework (33:26-
29), which continues with the imagery of the divine warrior. But the

5. Michael Fishbane, *Biblical Interpretation in Ancient Israel* (Oxford: Clarendon,
1985), 384, 546.

content of the blessings has transformed the warrior God into a God who works primarily in and through the weapons of *torah,* worship, and words. This reconstituted warrior language will lead Israel to victory over its enemies and to the blessings of life, safety, and prosperity. The pastoral images of "a land of grain and wine, where the heavens drop down dew" return to the expectations of a pastoral poem in the Song of Moses in chapter 32 (cf. 31:20; 32:1-2). Moses prays in chapter 33 that the seemingly antipastoral Song of Moses become again a pastoral, a poem about the assured blessings of Yahweh in spite of the rebellions of the people. Moses' prayers to God on behalf of the people had been effective before (9:25 – 10:5), and so Moses leaves with his people his most powerful legacy, his words of blessing and hope:

> Happy are you, O Israel! Who is like you,
>   a people saved by the LORD,
> the shield of your help,
>   and the sword of your triumph! (33:29)

Blessing, promise, and hope are the last words of Moses to Israel.

DEUTERONOMY 34: THE DEATH OF MOSES
OUTSIDE THE LAND

The lavish images of happy blessing and victory in Deuteronomy 33 pulsate with life and hope in the face of an open future. Combined with this chapter of blessing is chapter 34, the poignant scene of the death and burial of Moses before he reached his life's goal of setting foot in the promised land. The blessing is promised but not achieved. The end has arrived, but the goal has not been reached. What is the meaning of Moses' death in this last chapter of Deuteronomy?

Recall that the present form of Deuteronomy has understood the significance of Moses' death in various ways. Earlier in Deuteronomy, the motif of Moses' death outside the land in some way opened up the possibility for the hope and life to the rest of Israel promised in chapter 33. Moses would die because of the people's sin (1:37; 3:26; 4:21). A new generation of Israelites would enter the land of promise because of his death, a land into which he could not go. But Deuteronomy makes clear that Moses does not die as a substitute. He does not die *instead* of the people but rather *ahead* of them. The structure of the new Moab covenant (chaps. 29–32) moves from God's merciful election of Israel through God's judgment and finally to God's vindication and saving of the people. Like Moses, this community of Israel will experience its own suffering and judgment. But Moses' death in some way contributes to the possibility that Yahweh will ultimately restore the community after it has passed through the trauma of an exilic death.

A later editor of Deuteronomy (perhaps a Priestly or later Deuteronomic redactor) had explained Moses' death as the result not of the people's sin but of his own human failure. Moses had once "broken faith" at Meribath-kadesh (Deut. 32:48-52). Moses had failed to maintain God's holiness and thus joined the ranks of rebellious Israel against God. Moses in this view was a sinner and rebel like the others, if only for one brief lapse of faith.

Interestingly, the account of Moses' death in Deuteronomy 34 does not mention either of these two prior explanations for the meaning of Moses' death. As such, chapter 34 provides a third and crucial stage in Deuteronomy's reflection on Moses' death that affects and redirects one's reading of the whole book. A close reading of the chapter helps one see where Deuteronomy finally wishes to leave the reader. My reading of Deuteronomy 34 divides into three parts: verses 1-6 — Moses' survey, death, and burial; verses 7-9 — Moses' vigor, the people's mourning, and Joshua's leadership; verses 10-12 — Moses' unique power and relationship to Yahweh.

DEUT. 34:1-6: MOSES' SURVEY, DEATH, AND BURIAL

In their present form, these verses are largely the product of a later Deuteronomistic writer or editor.[6] The scene is a fulfillment of the LORD's statement in 3:27 and 4:22 — Yahweh tells Moses that he will see the land but die before actually setting foot on its soil. Standing on Mount Nebo across the Jordan River from Jericho, Yahweh shows Moses the promised land from its northern extremity in Dan to the southern reaches of the Negeb (34:1-3). God reaffirms the continuing validity of the pentateuchal promise of the land to the ancestors ("to Abraham, to Isaac, and to Jacob"). But the promise remains for Moses only a distant sight, not an actualized fulfillment: "I have let you see it with your eyes, but you shall not cross over there" (34:4).

Moses then dies in the land of Moab "at the LORD's command." Moses' demise is not a natural death but a premature and divinely imposed limit on Moses' life. The Hebrew text reports that "he

6. For example, Martin Noth, *The Deuteronomistic History,* JSOTSup 15, 2d ed. (Sheffield: JSOT Press, 1991), 28, 60; and Mayes, *Deuteronomy,* 411. Mayes argues that the references in v. 1 to "the plains of Moab" and "Mount Nebo" are Priestly additions to the otherwise Deuteronomistic section. They may also be post-Deuteronomic additions by a redactor who was editing the entire Pentateuch. The same may be true of the references to "Abraham, to Isaac, and to Jacob" in v. 4.

[Yahweh] buried him [Moses] . . . but no one knows his burial place to this day" (34:6). God returns Moses back to the dust from which God originally created all humans (Gen. 2:7; 3:19). Moses' burial place is hidden and thus unable to become the site of a shrine or cult of a dead human ancestor, a practice strictly forbidden by Deuteronomy's own laws (Deut. 14:1; 18:11; 26:14). Moses is not a god but a "servant of the LORD," an honored title but clearly distinguished from the divine majesty of Yahweh, who alone is to be worshiped.

This last chapter of Deuteronomy makes no attempt to explain or to rationalize Moses' death. Moses' death is not presented as an atoning sacrifice, a precursor of the people's judgment, or punishment for Moses' own sin. The reader no longer hears Moses begging God to let him enter the promised land (Deut. 3:23-26). The straightforward narration of Moses' death without explanation simply underscores the inevitable reality of human death and limitation. The text allows the mystery of human suffering and death to remain unanswered. After Moses "went up" to Mount Nebo, Yahweh takes over the action of the verbs — showing, speaking, commanding, and burying. The only action that Moses does is "die." This section of chapter 34 is in tune with the emphasis of the Moab covenant in chapters 29–32, stressing the priority of divine over human action.

DEUT. 34:7-9: MOSES' VIGOR,
THE PEOPLE'S MOURNING, AND JOSHUA'S LEADERSHIP

A Priestly or later Deuteronomistic editor has probably added verses 7-9 as a supplement to 34:1-6.[7] The verses begin by noting that Moses died at the age of 120 years, a long human life but not an exception in the biblical tradition (e.g., cf. Gen. 25:7; 47:28; 50:26). But at 120, Moses remains exceptionally strong and healthy: "His sight was unimpaired and his vigor had not abated" (Deut. 34:7). Unlike the ancestor Isaac, whose eyes were dim in his old age (Gen. 27:1), Moses is able to see clearly the land that God has showed him. Moreover, Moses' "vigor" remains strong. The word for "vigor" is rare in Hebrew

---

7. Mayes, *Deuteronomy*, 413. The reason Mayes and others trace these verses to the Priestly redactor is their correspondence to Priestly material about Aaron's death and Joshua's succession in Num. 20:29 and 27:18-23. Moreover, the reference to Moses' "vigor" seems to conflict with the Deuteronomic note in Deut. 31:2 that characterizes Moses as feeble in his old age, thus suggesting it may be from a different hand. In a thorough treatment of the question, Lothar Perlitt ("Priesterschrift im Deuteronomium?" *ZAW* 100 [Supplement 1988]: 65–88) argues against any traces of a Priestly source in Deuteronomy. Perlitt would attribute these allegedly Priestly texts to a Deuteronomistic editor who knew the Priestly material and worked it into the final form of Deuteronomy.

but is associated with the fresh, moist property of young trees and fresh fruit. At 120, Moses remains strong, young, and supple. These claims about Moses' extraordinary strength and youthfulness are common legendary motifs associated with heroes in ancient literature.[8] This heroic depiction of Moses seems to contradict the portrait of Moses as feeble and weak in Deut. 31:2: "I am now one hundred twenty years old. I am no longer able to get about." While the contradiction may be explained away as coming from two different sources, their presence together in the final form of Deuteronomy suggests a meaningful tension in the portraiture of Moses. Moses is heroic and legendary and at the same time subject to the limits and weaknesses of all human beings. This same dialectic is at work in the juxtaposition of the stress on the inevitable reality of Moses' death on the one hand (34:1-6) and on the undiminished vigor and sight of heroic Moses on the other (34:7).

The section continues in 34:8-9 with the people's mourning of Moses for thirty days, the usual period for mourning the dead. This period of mourning marks the transition from one stage in life to another (21:13). The weeping and anguish lasts for a month and "then the period of mourning for Moses was ended" (34:8). Respect is granted to Moses, but the yearning for the days of his unparalleled leadership must end and give way to a new generation, new leadership, and new struggles. Thus, Joshua takes over as leader of the community of Israel: "the Israelites obeyed him, doing as the LORD had commanded Moses" (34:9). Joshua is not an exact and full replica of Moses. He has the "spirit of wisdom" because Moses laid his hands on him, but Joshua does not have the spirit of Moses himself. Joshua does not lead as Moses did according to his own personal interpretation or meditation of God's words. Rather, Joshua leads according to the Mosaic interpretation of God's commands and words now recorded in the book of the *torah* (cf. Josh. 1:7-8). In the transfer of leadership recounted earlier in Num. 27:12-23, God instructed Moses concerning Joshua, "You shall give him *some* of your authority," meaning presumably not all of it.[9] Joshua is a legitimate leader of Israel but not of the same stature as Moses.

---

8. George W. Coats, "Legendary Motifs in the Moses Death Reports," *CBQ* 39 (1977): 34–44. Cf. also idem, *Moses: Heroic Man, Man of God,* JSOTSup 57 (Sheffiield: JSOT Press, 1988).
9. Coats, "Legendary Motifs," 37.

DEUT. 34:10-12: MOSES' UNIQUE POWER
AND RELATIONSHIP TO YAHWEH

This text is commonly thought to be one of the latest additions to the Pentateuch, and its language affirms the absolute incomparability of Moses as a "prophet" of God (34:10). The uniqueness of Moses stems in part from his unparalleled intimate relationship with Yahweh; Moses was one "whom the LORD knew face to face." To "know" another person in Hebrew denotes an intimate relationship. To know "face to face" pushes the level of intimacy even higher, straining to express near parity or equality. A similar expression of the closeness of God and Moses occurs in Exod. 33:11, where God speaks to Moses "face to face, as one speaks to a friend."[10] The prophet Jeremiah as a new prophet like Moses (cf. Deut. 18:15) is perhaps the closest analogue to the uniquely intimate relationship of God and a human prophet (Jer. 1:5; 12:3). Nevertheless, Moses stands out as the prophet par excellence, without equal or rival.

Moses' uniqueness derives not only from his intimate relationship to Yahweh but also from his unmatched powerful "signs and wonders" done in Egypt and "all the mighty deeds and all the terrifying displays of power" that Moses did for all Israel (Deut. 34:11-12). What is truly remarkable here is that these words ("signs and wonders," "mighty deeds . . . terrifying displays of power") are technical terms applied consistently in Deuteronomy to *Yahweh* alone (4:34; 6:22; 7:19; 11:3; 26:8; 29:3). Yet in the end these powerful deeds of saving Israel are attributed to Moses.

One could simply dismiss this shift of subject from Yahweh to Moses as an editorial addition and thus dissolve the seeming tension between attributing "signs and wonders" to Yahweh and then to Moses. But the text is profoundly meaningful if one takes seriously its role in the movement of the entire book of Deuteronomy and in the context of chapter 34. Deuteronomy has moved from the past story of God's faithful actions (chaps. 1–4) to the present and near future commandments and laws directing human activity and life (chaps. 6–28) to the new covenant of Moab, which returns to the theme of God's faithful actions to save and to vindicate a rebellious Israel (chaps. 29–32). It is *God's* faithfulness and action that stand at the beginning and end of the life of the community. What role then do the law and human obedience

---

10. The motif of the shining face of Moses and the necessity of the veil in the book of Exodus reflects this same uniquely close encounter and relationship with God that sets Moses apart from the rest of the community (cf. Exod. 34:29-35). The episode in Numbers 12 likewise affirms Moses' uniqueness as a prophet or mediator of God's word (Num. 12:8).

play in the light of consistent human rebellion and the need for God's undeserved mercy? The concluding paragraph of chapter 34 responds to these questions by affirming Moses' crucial role as the human agent of divine activity. Moses and Yahweh are virtually identified in functional terms. Moses' life and words are remembered in retrospect as mediating the very words and actions of God. Human life and obedience can embody the real presence of God in the world. The blessing in chapter 33 is *God's* blessing, but it is mediated through the *human* words of Moses.

Yet it is clear in the context of Deuteronomy that Moses must join the fate of all humanity in sin and death. Moses was not God during his lifetime, nor can he become an ancestral god to be worshiped in his death (34:6). Moses will die outside the promised land because of the people's sin (3:26), because of his own failure (32:51), and because death is simply the undeniable fate of all humans (34:5). But as a servant of God, Moses has been a vehicle for redemptive, healing, and saving actions that will open the future for the sake of others. Human gifts and achievements are affirmed even as the inevitability of limits and failures is acknowledged. Life and death, sacrifice and tragedy, heroic accomplishments and deeds, unfulfilled hopes and dreams — these are the ultimate components of the realistic mixture of human struggle and divine purpose that make this last scene in Deuteronomy one of the most moving in all of Scripture.

SUMMARY: DEUTERONOMY 33–34
AND THE DEATH OF MOSES

The relationship of these last two chapters to the Deuteronomic theme of the death of Moses is self-evident and requires little additional explication. Chapter 34 narrates the actual account of Moses' death, a climactic and bittersweet end toward which Deuteronomy has been building from its opening chapter. But an important nuance has been added to the theme of Moses' death. The mourning over the human mortality of Moses (34:8) joins with the celebration of the wondrous and profound ways in which God has used Moses to guide and save the people of God. As Moses draws his last breath on Mount Nebo with the vision of the promised land still alive in his eyes, the tragic and the noble intermingle. Moses' life is a life whose end is too soon but whose legacy lingers on in a text which is still read and a song which is still sung across the ages among "us, who are all of us here alive today."

One modern embodiment of the realistic and empowering hope modeled by Moses was a person who sought a day when all God's children would be free together. One night, after recounting how he had seen glimpses of God's will being worked out as black Americans in Selma, Birmingham, and Memphis began to take their places in a society that was not willing to acknowledge that place, Martin Luther King, Jr., spoke of the threats made against his life:

> Well, I don't know what will happen now. We've got some difficult days ahead. But it really doesn't matter with me now—because I've been to the mountaintop. I don't mind. Like anybody, I would like to live . . . but I'm not concerned about that now. I just want to do God's will, and God's allowed me to go up to the mountain. I've looked over and I've seen the promised land. I may not get there with you, but I want you to know tonight that we as a people will get to the promised land. So I'm happy tonight. I'm not worried about anything, I'm not fearing any man. Mine eyes have seen the glory of the coming of the Lord.[11]

Within a week of speaking those words, he was dead. But Martin Luther King, Jr., was ready. In simple things like people taking different seats on buses or garbage collectors standing up for their rightful dignity, King had been to the mountain. He knew God would one day overcome. Moses, King, and countless other faithful servants of God have had visions of an end they would not see. But the little bit they tasted gave them courage to carry on with their life and work. They trusted that God would work in and through their lives, and they knew God would continue to work to bless and save long after they were gone. Deuteronomy calls its readers "today" to a similar vocation of working and hoping for the promised land, knowing that its accomplishment will finally be God's doing, not theirs. In this way, Deuteronomy proclaims the limits of human law and the triumph of divine love.

> Happy are you, O Israel! Who is like you,
>   a people saved by the LORD,
> the shield of your help,
>   and the sword of your triumph! (33:29)

11. *A Testament of Hope: The Essential Writings and Speeches of Martin Luther King, Jr.,* ed. James M. Washington (San Francisco: Harper & Row, 1986), 286.

CHAPTER 9

Centering and Decentering: Deuteronomy, The Death of Moses, and Biblical Theology

The author should die once he has finished writing, so as not to trouble the path of the text.

—Umberto Eco[1]

The death of Moses, the "author" of Deuteronomy, freed the text and opened its horizons to a long and winding path of interpretation through generations upon generations of reading. We are invited again to join the path of the text as we seek Deuteronomy's meaning in our contemporary place and time. In this concluding chapter, I reflect briefly on the theology of Deuteronomy and the implications of the book for the task of biblical theology in our so-called postmodern context.

Twentieth-century biblical theology has been marked by repeated attempts to find the "center" for the theology of the Hebrew Scriptures. Scholars have rummaged through the various historical and thematic overlays of ancient Israel's literature in the quest for the one normative and foundational "concept" or "bipolarity" of concepts. Numerous proposals have ranged from Eichrodt's "covenant"[2] to more recent

1. Umberto Eco, *Postscript to the Name of the Rose* (Orlando: Harcourt, Brace and Jovanovich, 1983), 7.
2. Walter Eichrodt, *Theology of the Old Testament,* 2 vols. (Philadelphia: Westminster, 1961, 1967); originally published in three volumes as *Theologie des Alten Testaments* (Leipzig: Hinrichs, 1933–39). Eichrodt sought to steer a middle path between historical-critical inquiry and systematic analysis by isolating the theme of "covenant" as "a living process" (not a static or dogmatic idea) that undergirded "the structural unity of the Old Testament message" (p. 17). Nevertheless, Eichrodt's "covenant" functioned as his conceptual center for all of the Old Testament.
    Examples of other proposals include "I am Yahweh your God" by Walther Zimmerli, *Old Testament Theology in Outline* (Atlanta: John Knox, 1978); "the holiness of God" by E. Sellin, *Theologie des Alten Testaments,* 2d ed. (Leipzig: Hinrichs, 1936), 19–23; "the universal dominion of Yahweh in justice and righteousness" by Rolf Knierim, "The Task of Old Testament Theology," in *Horizons in Biblical Theology* 6 (1984): 25–57;

bipolarities such as Westermann's "deliverance and blessing," Brueggemann's "structure legitimation and embrace of pain" or Terrien's "presence in absence."[3] Such quests for a timeless and foundational conceptual "center" or "bipolarity" in biblical theology have come under attack from two fronts. On one hand, historical-critical study of Israelite religion has highlighted the broad diversity of biblical traditions and theologies that resist summarizing under one conceptual or bipolar umbrella. On the other hand, the emerging postmodernist critique of any notion of a timeless or foundational "center" for any text would reject the possibility of an authoritative and universal center of biblical theology. Such quests, fueled by the Enlightenment and modernity, it is argued, merely reflect the illusory human yearning to define, control, and master everything from nature to technology, from history to texts.[4] Is our only option then to float aimlessly among the various theologies and histories of Israelite religion or among the

---

"promise" by Walter C. Kaiser, "The Center of Old Testament Theology: The Promise," in *Themelios* 10 (1974): 1-10; and "creation faith" by H. H. Schmid, "Schöpfung, Gerechtigkeit und Heil. 'Schöpfungstheologie' als Gesamthorizont biblischer Theologie," *Zeitschrift für Theologie und Kirche* 70 (1973), 1-19.

3. Claus Westermann, *Elements of Old Testament Theology* (Atlanta: John Knox, 1982); Walter Brueggemann, "A Shape for Old Testament Theology, I: Structure Legitimation; II: Embrace of Pain," in *Old Testament Theology: Essays on Structure, Theme, and Text*, ed. Patrick D. Miller (Minneapolis: Fortress Press, 1992), 1-44; and Samuel Terrien, *The Elusive Presence: Toward a New Biblical Theology* (San Francisco: Harper & Row, 1978).

Examples of other bipolar proposals include "the rule of God and communion between God and humans" by Georg Fohrer, *Theologische Grundstrukturen des Alten Testaments* (Berlin: de Gruyter, 1972); "Yahweh the God of Israel, Israel the people of God" by Rudolf Smend, *Die Mitte des Alten Testaments* (Zurich: EVZ-Verlag, 1970); and "the covenant of Sinai and the covenant of David" by F. C. Prussner, "The Covenant of David and the Problem of Unity in Old Testament Theology," in *Transitions in Biblical Scholarship,* ed. J. C. Rylaarsdam (Chicago: Univ. of Chicago Press, 1968), 17-41.

4. Postmodernism is a notoriously difficult term to define. Patricia Waugh observes that the term is used in at least three senses: (1) "as a term to designate the cultural epoch through which we are living and largely viewed in apocalyptic terms," (2) "as an aesthetic practice which is seen variously as co-extensive with the commodified surfaces of this culture or as a disruption of its assumptions from within," and (3) "as a development in thought that represents a thoroughgoing critique of the assumptions of Enlightenment or the discourses of modernity and their foundation in notions of universal reason" (*Postmodernism, A Reader,* ed. Patricia Waugh [London: Edward Arnold, 1992], 3). Postmodernism generally attacks three kinds of targets: "empiricist objectivism" where "the 'meaning' of a text consists in the way that it refers to this world"; a "conceptualist objectivism" where the "meaning" of a text is judged by its conformity to a set of concepts "which has an absolute and privileged character"; and a "subjectivism" that equates the meaning of a text with "understanding the mind of the author" (Michael LaFargue, "Are Texts Determinate? Derrida, Barth, and the Role of the Biblical Scholar," in *HTR* 81 [1988]: 341-57).

multifarious readerly interpretations that need to be deconstructed in an endless "play" of indeterminate meanings of texts?

The book of Deuteronomy, I believe, may help to offer a third option between the chaos of deconstructive relativity and the modernist ideal of some eternal humanly constructed foundational center. The German scholar Siegfried Herrmann proposed some years ago that the theological center of the Bible should not be an abstract concept but a biblical book, namely, Deuteronomy.[5] His suggestion was based on his observation that Deuteronomy was a concentrated repository of themes important to any Old Testament theology. In my judgment, Herrmann is both wrong and right. While Deuteronomy contains many important themes, it is certainly not exhaustive and thus is not an adequate summary of all important themes of biblical theology. But Herrmann is right in that Deuteronomy may indeed provide for our time a helpful center guiding the study of Old Testament theology, not only for its content but even more for its model of the *process* of theological interpretation.

Among all the biblical books, Deuteronomy appears the most reflective about the move from oral words and tradition to a written authoritative text and the process of interpreting that text in future generations. Deuteronomy wrestles with the role of texts, authors, interpretive communities, and God. As it does so, Deuteronomy holds together a creative dialectic between traditions that center Israel's theology and other traditions that *de*center the community and its theology. Our study of Deuteronomy has revealed several ways in which this dialectic between centering and decentering is played out.

THE COVENANTS OF HOREB AND MOAB

Behind much of our study of Deuteronomy is an implicit critique of widespread characterizations of Deuteronomy's theology as singular, flat, mechanistic, and focused entirely on rewards and punishments. Scholars tend to emphasize only the centralizing elements of Deuteronomy's theology. Werner Schmidt argues that "the intention of Deuteronomy may be summed up in a three-member formula: one God, one people, one cult. And we may add: one land, one king, one prophet."[6] James Crenshaw frequently refers to the "Deuteronomistic

---

5. Siegfried Herrmann, "Die konstruktive Restauration, Das Deuteronomium als Mitte biblischer Theologie," *Probleme biblischer Theologie,* FS Gerhard von Rad, ed. H. W. Wolff (Munich: Chr. Kaiser Verlag, 1971), 155–70.
6. Werner H. Schmidt, *Old Testament Introduction,* trans. Matthew O'Connell (New York: Crossroad, 1984).

theology of retribution" and "reward and punishment" where the people are promised blessings "provided that they will keep the statutes and ordinances of this law with complete faithfulness."[7] "The Deuteronomic theory of history," writes H. H. Rowley, "was that the nation always got what it deserved (cf. Dt 28)."[8] Thus, many argue that Deuteronomy's theology is summarized in the formula from Deut. 11:26: "See, I am setting before you today a blessing and a curse: the blessing, if you obey . . . and the curse, if you do not obey." But this is done only by discounting the later chapters of Deuteronomy as secondary or later "appendixes" that do not figure in the explication of Deuteronomy's full theology.[9] The effect of simplifying Deuteronomy into a flat, retributional theology is that it erroneously sets up Deuteronomy as a foil against which the wisdom tradition, especially Job and Qoheleth, argue. Job's friends become little "Deuteronomists" who espouse a rewards and punishment theology that Job rightly rejects.[10] Qoheleth's pessimism about knowing the ways of God or the secrets of life is allegedly "worlds apart" from Deuteronomy's naive claim to know the direct will of God and thus to know the reasons for all of God's actions.[11]

This study has demonstrated Deuteronomy's theology to be much richer, more nuanced, less naive, less singular or centralized, and more compelling than many past characterizations of its theology suggest. Indeed, the spirit of Deuteronomy, the recurring theme of Moses' death, and the willingness to face fully the horrors and tragedy of exile (Deuteronomy 28) suggest a level of engagement with the tragic and existential struggles of human life under God as profound as any in the wisdom tradition. The death of Moses casts its shadow over the whole of Deuteronomy in an unresolved but meaningful tension between human limits and human possibilities.

One of several ways by which this study illustrated Deuteronomy's richness and profundity involved the dynamic interplay between the

---

7. James Crenshaw, "The Human Dilemma and Literature of Dissent," in *Tradition and Theology in the Old Testament,* ed. Douglas Knight (Philadelphia: Fortress, 1977), 249; Crenshaw, *Story and Faith, A Guide to the Old Testament* (New York: Macmillan, 1986), 88. Cf. also W. Sibley Towner, *How God Deals with Evil* (Philadelphia: Westminster, 1976), 40–46.

8. H. H. Rowley, *Job,* NCBC (Grand Rapids: Eerdmans, 1976), 18.

9. For example, A. D. H. Mayes, *Deuteronomy,* NCBC (Grand Rapids: Eerdmans, 1979), 371, labels the last four chapters of Deuteronomy an "appendix."

10. Rowley, *Job,* 18; Daniel Simundson, *The Message of Job: A Theological Commentary* (Minneapolis: Augsburg, 1986), 16.

11. Robert Gordis, *Koheleth, The Man and His Word* (New York: Schocken, 1968), 44.

Horeb and Moab covenants. The juxtaposition of two simultaneous covenants — Horeb (Deuteronomy 5–28) "in addition to" Moab (Deuteronomy 29–32) — center on God's relationship to the people of Israel. The Horeb covenant emphasizes God's gracious election of Israel and the expected human responsibility for obedience to the will of God. The Horeb covenant, however, deconstructs itself through the ambiguities of its own statutes and ordinances that shipwreck in the end upon the curses of Deuteronomy 28, a literary text that resonates with Israel's sociohistorical experience of exile. The Moab covenant does not negate but decenters the Horeb covenant with an emphasis on the judging and saving action of God in the face of the failure and limitation of human obedience. Thus, Yahweh will be the one who will create obedience through the strategies of the Moab covenant, an obedience that humans could not achieve under the Horeb covenant (compare Deut. 10:16 and 30:6). Yet the Horeb covenant remains in effect and humans continue to struggle, however imperfectly, toward faithfulness. The two emphases on human obedience (the Horeb covenant) and divine promise (the Moab covenant) remain side by side in Deuteronomy, even as God's promise predominates and overcomes the limitations of human failure and rebellion.

THE ARK, THE STONE TABLETS, AND THE BOOK

The book of Deuteronomy contains an authoritative center, the Ten Commandments. Deuteronomy 5 reports that the Ten Commandments were spoken directly by God to the whole assembly. God "wrote them on two stone tablets," gave them to Moses and "added no more" (Deut. 5:22). Yet even this direct divine text was susceptible to deconstruction. Moses deconstructed the Decalogue text "written with the finger of God," smashing the stone tablets as a consequence of the golden calf apostasy (Deut. 9:10, 17). In response to Moses' pleas and intercession, God wrote a second text of the Ten Commandments and instructed Moses to put the new stone tablets *inside* the ark of the covenant to be carried with the people (Deut. 10:2-5). Moses then took stylus in hand and wrote his own text, the "book of the *torah*" (Deuteronomy). Moses instructed the Levites to place this book *beside* the ark of the covenant, which contained the stone tablets *inside* it (Deut. 31:26). The ark and its stone tablets formed a literary and authoritative center while the imagery of the book of Deuteronomy "beside" the ark marked it as a secondary and humanly mediated word from God through Moses to the people.

The first version of the stone tablets had already been deconstructed in the golden calf story. By the time of the Babylonian exile and the destruction of Jerusalem as described at the end of the Deuteronomistic History, the ark and the second edition of the stone tablets — disappeared off the stage of Israel's history. All that was left of that sacred tradition was the book of the *torah,* Deuteronomy, which was *beside* the ark but not in it. Deuteronomy thereby acknowledges that the words of God are always mediated, constructed through human interpretation. Deuteronomy's words are secondarily derived and not entirely equatable with the direct and full words of God. Yet they are all we have. The imagery of the broken and lost stone tablets undermines and decenters the foundation of human possession of God's direct word.

THE CENTRAL SANCTUARY: "THE PLACE THAT YAHWEH WILL CHOOSE AS A DWELLING FOR HIS NAME"

Deuteronomy 12 frequently refers to a central sanctuary for all Israel, but Detueronomy never names the place. The Deuteronomistic History names the place Jerusalem (1 Kings 8:29, 44, 48). But Deuteronomy's concern is not so much a particular city or place but its insistence on a place "that Yahweh will choose," whatever city that may be.[12] The city will not be a relativistic choice dictated only by humans "doing whatever is right in their own eyes" (Deut. 12:8, 13). God will choose the place and there the divine power will indeed be available through the presence of God's "name." But Deuteronomy recognizes that God's presence will not be exhausted or bound to any one place. God is present both "in heaven" — a realm not accessible to humans — as well as "on earth" where humans do live (Deut. 4:36, 39; 10:14; 26:15; cf. 1 Kings 8). The exilic portions of Deuteronomy 4 and 29–30 affirm God's presence will be with the people in exile: "from there you will seek Yahweh your God, and you will find him" (Deut. 4:29). God will scatter and decenter Israel, but God will also be present in those exilic places far away from the center (Deut. 4:27; 29:28). Thus, the place that Yahweh would choose for the divine name enabled God's presence to be centered provisionally in one place but ultimately decentered

---

12. It is often assumed that Deuteronomy has roots in northern Israelite soil. Thus, it is possible that "the place that YHWH your God will choose" may have once referred to a northern cult center like Bethel or more probably Shiloh. The strongest evidence for this possibility is Jeremiah's temple sermon where God speaks of Shiloh as the place "where I made my name to dwell at first" (Jer. 7:12). Gerhard von Rad in *Studies in Deuteronomy* (London: SCM Press, 1961), 38–39, notes that the identification of the "place" with the city of Jerusalem is only one possibility" since "Deuteronomy never speaks of the city of Jerusalem."

in any permanent sense from a given humanly constructed sanctuary or site.[13]

MOSES, GOD, AND THE DEUTERONOMIC NARRATOR: CENTERING AND DECENTERING NARRATIVE VOICES

Robert Polzin in his literary interpretation of Deuteronomy, *Moses and the Deuteronomist,* distinguishes three narrative "voices" within the book: God, Moses, and the voice of the narrator or implied author of the book. According to Polzin, these three voices overlap, blur, and ultimately compete in a struggle of narrative voices. One voice — the narrator — eventually wins the struggle and drowns out all other voices. The "voice" of the Deuteronomic narrator speaks in a total of only fifty-six verses in Deuteronomy. Most of Deuteronomy comprises simply a series of direct quotations of Moses. The narrator's "voice" occurs in the numerous frame breaks that typically introduce or conclude the words of Moses or of God (e.g., Deut. 1:1-5). Polzin argues that this "voice" of the Deuteronomic narrator engages in a subtle strategy of first exalting, then blurring, and finally subverting the voices of God and of Moses. Ultimately, the voice of the "narrator" or "implied author" emerges triumphant as the one remaining authoritative voice at the end of Deuteronomy. The reader is thus prepared to heed this authoritative narrator throughout the remainder of the Deuteronomistic History in Joshua–1 and 2 Kings.[14]

According to Polzin, the narrator's strategy involves several steps. The Deuteronomic narrator first blurs the distinction between the voice of God and the voice of Moses. Apart from the Ten Commandments, God's words in Deuteronomy are always mediated through Moses. The narrator next begins to break down the difference between Moses' voice and the narrator's own voice. Polzin argues that the repeated use of the phrase "this day" throughout Deuteronomy fuses the temporal horizons

---

13. On Deuteronomy's use of YHWH's "name" as the vehicle of divine cultic presence, cf. Gerhard von Rad, *Studies in Deuteronomy,* 37–44; Moshe Weinfeld, *Deuteronomy and the Deuteronomic School* (Oxford: Clarendon Press, 1972), 191–209; S. Dean McBride, "The Deuteronomic Name Theology" (Ph.D. diss., Harvard University, 1969); and more recently, Trygve Mettinger, *The Dethronement of Sabaoth: Studies in Shem and Kabod Theologies,* trans. F. H. Cryer (Lund: CWK Gleerup, 1982). Mettinger, among others, sees Deuteronomy's "name" (*šēm*) theology as an explicit corrective to the Jerusalem-Zion "glory" (*kābôd*) theology of the divine presence (expressed principally in the Psalms and Isaiah). J. Gordon McConville, "God's 'Name' and God's 'Glory,'" *TynBul* 30 (1979): 149–63, argues that the name and glory theologies of divine presence are compatible and not necessarily opposed to one another.

14. Robert Polzin, *Moses and the Deuteronomist. A Literary Study of the Deuteronomic History: Part One. Deuteronomy, Joshua, Judges* (New York: Seabury, 1980). The argument concerning the book of Deuteronomy is concentrated on pp. 25–72.

of Moses and the later narrator into one. The narrator and the Mosaic voice are also similar in being the only ones who quote the words of God directly.

Polzin contends that as Deuteronomy moves toward the final scene of the death of Moses, the teaching authority of Moses (and hence the authority of God) shifts *from* Moses and *to* the Deuteronomic narrator. The Deuteronomic narrator becomes the new "prophet like Moses" promised in Deut. 18:15.[15] With the death of Moses, Polzin argues, "the words of Moses are ended; the words of the narrator now take center stage in the history."[16] By the end of his reading of Deuteronomy, Polzin silences not only Moses but also God. For Polzin, what appears to be a dialogue of conflicting voices becomes a monologue. All that remains is the single voice of the Deuteronomic narrator who continues throughout the Deuteronomistic History in Joshua–Kings.

While Polzin's proposal is a sensitive and provocative literary reading, my reading of Deuteronomy would suggest a somewhat different understanding of the interplay of narrative voices in Deuteronomy. My own conclusion is that the voice of God emerges as the decentering center of Deuteronomy. First of all, I would disagree with Polzin and instead maintain that the voice of *Moses* and the voice of *God* are never fully blurred or fused in Deuteronomy. As we have already noted, the imagery of the ark illustrates the boundary between the direct words of God and the mediating words of Moses. The stone tablets upon which God's own hand wrote the Ten Commandments are *inside* the ark as a sign of their unique authority (Deut. 10:1-5). Deuteronomy, the book authored by the hand of Moses, is carried outside and *alongside* the ark as a secondary and mediated interpretation of God's direct words (Deut. 31:26).

The distinction between God's voice and the human voice of Moses is also explicitly made in Moses' observation in Deut. 29:29: "The secret things belong to YHWH our God; but the things that are revealed belong to us and our children forever, that we may do all the words of this *torah*." The full knowledge of God, "the secret things," remain elusive. Humans, including Moses, are given only a partial disclosure of the divine. There is overlap between the words of God and Moses but also dissonance. But within the diversity of human understandings of God and the world, Moses' words in Deuteronomy provide enough of a unified and coherent picture that a new generation may live and act faithfully: "that we may do all the words of this *torah*."

15. Ibid., 35–36.
16. Ibid., 72.

The distinction between God and Moses is portrayed most clearly at the end of Deuteronomy. As the persona of Moses begins to wane in the closing chapters, God's activity begins to move to the foreground. The Moab covenant in Deuteronomy 29–32 emphasizes God as final judge and deliverer. God is the one who transfers leadership from Moses to Joshua (Deut. 31:7-8, 14-15, 23). The movement of the poetic Song of Moses clearly ends with God at center stage (Deut. 32:39-43). Moses' prayer, which requests God's blessing upon Israel in Deuteronomy 33, entrusts Israel to God's care and oversight after Moses dies. Finally, it is God who is the subject of the verbs in the final chapter of Deuteronomy. On Mount Nebo, Yahweh shows, speaks, commands, and buries. The only action that Moses does is die. God puts Moses to death and buries his body in an unknown place (34:5-6).

Thus, the voices of God and Moses are not fully blurred or fused as Polzin tries to argue. Nor are the voices of *Moses* and the *Deuteronomic narrator* fused together as one. Deuteronomy's strong claim for the absolute uniqueness of Moses does not allow Moses' full authority to transfer to the Deuteronomic narrator: "*Never* since has there arisen a prophet in Israel like Moses' (Deut. 34:10-12). Even if Polzin is correct in identifying the Deuteronomic narrator as the new "prophet like Moses" promised in Deut. 18:15, that prophet must submit to the tests of true and false prophecy (Deut. 18:20-22). Moreover, future authority within the community will not be confined only to this one prophet's words. Authority will be distributed among several "voices" in the Deuteronomic program: judges, officials, priests, and king (Deut. 16:18-22). Just as Moses redistributed his centralized authority among tribal leaders in the first narrative of Deuteronomy (1:9-18), so the Deuteronomic narrator as prophet will also share authority with other "voices" in the community.

Indeed, there are many other "voices" within Deuteronomy beyond the three that Polzin isolates (God, Moses, narrator). The written text of Deuteronomy itself, the written "book of the *torah*," will exercise authority as an ongoing "voice" or "witness" in the community (31:9, 26). The "elders" and "priests" join Moses in speaking at the end of Deuteronomy (27:1, 9). The "elders" and "priests" will be the ones entrusted with the authority of teaching and interpreting the *torah* for future generations (31:9, 24-28). Parents will also have a "voice" as they teach their children (6:7, 20). "Heaven and earth" will have a voice as "witnesses" against Israel (31:28). Other forces of nature and the political powers of other nations will have a "voice" in the judgment (chap. 32) and the blessing (chap. 33) of Israel. Above all, the hidden but revealed God remains the final "voice" and arbiter of human life and destiny:

> See now that I, even I, am the one,
>   there is no god beside me.
> I kill and I make alive;
>   I wound and I heal;
> and no one can deliver from my hand. (Deut. 32:39)

In the world of Deuteronomy, no one can deliver even Polzin's human "narrator" from the divine hand. Like Moses and every human interpreter, the narrator will die outside the promised land.

In my judgment, Polzin's reading of Deuteronomy participates in the modernist illusion that the human voice and actor is the final arbiter of reality and meaning. For Polzin, all decentered dialogue and plurality finally merge into the one central human voice of the narrator. But Deuteronomy's perspective in our reading is quite different. Dialogue and plurality remain among diverse human and nonhuman voices and authorities. The promised land is never fully achieved. God retains competing idols and voices in the land of Canaan even after the conquest (Judges 2). The journey continues through the ongoing struggles of persuasion and catechesis among a variety of competing theologies and idolatries. In the Deuteronomic program, however, such plurality does not slide into the radical deconstruction of texts and reality where all interpretations are equally valid. Deuteronomy warns, "You shall not act as we are acting here today, all of us according to our own desires" (Deut. 12:8). God remains as the ultimate and single center of all of all that is: "Hear, O Israel: YHWH our God, YHWH alone" (Deut. 6:4). However, the human struggle to discern the full significance of that singular Reality will never be over. Like Moses, interpreters will never fully enter the promised land on this side of the grave. But also like Moses, every generation will be given the opportunity for enough of a glimpse of the promised land to continue the journey.

In the meantime, communities of interpretation will struggle and argue for provisional theological centers in the midst of a plurality of competing words and "voices." That plurality of voices exists within the biblical canon itself. It exists among the diverse communities of interpretation that read and wrestle with the biblical text, both communities of scholarship and communities of faith. If we take Deuteronomy's wisdom seriously, persuasive proposals for a theological center in our postmodern context will acknowledge their provisionality and limits. They will appeal to a variety of criteria and provisional foundations, recognizing that no human construction or ideology is timeless or universal. Proposals for a theological center will not claim to know all the "secret things" of God. But each new generation will seek to know enough of the "revealed things" to "observe all the words of this *torah*" for at least one generation more. That will be enough. As human interpreters, we are suspended in ambiguity between the boundaries of the modern and the postmodern, between the need for a center and the decentered reality of human life, between monotheism and the temptation of many gods, between the universal and the particular, between human ability to control and humanly unmanageable forces of politics and nature, between human responsibility and divine activity. Suspended in ambiguity on the boundary of the promised land, Deuteronomy nevertheless invites us to journey on.

Index of

Biblical Passages

Index of

Authors